WORLD WAR 3

WORLD WAR 3

**A MILITARY PROJECTION FOUNDED ON TODAY'S FACTS.
GENERAL EDITOR SHELFORD BIDWELL.**

PRENTICE HALL INC.
ENGLEWOOD CLIFFS, N.J.

MADE BY ROXBY PRESS PRODUCTIONS
98 CLAPHAM COMMON NORTH SIDE,
LONDON SW4 9SG

EDITOR: RICHARD HUMBLE
DESIGNER: DAVID PEARCE
PICTURE RESEARCH: JOHN MOORE
PRODUCTION: REYNOLDS CLARK ASSOCIATES LIMITED

PRINTED AND BOUND IN SPAIN BY TONSA,
SAN SEBASTIAN

D.L.: S.S. 403/1978

CONTENTS

PROLOGUE

IS THIS THE ROAD TO DISASTER?

The prospect of a third and infinitely destructive world war – an armed clash between the two superpowers of the United States and the Soviet Union and their client states and allies, using weapons of mass destruction – is both immediate and apparent.

Two facts are crystal-clear. The combustible matter is present; and human beings are predisposed to war. They will, for no apparent reason, choose war rather than peace. This is not a matter for argument: the history of this century alone provides abundant proof. So far this has been a matter for regret rather than for speculations about Armageddon. Warfare, brutal as it is, seems to be an essential element in human intercourse, and the human race has so far been sufficiently durable to repair the damage.

There has always been a connection between the means of waging war – the weapons lying to hand – and its outbreak. The USA and the Soviet Union together have 5,763,000 men under arms. Conventional weapons are infinitely more destructive than ever they were when World War 2 ended in 1945 (not only because of increased lethality, but the accuracy with which targets can now be located and weapons delivered). All the same, a conventional war could conceivably be halted and, conceivably, the damage done repaired. But nuclear warfare cannot.

If we are to believe the defence analysts (and we must at least listen to them), they forecast that by the early 1980s, which is as far forward as we attempt to peer in this study, the two superpowers will have between them 21,500 nuclear warheads ready to hurl at each other. And these are only the 'strategic' weapons, without taking into account the 'small' tactical weapons designed to be used against conventional forces on the battlefield. A substantial portion are in the megaton rather than the kiloton range – that is, their lethality is measured in millions of equivalents of ordinary high explosive rather than thousands. No elaborate calculations are required to establish the finality of a strategic nuclear exchange.

Such are the material factors predisposing towards war, and the danger is there, however much the nuclear strategic forces are regarded by both sides as a deterrent. A greater danger, perhaps, lies in the domain of emotions and ideas.

Judging only by the literate Western world, we seem obsessed with the subject of war and warfare. We dwell with extraordinary intensity on both the world wars we have endured; we write novels, plays and poems about them. The review pages of newspapers can be opened every week in the certainty of the mention of some publication or other dealing with war. Nor is this a literate or 'elitist' trend. The paperback market is supported by the demand for the crudest of war stories. Baron von Richtofen still flies, the US Marines still hold Guadalcanal and the US Army is still winning the Battle of the Bulge.

Science fiction has always been obsessed with war. The recent film 'Star Wars' made box-office history with its super-electronic warfare fought between super-warships using super-weapons. Only press the trigger and the adversary disappears. Given the means – and the means are there, as the dry pages of the ISS *Military Balance* and the statistics of the arms trade and arms diplomacy confirm – combined with this deep-rooted neurosis, it is reasonable to fear that it only requires a sudden, local convulsion to tip humanity over the rim of the crater into hell.

It can be argued that 'World War 3' is already taking place around us, and that, consolingly, a vast sustained conflict, with every activity suspended except to provide sufficient food and power for survival and the production of weapons, has been banished by the nuclear deadlock. As each of the two superpowers possesses twice, or five times, or ten times the number of nuclear warheads required to eliminate the other's population centres, and as there can be no defence against nuclear attack, universal war continues, affording an outlet for aggression, but damped down below the level at which any local conflagration can spread and become universal. This argument is, with certain qualifications, acceptable, but such a state of affairs is not, by definition, a 'world war'.

This must be described as a full-scale act of armed aggression by one side upon the other. And the scene of such aggression, it is believed, could only be in North-West Europe, where the forces of NATO and the Warsaw Pact face each other. It is there that a high concentration of nuclear weapons exists and the largest conventional forces confront each other.

Thus the condition of the world may be seen not as an existent, continuing 'World War 3' but as a *world-wide state of warfare*, first in one locality and then in another, encouraged and damped down according to the advantage likely to be gained or the danger incurred by the two superpowers. These localised conflicts have a variety of causes. One whole group, still in progress, arose from the break-up of the colonial empires, followed by civil war among the inheritors. Although on some levels they resemble guerrilla wars and embody guerrilla methods they are not small; the intervention of the superpowers as sponsors, advisers and purveyors of modern weapons converts them to large-scale wars. The Vietnam war was one of the most destructive in history apart from the world wars, and in number and quality of modern weapons the battles in Syria and Egypt in 1973 eclipsed many battles of World War 2.

We can congratulate ourselves on having avoided anything worse so far, by virtue of the nuclear strategic balance. Yet the present state of affairs is a genuine human tragedy, created and aggravated by the obsessive system of providing client states with massive supplies of sophisticated arms in order to obtain political leverage and to attract them into one of the two rival camps, or the immoral sale of arms for commercial gain.

As far as an extension from a local war to a global war is concerned it is fair to say that the nature of a *casus belli* has changed because of the nuclear deterrent. A complex structure of 'crisis management' has come into existence, with any major move by either of the superpowers carefully calculated to be an unmistakable signal of intention and warning, from which both sides can withdraw without excessive loss of face. In earlier, pre-nuclear times, such crises as the dispute over NATO's land access to Berlin, or the Cuban Missile Crisis of October 1962, might all have led inevitably to war.

All the same, the fear remains that the fomenting of wars and the provision of modern weapons is an intensely dangerous business, and that one day a conflagration or a group of conflagrations might somehow get out of hand, in spite of all the elaborate skills of crisis management. Even if this is unlikely, it is not a fear that can be dismissed out of hand.

When, therefore, the idea of this book was first discussed it was decided to concentrate on the prospects of a mighty, uncontrollable explosion which could shatter the precarious stability of the world we live in. The possibility of the emergence of India or China as a third superpower; of a Japan once more in a mood to flex her muscles in international affairs; of the gradual shift in the balance of power and influence towards one side or the other – all are formidable subjects for speculation but are pale and remote beside the ordinary man's fear of being destroyed in a world-wide nuclear holocaust in the next few years.

In this book we have adopted two dates of reference. Part I describes the world as we know it now. Part II covers imaginary events about five years in the future. It is to be hoped that they will never be anything else but imaginary. The distant date gives the authors reasonable latitude to extend some present trends to a worst case. The reader should not be carried away by this, but consider it in relation to Part I – the current world scene.

In Part I those factors making for war are examined, but we also take into account the stabilizing factors which serve to prevent the sudden outbreak of war. It is not in the interests of the superpowers or those of the second rank to allow it to happen, and the most elaborate arrangements exist to prevent it. It should also be noted that the Marxist world-view guiding the actions of the Soviet leaders does not prophesy the conquest of the capitalist world by force of arms. Instead it makes its contribution to fear by forecasting a Western attack on the Soviet Union, caused by the death-throes of the capitalist/ imperialist 'system'.

Part I also describes the military scene – not so much the weapons themselves, but also the military philosophies of the rival camps. Part II examines the nature of the *casus belli*: no mere spark, but a combination of circumstances interpreted as an unacceptable threat by one side. It may be regarded as extravagant; so much the better. The core of our argument is that the world as we know it will not slip into war as it did in 1914 and 1939, but only as the result of some intolerable provocation. The reader may also ask why,

in our imaginary situation, the first resort to the use of armed force does not come from the West. The short answer to this is that the balance of military resources favours the Soviet Union and its client states so overwhelmingly that offensive action by the West, whatever the provocation, would be a suicidal act. The Atlantic Alliance can only fight a defensive battle along the lines predetermined by itself, relying on the nuclear weapon as the ultimate deterrent against being completely overrun by superior numbers in a conventional attack. The imagined circumstances of 1983 are based on the deepest Soviet fears and on study of Soviet doctrine.

Part II is also fiction, but fiction, we believe, fairly based on the nature of conventional war in our time. Such a war will be enormously destructive, and self-destructive, even by the standards of past wars in this century. It is a fact to be grimly noted that the huge battles of 1973 in Syria and Egypt took place in barren or thinly-populated territory, whereas our assumed conflict is staged in a prosperous, urban, densely-populated part of Europe: the Federal Republic of Germany.

And yet it is by no means pure fiction. About the only thing that is uncertain about it is the scale of damage caused by its secondary effects on the population of countries remote from the actual scene of nuclear war. It is sufficiently dreadful in itself to make any discussion of the use of chemical or bacteriological weapons superfluous.

Forecasts of the future can only be a flight into imagination from the launch-pad of fact. The contents of this book may be dismissed, though not easily, as 'futurology'; but it is also a parable. The sure road to rendering its more horrible scenes and statistics invalid is to renounce totally the use of armed force and to dismantle the weapons of war.

SHELFORD BIDWELL

PART ONE

THE RIVALS AND THE WEAPONS

1. SHADOW OF THE SUPERPOWERS

The use of the term 'super-powers' to describe the world's most important and formidable nations was first popularised in 1944 by an American scholar, William Fox, writing in a book that took the term for its title. Fox distinguished the superpowers from other major powers 'which may enjoy the formal and ceremonial prestige of great power status but whose interests and influence are great only in a single theatre of power conflict'. The presence of the superpowers could be felt throughout the world, while that of lesser powers would be confined to particular regions. To be a superpower demanded more than great strength or even global interests: it was necessary to have the ability to support such interests by deploying preponderant power whenever and wherever needed. The terms of membership to the superpower club were 'great power plus great mobility of power'.

To Fox only three nations qualified for membership: America, Russia and Britain. By his criteria, and almost any other criteria, Britain no longer qualifies. In the decades after the war Britain's *relative* power declined and she disposed of her overseas possessions. Other candidates have come forward for superpower status. A few years ago it was common to hear talk of a 'pentagonal' world system based on Japan, the European Communities and China as well as America and Russia. Some would say that the control over international oil supplies exercised by Iran and Saudi Arabia is reason to elevate their international status. India has often presented herself as a potential superpower because of her large population, her incipient nuclear power and her role as leader of the non-aligned bloc of countries.

The United States and the Soviet Union are by no means omnipotent in all areas of international life. In matters of trade and finance the Soviet Union plays a marginal role while Japan and the EEC are right at the centre. The US and USSR stand out only on one basic measure – military strength. Their stature is based on armed forces of outstanding quantity, quality and mobility. Other nations, or groupings of nations, may be extremely important in a non-military sense globally, or militarily important at a regional level, but only the US and USSR are militarily important throughout the globe. Nevertheless, accepting this as the essential source of 'super' power, it will be necessary to discuss the constraints on the uninhibited application of this power, and its relative value compared with other instruments of foreign policy.

THE ESSENCE OF POWER

To explore this problem further let us look closely at the word 'power'. Though a useful means of conveying the importance of hierarchy in political life, it is a difficult concept. It is conventionally defined as the ability to get your own way. However, this varies according to what you are trying to do and the source of the impediments. If other countries oppose your plans, power is not only about what you can do to them but about what they can do to you. If military aims do not extend beyond defence of boundaries, power requirements are far less than if some neighbouring territory is sought. The weapons at your command may make one nation tremble while another, having found the perfect countermeasure, remains indifferent. The trembling nation, impressed

by overwhelming military strength, may still have an option of interfering with essential supplies of raw materials, so causing your economy to collapse.

Thus, though the word 'power' appears in the English language as a noun rather than a verb, it can only be understood properly in an active sense and in relation to the activities of others. Power is not a possession and so cannot be measured or quantified in any satisfactory way. It is, however, derived from key resources and so we can find out a lot about potential power by evaluating a nation's military, economic and political resources. But we must always bear in mind that as important as possession of valuable power resources is the ability to mobilize these resources and skill in employing them. Against an invading army, the best-trained collection of soldiers is of limited utility if asleep in barracks. Even when assembled and armed the advantages of preponderant strength can be dissipated by an incompetent general. Also, we need to look as much at areas of vulnerability as areas of strength.

Since the industrial revolution, wars have been battles of production; in consequence, military power has been based on

Top: *Big Three, 1945 – Attlee (Britain), Truman (USA) and Stalin (USSR).* Above: *From Big Three to Big Two – Brezhnev and Nixon in 1973*

the level of a society's industrialization. In the early 1920s the new leaders of Russia, feeling threatened by the persistent hostility of the capitalist world, directed their efforts towards industrializing this shattered and backward, agrarian country. Despite the enormous strains and sacrifices, industry was developed through a series of Five Year Plans with precedence being given to capital goods over the needs of consumers.

Since 1945 a new ingredient has become essential to military strength – the capacity to exploit rapid technological

THE SUPERPOWERS: ALLIES AND CLIENTS

USSR

WARSAW PACT AND CLIENTS

U.S.A.

NATO AND CLIENTS

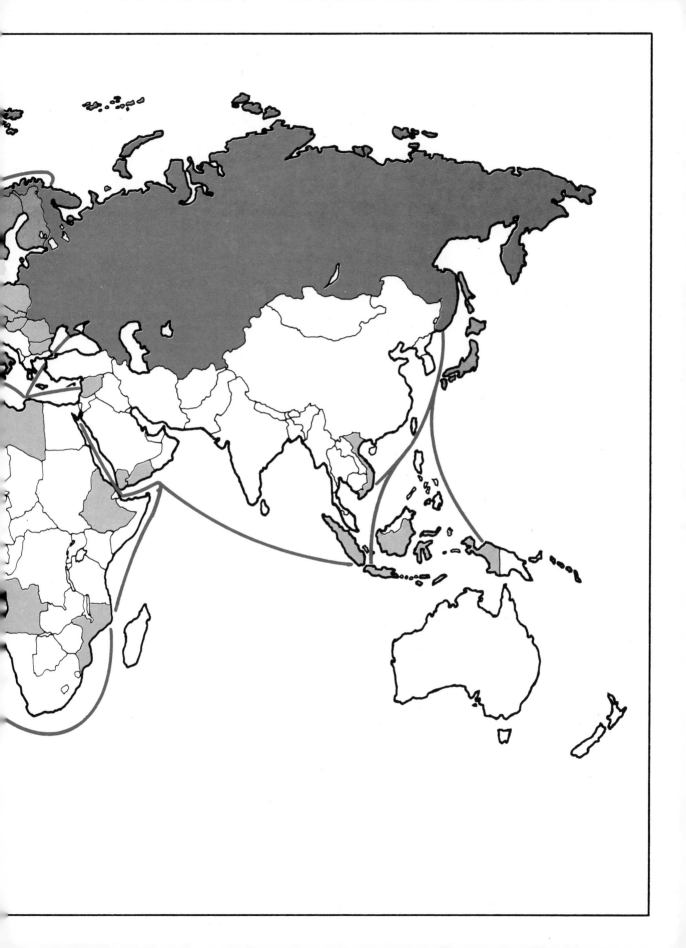

The traditional muscle of American technology: F4 Phantoms on the production-line in St Louis

advance. In quick succession radars, missiles, nuclear energy, computers, artificial satellites and micro-electronics have transformed the character of armed force. To start with this worked to the advantage of the United States – blessed with large numbers of scientists and engineers, the funds and facilities to get the best out of them, as well as a culture sympathetic to the notion that national security should be based on the sophisticated application of brains rather than the crude application of brawn.

To the great surprise of many Americans the Soviet Union kept on catching up with the Americans, albeit after a few years, in the development and manufacture of the most advanced weapons systems. When the first Soviet atom bomb was tested in 1949, only four years after Hiroshima, there was a common tendency to decry the achievement as the result of successful espionage. It took the Soviet triumph of the first successful launch of an earth satellite – Sputnik I in October 1957 – to bring home to the Americans that they were facing a competitor with significant technological skills.

Since then the United States has continued to set a tough pace in the development of modern weapons and the Soviet Union has not always found it easy to keep up. But the Russians have shown a remarkable tenacity, anxious to deny the Americans strategic advantage and to demonstrate that a socialist state can be as sophisticated as any capitalist state. To this end some 10–15% of the GNP, and most of the best brains, of the Soviet Union have been devoted to military work. Whereas advanced weapons come naturally to the Americans, reflecting the innovatory nature of the whole society, it has been a concentrated effort for the Russians, requiring a sacrifice from the non-military sectors.

THE NUCLEAR MENACE – AND SHIELD

The superpowers are not alone in their ability to exploit nuclear energy for military purposes, but the quality and quantity of their arsenals set them apart from Britain, France and China. Only the superpowers have the capability to destroy as viable entities *any* other nation on earth, including each other. This is not to dismiss the smaller nuclear powers. They could cause considerable hurt and disruption, even to the superpowers, but it would be more comparable, to use de Gaulle's phrase, to 'tearing off an arm' than a mortal wound. Furthermore, the superpowers can detonate nuclear weapons at almost any spot on the globe, these days with considerable accuracy. Britain and France have no spare capacity for purposes other than the national deterrence of the Soviet Union. China can only threaten nations within a restricted radius.

The distinguishing feature of the superpowers' position is their ability to offer other states the protection of their nuclear umbrella. Western Europe, Japan, Australia and New Zealand all shelter under the American umbrella, while Eastern Europe is protected by the Soviet Union. Occasionally it is suggested that Britain and France could combine forces to provide an indigenous nuclear defence for Europe, but there is little confidence that a sufficiently imposing force would result. Nevertheless, there is a persistent disquiet surrounding dependence on US nuclear protection. When the protection was first offered, America was so superior to the Soviet Union that if a conventional invasion of Western Europe triggered the nuclear devastation of the Soviet Union, the Kremlin would have little to offer by way of retaliation. By the end of the 1950s it was becoming apparent that a future Soviet nuclear retaliation was likely to be every bit as devastating as any American attack. It took no great political insight to realise that a rational American president might think twice before unleashing the nuclear forces at his command if this was liable to result in national suicide.

For some time it was thought possible that retaliation might be escaped through what became known as a 'first-strike capability'. This would involve a surprise attack which would disarm the enemy by destroying his retaliatory forces before they could be launched, combined with an effective air defence and anti-ballistic missile (ABM) system which would neutralize any bombers and missiles that did get away. Neither side has proved able to develop such a capability. No efficient or economical ABM system could be designed to cope with the speed, variety and magnitude of plausible nuclear attacks.

Meanwhile, though it has become possible to target missiles or aircraft based on land and perhaps destroy a considerable number in a surprise attack, the growth of the relatively invulnerable submarine-based nuclear forces put paid to any aspirations of fully disarming the enemy. Both superpowers, now and for the foreseeable future, will still be able to devastate the enemy in a retaliatory second strike even after absorbing a full-blooded first strike. The state of affairs in which both sides enjoy a secure second-strike capability has been described as one of 'mutual assured destruction', a reasonably self-explanatory phrase. Given this state of affairs, neither superpower is in a position to take great nuclear risks against the other. Hence the concern of some of America's allies that she would not prove to be wholly reliable if she should ever be called upon to honour her obligations to her allies, and respond to a Soviet conventional invasion.

The Soviet Union is not subject to the same questioning as in the United States. Her dependencies in Eastern Europe are sufficiently well orchestrated for there to be no *public* scepticism concerning any Soviet policies. However, a central argument during the early stages of the Sino-Soviet split was over the extent to which the Soviet Union was providing adequate nuclear cover for China. In 1958 when the Chinese, who believed the Soviet Union to be stronger than she actually was, began to attempt to gain control of the last territory controlled by Chiang Kai-shek's Nationalists, the Russians made a point of reminding the Chinese that nuclear protection was provided to defend them from attack and not to support their adventures. Chastened by this experience, the Chinese began to develop their own nuclear weapons. Impeded by their erstwhile comrades in this enterprise, their hostility to Moscow grew.

In NATO only the French actually reoriented their national strategy in response to doubts over the value of the US nuclear guarantee. Other allies have preferred to believe in the reliability of the guarantee, however much of an act of faith this may be, on the positive grounds that so long as the Soviet Union believes there is even the slightest risk of receiving the full brunt of American nuclear might she will be deterred from any provocative actions, and on the more negative grounds that there is no credible alternative, at least at a level the Europeans could afford. America's allies, in an effort to maintain this act of faith, continually require of the United States reassurances of her willingness to use nuclear weapons on

behalf of Europe. In order to symbolize the commitments US nuclear forces are kept in European bases though it is no longer essential to base such weapons so close to Russia to ensure that she can be attacked.

The Western European dependence on America is not solely confined to the nuclear area or even to support in conventional arms. There is a great dependence upon America for intelligence information. Both superpowers maintain a close watch over the development and disposition of the military forces of their potential adversaries through the regular orbiting of reconnaissance satellites. High-powered radars pick up crucial information on the testing of Soviet weapons. Satellites are now also used for the crucial functions of surveillance, navigation, command, control and communications – and all but a few of the relevant satellites are owned by the superpowers. The value of this space-based infrastructure is considerable, though often neglected because of the normal focus on earth-based weapons. Instant intelligence and fast communications could well make the difference in any war, nuclear or otherwise, and can be

Long arm at sea: the American nuclear-powered aircraft-carrier USS Enterprise, *the largest warship ever built when laid down in 1958, here shown with her massive air group off Vietnam in 1969*

a source of strength in crises, helping to avoid hasty actions based on incomplete evidence.

'SHOWING THE FLAG', SUPERPOWER-STYLE

The final feature which distinguishes the superpowers from the crowd is their ability to put on a show of force around the globe. A show of force can mean anything from a direct military intervention to material support for an ally or client, to a piece of old-fashioned gunboat diplomacy. For reasons which will be discussed below, both superpowers are reluctant to get too involved in military conflicts far away from home. The traumatic experience of Vietnam, in which over 46,000 Americans lost their lives, has made US politicians think twice before making any further commitments of troops abroad. President Nixon

enunciated a new doctrine in which the United States 'will look to threatened countries and their neighbours to assume primary responsibility for their own defense, and we will provide support where our interests call for that support and where it can make a difference'. During the 1970s the American emphasis has been placed on providing the most modern military equipment, short of nuclear weapons, to those in need, with some training and technical advice thrown in for good measure. (The numbers of US personnel involved in training and advice abroad is growing considerably – to some 150,000 by 1980 in Iran alone.)

The Soviet Union's capacity to operate at long distance is a more recent development. Throughout most of the post-war period it has lacked significant overseas bases or a large ocean-going navy. At the time of the Cuban Missile Crisis of October

Long arm in the air: this is an American B-52 intercontinental bomber
of Strategic Air Command, carrying two
'Hound Dog' stand-off weapons armed with nuclear warheads

One of the acid-tests for superpower status:
the ability to airlift military muscle with speed and abundance.
Here Soviet helicopters bring in back-up equipment during 'Dniepr', a Warsaw Pact exercise

1962, the Russian leaders became aware of their inability to challenge American conventional dominance outside of Europe. Since then, however, though there has not been much success in securing permanent overseas bases, the Soviet Navy has expanded at a remarkable rate. One impulse behind this expansion has been the desire to counter US nuclear submarines, but another, in recent years, has been the wish for some means of visibly projecting Soviet power. However, when it comes to the speedy provision of arms for a client state in trouble, aircraft are the most useful transports. The massive airlift of Russian arms to Ethiopia in late 1977 and early 1978 involved regular flights of some 225 aircraft.

In the October 1973 war in the Middle East, both superpowers provided a spectacular demonstration of the importance of their airlift capabilities. From 14 October to the cease-fire on 25 October approximately 11,000 tons of equipment were delivered to Israel from America, mainly by C-5 and C-141 transport planes. A country at any level other than a superpower could not have mounted such an operation. Even if the air transports were

available, there would not have been the spare stocks of equipment available for transfer. The ability to turn these military supplies on and off as the occasion warrants presents the superpowers with a source of considerable influence over countries that have got themselves, or are about to get themselves, into a scrape. In the case cited above, of the October War, the American government held back supplies from Israel, even as her position began to look desperate, in order to make her more receptive to American guidance on the conditions for a cease-fire.

THE LIMITS
OF MASS DESTRUCTION

Superpower status is therefore derived from the possession of immense military capabilities and the ability to use these capabilities to help a wide range of other states, including some of the great powers of the past, to solve their most pressing security problems. The most substantial and imposing military capabilities of all are nuclear weapons, which have been collected by both superpowers in abundance.

Yet the apparent military supremacy

of the superpowers has to be qualified in some important respects, not only because of the capabilities of other powers but also because of the limited utility of nuclear power itself.

The trouble with nuclear weapons is that they are *too* powerful. They are capable of killing and destroying on an unimaginable scale, and no convincing method has yet been devised – or is ever likely to be devised – to block or neutralize a nuclear attack. The official Soviet view is that a socialist society is better designed to survive nuclear war than a capitalist society. It is doubtful that this official basis for confidence (the eventual triumph of socialism under all circumstances) is allowed by Soviet leaders to influence their plans unduly when it comes to calculating the risks attendant on any moves in the international arena. Both superpowers have secure second-strike capabilities, so neither can attempt to destroy the other without a very good chance of itself being destroyed in the process.

Despite the fact that neither side can hope to achieve a decisive strategic advantage, both undertake energetic development and production programmes to improve and augment their means of nuclear destruction. Part of this effort is prompted by the need to assure a second-strike capability, for example to keep submarines invulnerable or to penetrate ABM defences. It is also prompted by a sense that an appearance of nuclear superiority can be an important asset in international politics, even though this apparent superiority could never be translated into a genuine military victory.

Nuclear weapons are very much subject to a law of diminishing marginal returns, at least in the military sphere. After a while additional nuclear blasts will only, to use Winston Churchill's phrase, make the 'rubble bounce'. Nevertheless, a well-stocked arsenal of the most advanced nuclear weapons, even if most of them would be no more than 'rubble-bouncers', is thought by many politicians to offer a

*Test firing of a 'Minuteman' American ICBM at Cape Canaveral in May 1961.
Any addition to a superpower's arsenal must be announced or demonstrated
if full deterrence credibility is to be obtained*

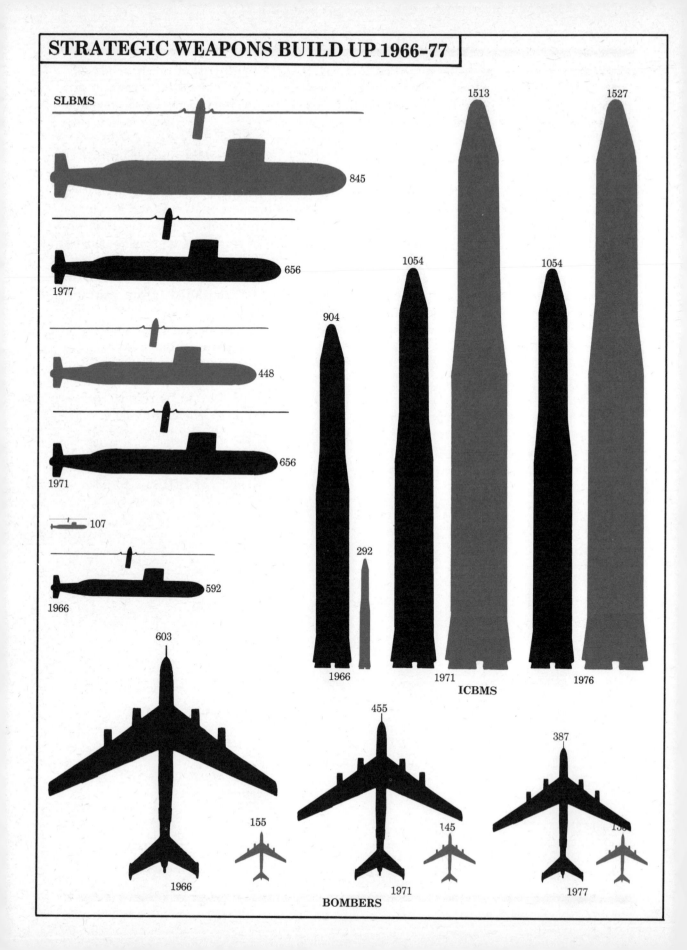

STRATEGIC WEAPONS BUILD UP 1966–77

psychological boost: citizens and allies are reassured, potential adversaries intimidated and waverers impressed.

Unfortunately, because the force structures of the two superpowers are asymmetrical, with great varieties in the quantities and qualities of the different types of weapons, there is no straight-forward method of assessing superiority. The Soviet Union has emphasized land-based weapons and quantity; the United States has a more balanced force, at a higher level of sophistication, but in fewer numbers.

Table I, opposite, shows the buildup of forces since the mid-1960s. Until one looks at the number of warheads, the strongest impression is of the Soviet Union catching up and overtaking the United States in a dramatic fashion. But the United States was the first to develop the technique of MIRVing (through which a warhead is divided into a number of independently-targettable parts) thus gaining, for the moment, a superiority in individual warheads. Because the Russians' missiles are larger and can carry more, they will, as their MIRVing programme proceeds, take the lead by this measure as well. On the other hand the American missiles tend to be more accurate and the American submarine-launched ballistic missile force, though numerically the smaller, is more sophisticated and efficient than the Soviet force.

The Strategic Arms Limitations Talks (SALT) have been preoccupied since 1969 with finding some means of measuring strategic strength so as to get the superpower forces into 'balance'. In the first SALT agreement of 1972 there was a trade between Soviet quantity and American

GROWTH IN US AND USSR STRATEGIC WEAPONS

	1966 US	USSR	1971 US	USSR	1976 US	USSR	1977 US	USSR
ICBMs	904	292	1054	1513	1054	1527	1054	1477
SLBMs	592	107	656	448	656	845	656	909
Bombers	630	155	455	145	387	135	373	135
Total Delivery Vehicles	2126	554	2165	2106	2097	2507		
MIRVed Missiles	—	—	164	—	1046	140		
Independent Warheads on missiles	1496	399	2446	1961	7274	2970		

Source: IISS 'Military Balance, 1976–77'; all figures are for mid-years.

LIKELY SALT II AGREEMENT

1. TREATY TO 1985

Reduction to 2,160–2,250 delivery vehicles.

of which 1,320, MIRVed missiles
or aircraft with cruise missiles
of which 1,200–1,250 MIRVed missiles
of which 820 MIRVed ICBMs

2. PROTOCOL TO 1980

Ban on deployment of mobile ICBM launchers.
Limitations on flight testing and deployment of new types of ballistic missiles.
Limitations on flight testing and deployment of all cruise missiles of range over 2,500 Km and sea and land launched cruise missiles of range over 600 Km

quality. This was not too popular with the American Congress, which wanted quantitative parity. At the time of writing a new SALT II agreement has still to be reached, though there are signs of a compromise formula which will require few adjustments of either sides' current or projected forces and will demonstrate an essential equality (see Table II). If the Americans and the Russians can sort out the finer points, a signed and sealed agreement should have the virtue of dampening the pointless debate over who is really 'ahead'.

The second key limitation on the value of nuclear weapons is that they are only of use in a somewhat narrow range of circumstances. They suffer from what might be called the 'sledgehammer syndrome'. Most military challenges appear as nuts far too small to be cracked with such overwhelming power. Nuclear means can be justified by references only to the rarest of ends, the need to block or deter a direct threat to the survival of the nation – a nuclear attack or a full-blooded conventional invasion. To their employment is attached a particular horror, almost a sense of taboo. So inhibited, the superpowers find their nuclear strength of only marginal importance in many of the crises and challenges they face. It sets them apart from other nations, ensures they can respond in kind to ultimate threats, and results in them taking on the responsibility to cover other nations against such threats. For all threats of a less-than-ultimate nature it has become necessary to resort to more conventional means.

CONVENTIONAL WEAPONS

As for more conventional modes of warfare, the superpowers still have the advantages of numbers and quality which can be used either for their own benefit, or for the benefit of allies. In the Middle East, well-equipped client states have fought battles of a traditional kind to a clear conclusion. But many of the contested regions of the world are agrarian rather than industrial, and warfare is often fought according to ways and means for which large industrial nations are either physically and/or temperamentally unsuited. In Vietnam the United States, materially supreme against all comers, could not overcome the political disadvantages of unpopular and corrupt clients, nor the military disadvantages of being geared to more open and decisive forms of fighting than a protracted guerrilla struggle. Even when, as in Angola, one side apparently triumphs in battle, an opposition that knows its local terrain and has a strong popular base can persist in an irritating and harmful guerrilla warfare. When Russian troops invaded Czechoslovakia they met little armed opposition and so could impose the Kremlin's will. But a similar exercise against an armed population, perhaps in Yugoslavia, could result in a frustrating and costly campaign.

MILITARY FORCE: RUSSIA'S BEST EXPORT?

The Soviet Union needs the military instrument more than the United States. The devotion of so many scarce resources to the creation of a military base comparable to that of the United States has left many sectors of the Soviet economy underdeveloped. Since the late 1960s, the Russians have found it necessary to import Western civilian technology in an effort to modernise their economy. With a controlled home market, operating on the periphery of the international economic system, and providing only meagre financial and technical aid to non-Communist countries, the Soviet Union presents few economic attractions. She can be an extremely valuable ally in the midst of a conflict, providing equipment and advice. Once the fighting stops her value diminishes, with no significant trade, spare foreign exchange, or economic know-how to offer. Here the West scores heavily against the East. Soviet influence in most regions of the world is thus dependent upon a reasonably high level of conflict. When it comes to peacemaking the USSR is often left out in the cold. It is the United States, not the Soviet Union, who is most active in the search for political settlements in the Middle East and Africa.

We noted earlier that in assessing a nation's overall power it is as important to look at areas of vulnerability as areas of strength. We have seen that the two superpowers are only vulnerable in a military sense to each other. This does not mean that everyone else can be taken on with equanimity. The costs of any action, which might involve getting bogged down in a rural or urban guerilla war or a close attachment to a weak and failing regime, have to be weighed against the prospective gains.

Military measures are not the only type of sanctions one state can impose on another. Populations need to be fed; industries need raw materials and energy. The capability to deny the basic essentials of life can be as potent a source of power as preponderant military strength. In terms of food, basic raw materials and energy both superpowers probably have just enough to remain self-sufficient in war-time, given some sacrifices and the use of strategic stockpiles. However, in times of relative peace, when populations are ill-prepared for sacrifices, both superpowers have certain import requirements, which could make them vulnerable to action by the suppliers.

The United States is self-sufficient in food and most raw materials. The major vulnerability is in the area of oil supplies. Demand for oil has now outstripped home supply. Imports, mainly from the Middle East, now meet some 20% of its requirements. The Arab oil embargo that began during the October 1973 war showed how this could be used to coerce the United States. Then only 12% of US oil was imported and the main sufferers were Europe and Japan, but the US position has now deteriorated. Despite attempts by President Carter to reverse this trend, the United States is liable to be dependent upon the goodwill of the oil exporters, particularly Saudi Arabia, for some time to come.

The Soviet Union is self-sufficient in energy. There have been some disputed projections which suggest that she will become an oil importer during the 1980s. The Soviet Union occupies a large portion of the world's crust which makes her wealthy in most minerals. The main physical weakness has been the unimpressive performance of the Soviet agricultural sector. This performance varies from year to year, but in 1973 and 1976 bad harvests forced the Russians to buy from the United States, the world's largest exporter of agricultural produce, pushing up world prices in the process.

The main weakness of the Soviet Union, oddly enough, is political. The Communist Party of the Soviet Union presides over a vast empire, including the satellites of Eastern Europe, which brings together many diverse nationalities and interests. There are many frustrations and resentments simmering away which, perhaps when compounded by economic difficulties, could result in pressure for political change. Much domestic and diplomatic Soviet policy is geared to maintaining tight control of political life in her domain. This includes resisting Western demands for the 'free flow of people and ideas'. Twice in the years since the war, the Kremlin has resorted to military intervention to crush a dissident regime.

Few other problems are susceptible to solution by military means. In order to secure grain the Russians offered diplomatic concessions, and the deal itself reinforced the process of detente by showing that the United States would not take

American wheat for Russia is shipped at Norfolk, Virginia, in 1974 –
a good example of one superpower turning down the chance
to exploit a momentary embarrassment on the part of the other

advantage of a moment of Soviet weakness. In 1974 there was some talk in America of military action to take over Arab oilfields in the event of another embargo; but cool analysis revealed that this would probably worsen the situation, given the opportunities for sabotage of the pipelines or the difficulty of holding on to and running the wells for perpetuity in the middle of a hostile population. The policy is now to rely on the substantial links between the oil-rich Arabs and the Western economies, as a source of moderation.

INVOLVEMENT OR ISOLATION?

In the military sphere the superpowers are pre-eminent. When there is fighting or the prospect of fighting anywhere on the globe both superpowers have to make a policy decision whether or not to get involved because they usually have the capability to get involved. If they do intervene (usually, these days, with equipment, supplies and advice rather than troops), they can usually prevent their side from losing, though they cannot always guarantee that it will win. The recognition that neither superpower could hope to 'win' a nuclear war results in caution. Confrontation between the two usually results in stalemate. Elaborate mechanisms of crisis management have now been developed which allow them to keep most conflicts under control. The whole process of detente requires a modicum of mutual accommodation and a relaxation of tension.

The real danger is that client states will get out of control. Conflicts can develop their own momentum and defy attempts at restraint or peacemaking. In most regions new powers, often the oil-rich, have emerged which can play a complicating role. The superpowers are central to either the continuation or the resolution of most international problems, but their control over events is limited.

If World War 3 begins it is unlikely to be a conscious decision of superpower leaders. More likely they will be dragged into it by ambitious or irresponsible clients in circumstances they, the superpowers, do not fully understand.

2. CRISIS MANAGEMENT

To regard international crises as examples of co-operative action would, at first sight, appear to be absurd. Yet such an assessment would not be wholly inappropriate in relation to confrontations which have occurred between the United States and the Soviet Union during the period since 1945. Crises such as those over Berlin in 1948 and 1961, Cuba in 1962, and the Middle East in 1973, significantly increased the probability of hostilities occurring between the two superpowers. Yet it was precisely because of this heightened danger of war that the Soviet Union and the United States had an incentive to co-operate. As well as being adversaries pursuing conflicting objectives, they were virtually compelled to become partners in the common task of 'disaster avoidance'. The recognition that a large-scale war between them would almost certainly be mutually disastrous led to the development of what can be described as tacit rules of behaviour or codes of conduct designed to facilitate the peaceful resolution of their crises on terms which, if not completely satisfactory, were not wholly unacceptable to either party.

These codes have developed largely on an informal and intuitive basis and have no legal or formal standing. Nevertheless, they have been essential to the regulation, moderation, and control of confrontations which in an earlier period might well have precipitated large-scale hostilities. In certain ways, of course, the rules could be regarded as no more than the art of prudent statesmanship – and to reduce them to a set of simple axioms is not only to oversimplify the complexities involved but also to overlook the wisdom, skill, and expertise of the decision-makers.

There is no ready-made formula for crisis management. Yet the systematic and rigorous way in which these codes of conduct appear to have been followed suggests that there has been an implicit prohibition of certain kinds of action together with an explicit recognition that particular restraints and limitations are essential to the avoidance of war.

Furthermore, the importance of such restraints has been acknowledged by *both* superpowers. Claims that the decision-makers in Moscow are reckless or oblivious to the dangers of nuclear war are hardly borne out by Soviet behaviour. Indeed, successive Soviet leaders have demonstrated an innate caution and a degree of conservatism similar to that of their American counterparts. While both superpowers have been prepared to initiate policies or take actions which carry the risk of precipitating a confrontation, once in a crisis they have shown a marked reluctance to run the risk of war. Perhaps even more remarkable is that this pattern of behaviour prevailed at the height of the Cold War and is far from being a recent innovation. The Berlin Crisis of 1948 established some of the ground rules and, possibly inadvertently, set precedents which were to prove important in subsequent confrontations. What then are these rules.

CODES OF CONDUCT

The first, and one of the most basic, rules of crisis behaviour in the nuclear age concerns the avoidance of overt violence by the participants. In the confrontation over Berlin in 1948 each superpower not only took great care to avoid initiating violence on its own behalf, but also spurned altern-

Eyes across the Wall in divided Berlin –
two East German frontier guards peer through the wire
during the visit to the city in 1965 of Britain's Queen Elizabeth

atives likely to provoke a violent response from the opponent. Thus the Soviet blockade of West Berlin was imposed very gradually and justified on the grounds of 'technical difficulties' with the access routes. Similarly, the United States rejected the option of an armed road convoy to break the blockade. It was felt that this would be a direct challenge to Moscow and one that might result in both Soviet and American soldiers being killed – with dangerously unpredictable consequences. The airlift was a preferable option which allowed President Truman to avoid such a challenge yet simultaneously demonstrate the depth of the American commitment to retain West Berlin. Its other advantage was that it placed the onus for opening hostilities firmly back on the Soviet Union. And 'to disrupt the airlift, which soon acquired its own momentum, Stalin would have had to resort to shooting down planes in the air corridors, that is, to military measures paralleling those Washington had rejected'. It is perhaps not surprising, therefore, that the airlift was not subjected to sustained interference or serious disruption. In a curious sense, caution was contagious. It was also cumulative in its effect. A non-violent Soviet move met by a non-violent American reaction set the pattern for the crisis – and for Stalin then to have changed the rules would have meant a serious intensification of the conflict. Further, had one of the participants resorted to violence it would have been much easier for the opponent to do the same. And to the extent that each of the participants was relying upon the restraint of the other, such a move could only be self-defeating.

AFTER THE AIRLIFT: THE PATTERN REPEATED

By a mixture of good fortune and good judgement the superpowers arrived at a limitation, the significance of which went far beyond the specific circumstances of 1948. Indeed, the threshold between threats or coercion and overt violence was equally central to the peaceful resolution of the Cuban Missile Crisis in October 1962. When considering how to respond to the clandestine installation of Soviet missiles in Cuba, President Kennedy rejected the alternatives of an invasion or an air strike – in large part because the 'quarantine', as it was called, carried a lower prospect of killing Russians. Nor did the Soviet Union make any serious attempt to challenge the blockade, probably because to have done so would have meant provoking an armed clash. As in 1948, each side reciprocated and amplified the desire of the other to avoid hostilities. Both superpowers appear to have believed that to initiate violence would be to spark off a process over which they had little direct control and which might lead ultimately to disaster.

It is understandable, therefore, that in addition to rejecting a calculated resort to violence the superpowers have also been preoccupied with preventing its inadvertent or accidental outbreak. Thus in August 1961, when the Soviet Union sealed off East Berlin it was done in the early hours of a Sunday morning. The timing of the operation was almost certainly deliberate and appears to have been designed to minimise public confusion and popular protest. Uncontrollable riots in East or West Berlin could only exacerbate an already tense situation and this was something that the Soviet leaders wanted to avoid. So concerned were they to minimise the possibility of a dangerous incident that the troops who erected the barriers were not issued with ammunition. Similar anxieties were manifest during the Cuban Missile Crisis; President Kennedy and Secretary of Defense Robert McNamara were not content with merely *formulating* a response but supervised as closely as possible the *implementation* of the blockade in an attempt to ensure that 'needless incidents or reckless subordinates' did not spark off a violent clash at sea.

The prevention of violence is part of a wider problem facing the superpowers – namely, how to maintain control over events. Accordingly, the decision-makers have tended to choose options which enable them to retain at least a degree of control over the developing crisis. Alternatives which have irreversible consequences, which unnecessarily speed up the pace of

The focal-point of a crisis: American and Soviet tanks
stare down each others' gun-barrels at the Friedrichstrasse checkpoint in Berlin
before the Soviet fait accompli *was accepted by the West*

events or which restrict the adversary's freedom to retreat have not readily found acceptance. Nor have high-level policy-makers in Washington and Moscow been willing to relinquish their *own* freedom of action in order to allow allies or sub-ordinates scope for independent initiatives.

It seems probable, for example, that one of the main tasks of the 22,000 Soviet troops present in Cuba in 1962 was to ensure that the missiles remained very clearly under Soviet domination. The last thing Khrushchev wanted was to allow Castro any say in how, when, or if these weapons were to be used. In the 1961 crisis over Berlin the Soviet Union had been careful not to delegate too much authority to the Ulbricht government in East Germany; in October 1962 it was even more careful to relegate Castro to the sidelines and ensure that he could do nothing to intensify the crisis. There was nothing novel about this, however. In the 1958 Quemoy Crisis the Soviet Union had given only very limited support to Peking. Although Khrushchev publicly declared that the United States would not be allowed to attack the Chinese mainland with impunity, he was not prepared to support a Communist invasion of the offshore islands of Quemoy and Matsu. The commitment was very clearly circumscribed. In other words, the over-riding common interest of the superpowers in avoiding war takes precedence over the sensitivities and aspirations of allies, particularly where there is a possibility that authorized actions by these allies can entangle the Soviet Union and the United States so deeply that their room for manoeuvre is limited.

CRISIS BARGAINING

The desire to maintain freedom of action has also had a significant impact on the bargaining process during crises. Although both superpowers want a peaceful outcome of their confrontations, they also have certain objectives for which they are pre-pared to adopt coercive bargaining tactics. At the same time they cannot ignore the dangers inherent in the widespread or in-discriminate use of tactics such as brink-manship or escalation. Thus they have endeavoured to regulate their interactions in a way which not only minimises these dangers but, paradoxically, also renders the bargaining process more effective.

One of the most basic rules of crisis bargaining is not to demand too much of the adversary, not to require him to capit-ulate while conceding nothing in return. Excessive demands are likely to breed intransigence, and if the only alternative to escalation is virtual surrender then the opponent may feel compelled to intensify the conflict. The superpowers have recog-nised this and implicitly acknowledged that traditional notions of 'winning' or 'losing' have little relevance to their con-frontations. So far as possible the adver-sary must be allowed to make some 'gains' as a result of the crisis. Even if these are only token gains they can go a long way to avoiding one side or the other feeling humiliated. As one commentator has ob-served, 'making threats is not enough'.

The bargaining process is not purely coercive: inducements and rewards are an equally important element. Khrush-chev's withdrawal of Soviet missiles from Cuba in 1962, for example, was made easier by the fact that, in return, the United States gave a guarantee not to invade the island. The Middle East Crisis of 1973 saw a similar pattern. Israeli advances prior to, and after, the United Nations cease-fire of 22 October, placed the Egyptian 3rd Army in an extremely vulnerable position and aroused great anxiety among Soviet leaders that a repetition of the crushing Egyptian defeat of 1967 was imminent. When the Americans rejected the Soviet proposal for a joint superpower force to police the cease-fire, Moscow made prepar-

Top: *Caught by America's airborne cameras: Soviet missiles for Cuba, 1962.* Above: *Kennedy announces his reply to Krushchev's Cuban venture: the carefully-worded American 'quarantine' of Cuba*

ations for a unilateral intervention designed to prevent further Israeli gains. The American response was a mixture of conciliation and firmness. United States military forces were alerted in an attempt to *deter* the introduction of Soviet combat forces into the area. At the same time an attempt was made to *reassure* the Soviet Union that there was no need for intervention. Secretary of State Kissinger not only reiterated that the United States was trying to obtain a much stricter observance of the cease-fire, but also agreed to the creation of a special UN force to supervise the cease-fire – so long as Soviet and American forces were not included. This helped to defuse what was potentially a very explosive situation.

It also demonstrated that, in the last analysis, the United States was not in-

sensitive to Soviet vital interests. Indeed, another major rule of crisis bargaining is to avoid trespassing upon the adversary's vital interests. Adherence to this principle was one of the main reasons why the Western response to the erection of the Berlin Wall in 1961 did not go beyond rather perfunctory verbal denunciations. The United States recognized that if the Soviet Union failed to stem the exodus of refugees from East Germany, the viability of the German Democratic Republic could be seriously undermined – with all sorts of resulting instabilities throughout Eastern Europe. The Wall offered the best prospect of eliminating the refugee flow and containing the situation. Consequently, there was no attempt by the United States to interfere with the barricades dividing the city; such a move would have been regarded by the Soviet Union as highly damaging and very provocative. As a result it would almost certainly have elicited a vigorous reaction. The balance of interests in this instance was clearly in favour of Moscow, just as the following year in Cuba it worked to the advantage of Washington. Khrushchev's decision to withdraw the missiles from Cuba was an acknowledgement that while it would have been *advantageous* for the Soviet Union to have the missiles remain there, it was deemed *essential* by the United States that they be removed. This asymmetry of interest was decisive in facilitating the peaceful resolution of the crisis.

CLARIFYING THE ISSUES

Problems arise, however, because such asymmetries are not always apparent at the outset of superpower crises. Consequently, many moves by the participants can be understood as attempts to reveal and accentuate the basic structure of the crisis. Each side has to make clear just how much importance it attaches to the issue in dispute. There is some scope for

manipulation here, of course, as either protagonist may benefit from appearing to have more at stake than is actually the case. The temptations of temporary advantage, however, have not been sufficient to override the common interest in establishing acceptable limits to the bargaining process. Consequently, the superpowers have been concerned far more with clarifying than with obscuring the extent to which their respective interests are involved.

It is in connection with this that communication between the superpowers is so important. Although a great deal of this communication ostensibly takes the form of threats, the purpose is not so much to frighten the adversary as to convey to him the depth of one's concern. Soviet preparations for intervention during the Arab-Israeli war of 1973, for example, were designed primarily to make clear to the United States that the USSR was not prepared to tolerate another victory for Israel on a par with that of 1967. The preparatory military measures were not a substitute for diplomatic communication – rather were they an adjunct to it, re-

Another form of 'quarantine', this one keeping people in, not out:
East German soldiers hard at work strengthening the minefields
and barbed-wire defences of the German People's Republic

inforcing as they did Brezhnev's 'very firm' messages to Washington demanding a greater degree of Israeli restraint.

A further advantage of 'communication moves' of this kind is that they do not restrict either superpower's range of alternatives. Had the Soviet Union actually intervened rather than merely indicating its intention of doing so, the United States could hardly have refrained from responding in kind, with the result that a localized clash between the armed forces of the two superpowers would have been extremely difficult to avoid. Becoming enmeshed in a highly fluid and unstable military situation over which they had little direct control, however, was not something which appealed to the Soviet leaders who were careful to avoid irrevocable actions. Their caution and restraint was underlined by Kissinger in his press conference on 25 October when he stated that the United States was not demanding that the Soviet Union 'pull back from anything it has done'. It had done nothing to pull back from. Furthermore, the United States alert of nuclear and conventional forces mirrored the Soviet move perfectly. Although the decision has sometimes been criticised as a gross over-reaction by the Nixon administration such a charge seems unwarranted. For not only did the alert demonstrate that Washington was not prepared passively to accept a unilateral intervention by Moscow, but – and this is where its value lay – it did so without in any way escalating the conflict or taking it out of the control of the decision-makers on either side.

'Communication moves', then, are a useful substitute for more drastic bargaining tactics which would put the superpowers irretrievably on a collision course. They depend for their success less on their coercive effect than on their ability to highlight the underlying structure of the crisis and the limits of tolerance of the participants. This is not to suggest that more dangerous escalatory and committal tactics are prohibited or excluded completely from either superpower's repertoire. They have, of course, been used, but only in support of the *status quo* or in circumstances where there was a clear asymmetry of interest in favour of the government adopting them.

The Cuban Missile Crisis again provides a good example. The Soviet Ambassador in Washington was given an ultimatum that unless the missiles were withdrawn voluntarily the United States itself would have to remove them. But by this time President Kennedy, both through public statements and the establishment of the blockade, had demonstrated that he meant business. Consequently, there was little room for the Soviet Union to dismiss the threat of escalation as a bluff.

ASSESSING THE OTHER SIDE'S MOTIVES

It should be apparent from this that communication is a vital factor in minimizing the possibility of miscalculation. Success in this task, however, does not depend on communication alone. Above all it demands an ability and willingness to place oneself in the adversary's shoes, to consider how the situation appears from his perspective, and to pay proper regard to his legitimate interests, aspirations and anxieties. Only if a degree of empathy is attained will it be possible to evaluate and interpret signals from the adversary in any meaningful way. Moreover, without this capacity to project oneself into the opponent's 'frame of reference' assessing the implications of one's own actions becomes extremely difficult – and forecasting the adversary's possible response with any degree of success becomes well-nigh impossible. Recognition of this danger has ensured that the superpowers have taken steps to overcome it. For example, it is claimed that during the Cuban Missile

Crisis 'President Kennedy spent more time trying to determine the effect of a particular course of action on Khrushchev or the Russians than on any other phase of what he was doing'. One manifestation of this was the search for a legal basis for the quarantine. Because the Soviet Union was known to respect 'legalities' the United States tried hard to give the blockade a degree of legitimacy – and to a large extent succeeded when the Organisation of American States voted overwhelmingly to support it. That any legal justification for the measure was spurious did not matter so long as the Soviet Union took it seriously.

Sensitivity to the opponent's position and values was an important factor facilitating the communications process during the Cuban Missile Crisis. Yet the process was not without difficulties caused by delay and ambiguity. Thus it is hardly surprising that in the aftermath of the crisis a direct communications link or 'hot line' was installed between Washington and Moscow. The importance of this is difficult to over-estimate. Although it has not outmoded communications through public statements or symbolic actions, it does provide an opportunity for each side to reassure the other about its intentions – and to do so quickly, easily, and privately. Its value was illustrated during the Middle East War of 1967 when a United States communications ship off the Syrian coast was attacked by the Israelis. At first President Johnson and his advisers were uncertain about who was responsible and there was some speculation that the vessel had been attacked by Soviet forces which were about to intervene against Israel.

Nevertheless, when Johnson ordered carrier planes to investigate he used the 'hot line' to inform the Soviet leaders of his action so that *they* could not misinterpret it as the beginning of direct American involvement. And as soon as the United States discovered that Israel was responsible, this too was communi-

cated to Moscow. In other words, communication with the adversary is essential if mistakes, miscalculations and misinterpretations are to be avoided. Keeping open the channels of communication is, therefore, a *sine qua non* of successful crisis management. The same could be said for the other techniques and codes of conduct discussed on previous pages.

KEEPING TO THE RULES

Indeed, these tacit rules of behaviour have been accorded great respect in past confrontations. Skilful and prudent statesmanship, precedent and tradition, the obvious need for restraint, and the fact that transgression by one side would probably lead to similar or further violations by the adversary, have all been important considerations encouraging the emergence and consolidation of certain proprieties and norms of crisis behaviour. Yet such norms have an inherent weakness or vulnerability. If policy-makers in either Washington or Moscow calculate that ignoring them will be more advantageous than continuing to observe them, then disregarded they will be. In other words, they depend for their validity upon the consent of both superpowers; should the consent of either one be withdrawn, the effectiveness of the rules would be totally undermined.

Nor is this the only problem of crisis management. Decision-makers in a crisis are subject to a considerable degree of stress and – although in the past they have coped very well with this – if it is intense enough for long enough it can have a severely debilitating effect, degrading the capacity for fine, discriminating judgement and careful calculation. Furthermore, policy-makers' control over events can never be total. It is enormously difficult to prevent subordinates having at least some discretion in implementing the chosen options, while allies can prove not only devious and unpredictable but also highly resistant to direction by the superpowers. And there is always the possibility of miscalculations and mistakes in bargaining. Even if these pitfalls are avoided the superpowers could still find themselves in a crisis lacking the asymmetries of interest which have proved so essential to the peaceful resolution of previous engagements. Although such dangers were contained in the Cuban Missile Crisis it was the events of October 1962 which, more than any other occurrence, brought home to the superpowers the real possibility of a nuclear holocaust. It is hardly coincidental that the first serious steps toward superpower detente were made in the aftermath of the confrontation. The idea of detente and its various ramifications, therefore, must now be explored more fully.

FROM CRISIS MANAGEMENT TO CRISIS PREVENTION

In the popular mind the idea of detente is probably associated most strongly of all with the existence of on-going arms control negotiations between the two superpowers. The Strategic Arms Limitation Talks, in fact, have become virtually the barometer of detente. When progress is being made in SALT, detente itself is generally regarded as going well; when difficulties or delays arise in the negotiations this is similarly seen as a setback for detente. Certainly the importance of the negotiations should not be under-estimated. Yet their significance lies not only – and perhaps not even primarily – in their concrete achievements but in their very existence. They are a continuing acknowledgement that a meaningful and constructive dialogue between the ideologically opposed superpowers is possible. At the same time it can be argued that the Strategic Arms Limitation Talks have been required to bear too great a burden and have been promoted to the centre of detente

even though they are not fundamental to it.

It is suggested here that the superpower accords reached between 1971 and 1973 – the 'Agreement on Reducing the Risk of Nuclear War' signed in September 1971, the 'Declaration on Basic Principles of Relations' of May 1972, and the 'Agreement on the Prevention of Nuclear War' of June 1973 – are actually more significant than agreements on limiting strategic armaments. Indeed, these accords embody the very essence of detente, which lies in the attempt by the superpowers to transform their relationship from one of mutual emnity moderated only by co-operation during crises to one based on more pervasive collaboration to avoid confrontations.

One of the fullest expressions of this can be found in the 'Basic Principles of Relations' which states, among other things, that 'the USA and the USSR *attach major importance to* preventing the development of situations capable of causing a dangerous exacerbation of their relations. Therefore, they will do their utmost to avoid military confrontations and to prevent the outbreak of nuclear war. They will always exercise restraint in their mutual relations, and will be prepared to negotiate and settle differences by peaceful means'. In June 1973 the superpowers reiterated the same theme but were, if anything, even more explicit and agreed formally to '*act in such a manner as to prevent* the development of situations capable of causing a dangerous exacerbation of their relations'.

The actions and pronouncements of the United States and the Soviet Union during the Yom Kippur War, however, seemed to many critics to cast doubt on the sincerity with which the superpowers regarded these principles. Yet not only is it possible to argue – as is done above – that superpower behaviour during the crisis was marked by caution and prudence rather than recklessness or irresponsibility, but to go even further and suggest that most of the moves made by the United States and the Soviet Union were essentially precautionary. They were designed primarily to ensure that the situation did not deteriorate in a manner liable to drag them into a more direct confrontation. Paradoxically, by the very act of creating a crisis atmosphere, Moscow and Washington underlined their mutual need for co-operation to avert further misunderstandings or miscalculations. Their actions, therefore, can be seen as a mixture of crisis management and crisis prevention.

This point emerges more clearly when the episode is compared with the crisis of October 1962. Kissinger himself, in fact, was quick to state 'we are not talking of a missile crisis type situation'. Perhaps the major difference was that in 1973

neither side tried to achieve a *fait accompli* at the expense of the other. In 1962 the Soviet Union had attempted, but failed, to present the United States with a *fait accompli* through the installation of the missiles in Cuba. Because the missiles were discovered before the process was completed, the United States was able to achieve a surprise of its own with the establishment of the naval blockade. In other words, the actions of the superpowers preceded any serious diplomatic communication between them as each side attempted to strengthen its own negotiating posture to the detriment of the adversary's.

The 1973 crisis saw a very different pattern, with diplomatic communications preceding actions, far less jockeying and clandestine manoeuvring for advantageous positions and no serious attempt by either superpower to make substantial unilateral

Crisis management in action: Henry Kissinger flies in to Tel Aviv in October 1973,
his mission to defuse the crisis
caused by excessive Israeli successes in the Middle East War

gains at the expense of the other. Furthermore, it is significant that the problem was created not by the decisions and actions of the superpowers themselves but by their allies. It was, to a large extent, thrust upon Moscow and Washington by Israeli military success. And whereas earlier crises had been regarded as a mixture of danger and opportunity, the exchanges that occurred between 24–26 October 1973 suggest a far greater preoccupation with minimizing dangers than with maximizing opportunities for advancement. A plausible case can even be made that Soviet and American actions towards the end of the Yom Kippur War were fully in accordance with the clause in the 'Basic Principles of Relations' which acknowledged that 'attempts by either one to obtain unilateral advantage at the expense of the other, directly or indirectly' would be inconsistent with their objective of crisis avoidance.

At the same time, this clause should not be interpreted as a complete prohibition of continued competition between the superpowers. In those circumstances where either side can extend its influence and obtain 'unilateral advantage' without provoking the other sufficiently to bring about a confrontation, then almost certainly it will do so. To expect otherwise would be wishful thinking. Events in Angola demonstrated this very clearly, and it is significant that Soviet involvement there deepened considerably when it became apparent that the Ford administration had been placed in a strait jacket by a Congressional edict cutting off further aid from the United States. Indeed, it has to be acknowledged that superpower recognition of a fundamental common interest in survival does not mean that they have no conflicting interests. The superpower relationship is best understood as an 'adversary partnership'. The United States and the Soviet Union were partners in the task of 'disaster avoidance' even at the height of their hostility in the period up to 1962; by the same token they remain adversaries even during a period of greatly reduced tension.

There may well be occasions, therefore, when despite their genuine desire to avoid crises the superpowers will find themselves unable or unwilling to do so. The 'pressures for confrontation' and the 'temptations to conflict' cannot be discounted; the desire to extend one's influence, the need to prevent encroachments on one's interests, or the need to fulfil obligations to one's allies may prove compelling. And to expect the superpowers to remain merely disinterested spectators when regional conflicts occur is to ignore the dynamics of such conflicts. As S. L. Spiegel comments in *Dominance and Diversity*:

> *'The injunction to avoid involvement on opposite sides is difficult to fulfil because present conditions facilitate progressive commitment, because local conflicts often provide opportunities for superpower gains, because local leaders often manoeuvre to commit one or both of the superpowers to their side, because secondary powers may make tacit superpower collusion difficult, and because the ideological dispositions of local regimes may naturally divide the superpowers'.*

Furthermore, there is always the danger that one of the superpowers will adopt a course of action in the firm belief that it is unlikely to provoke the adversary – only to find that its judgement is mistaken. Although detente has diminished the likelihood of superpower crises, therefore, it does not exclude the possibility of their occurrence. Consequently, the prevention of World War 3 may continue to depend ultimately upon skill in the art of crisis management. It is comforting that in the past the superpowers have proved extremely adept in this task.

PHIL WILLIAMS

3. WEAPONS FOR SALE

ince 1945 (there is little point in going into the more distant past) the United States, Soviet Union, and a few other industrialized states have supplied some of the poorest – and, lately, *per capita* richest – unindustrialized countries with increasingly destructive weapons. In certain strategic conditions, this process could be a contributory cause of, or might even precipitate, World War 3. The supply of such weapons, and of systems designed to aid or outwit them, has accelerated sharply in recent years, and is continuing to do so, as the table on pages 38–9 indicates. Even if the probability of such an arms race causing World War 3 is remote, the possibility certainly exists, particularly if the export of reprocessed nuclear fuels, ostensibly intended for civil purposes, is brought within the meaning of 'supply'.

The process is not adequately described by the phrase 'international arms trade'. In the first place, the process is essentially between governments, not individuals or companies. Anthony Sampson's book *The Arms Bazaar* produces convincing evidence that not more than 5% of the global total supply of weapons is carried on by *entrepreneurs*, or by companies attempting to operate without any form of government backing. Second, although both the United States and Soviet Union sell arms, directly or indirectly, to the Third World, a very high if varying percentage of their deliveries is by way of gift, loan, or barter, needless to say with strings attached. Third, the supply of arms within the two major or strategic alliances of NATO and the Warsaw Pact far exceeds that to the unindustrialized countries. Moreover, although this internal supply

may be economically wasteful and, potentially, strategically dangerous, it is governed by certain concepts of strategic balance and, *between* the alliances, communications, which do have deterrence and conflict limitation value. Further, as a standard work points out: "Within the main alliances, arms supplies are not used as instruments of policy in the same way as in trade with third world countries.'

The unindustrialized Third World countries have not, on the whole, reached the stage where the concept of strategic balance is either understood or forms part of policies. The arms are for *use*, and restraint is more likely to be due to superpower pressure in terms of refusal to supply than fear of escalating conflict as such. It should be remembered that although the policies of Third World countries vary, the most active among them share certain characteristics. They seek territory, or prestige, or regional power, or all three, disguising these ambitions in terms of (sometimes legitimate) 'national security interests'.

Broadly speaking, as far as the supply of arms from the superpowers and others to the Third World is concerned, we may say that the World War 3 dangers from this process are twofold – and complementary. The greater danger is that a virtually unlimited *and unbalanced* supply of arms might lead to conflict which could only be limited by the direct but possibly competitive intervention of the superpowers. The lesser danger lies in a Third World country's inability to prevent internal conflict – intensified by a flow of arms to various contestants – causing regional conflict. The greater danger is illustrated by various aspects of the Middle East situation; the lesser by that in the Horn of

THE NUMBER OF STATES DEPLOYING ADVANCED MILITARY EQUIPMENT, BY REGION, 1965-75[1]	NATO		Warsaw Pact		Other Europe		Africa		East Asia		South Asia		Middle East[2]		Latin America		Oceania		Total	
	'65	'75	'65	'75	'65	'75	'65	'75	'65	'75	'65	'75	'65	'75	'65	'75	'65	'75	'65	'75
Supersonic aircraft	12	12	6	7	5	5	1	7	5	11	2	4	5	13	1	7	1	1	38	67
Submarines[3]	11	12	3	3	2	3	0	1	3	5	0	1	2	3	5	6	0	1	26	37
Major surface combatants[4]	10	10	1	2	2	2	1	2	4	7	2	2	1	2	5	6	2	2	28	35
Medium/heavy tanks	13	13	7	7	5	5	5	9	9	11	3	4	11	14	14	16	1	1	68	80
Anti-shipping missiles	0	11	4	5	1	4	0	2	2	10	0	1	1	8	0	6	0	1	8	48
Surface-to-air missiles	12	13	7	7	3	4	0	5	4	8	1	3	3	9	1	2	1	2	32	53
Surface-to-surface missiles[5]	9	9	7	7	0	0	0	0	2	4	0	0	0	3	1	1	0	0	19	24

[1]Figures for 1975 include states which have specified category of equipment on order, but have not necessarily received or deployed it.
[2]Includes Gulf states.
[3]Includes nuclear and conventional-powered types.
[4]Includes vessels exceeding 1,500 tons built or refurbished after World War II.
[5]Includes missiles with maximum ranges exceeding 20 statute miles.

Africa, and in Rhodesia.

With very partial exceptions, the Third World cannot produce its own arms at all, or unaided, except those needed for routine internal security tasks. This dependence on the major suppliers of arms has assumed a relationship of seemingly indefinite duration, as arms grow in complexity. (Whether they increase in overall effectiveness for the attainment of their users' objectives is another matter.) It often seems to be assumed, therefore, that the major suppliers are fully aware of the implications and consequences of this dependent relationship, and can control it by regulating the flow of arms to influence or coerce their clients, and to increase the security of both supplier and recipient.

This rather naïve 'Western' view of international security has been revealingly expressed in the doctrine set out by President Nixon in 1971: 'We will look to threatened countries and their neighbours to assume primary responsibility for their own defense, and we will provide support where our interests call for that support and where it can make a difference'. The weakness of the Nixon doctrine, however – and, in practice, it still operates today – is that it takes no account of the strategic motives of the Soviet Union, the economic motives of the non-superpower arms suppliers, or the commercial and domestic political power of the American arms industry.

The Soviet Union not only provides arms, but intervenes directly, or with satellite forces, when the gains appear to be worth the risks. The non-superpower suppliers sustain their domestic arms industries (and hence partly their domestic economies as a whole) by exports. In consequence, these suppliers seek markets, and security or strategic considerations are sacrificed in the process. The American arms industry, although dependent on government for orders – and much else – sells so aggressively abroad that security and strategic considerations are sacrificed by this process also. In short, not only is there a lack of strategic balance between Third World countries actually or potentially in conflict, but the understanding which exists between the United States and the Soviet Union in superpower terms (and their allies and satellites concerning NATO and the Warsaw Pact) is lacking when it comes to issues in the Third World.

So much for preliminaries. To consider what has actually happened since the Third World arms race accelerated requires a distinction to be drawn between the Middle East and all other areas. This distinction is important at all points –

20 YEARS OF ARMS IMPORTS: WHERE THE WEAPONS WENT

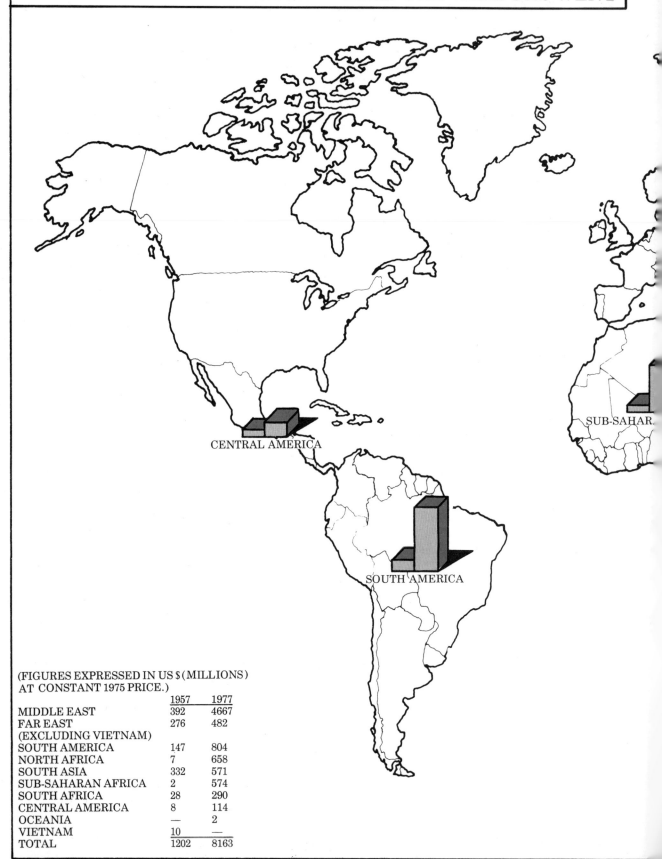

CENTRAL AMERICA

SOUTH AMERICA

SUB-SAHARA

(FIGURES EXPRESSED IN US $(MILLIONS)
AT CONSTANT 1975 PRICE.)

	1957	1977
MIDDLE EAST	392	4667
FAR EAST	276	482
(EXCLUDING VIETNAM)		
SOUTH AMERICA	147	804
NORTH AFRICA	7	658
SOUTH ASIA	332	571
SUB-SAHARAN AFRICA	2	574
SOUTH AFRICA	28	290
CENTRAL AMERICA	8	114
OCEANIA	—	2
VIETNAM	10	—
TOTAL	1202	8163

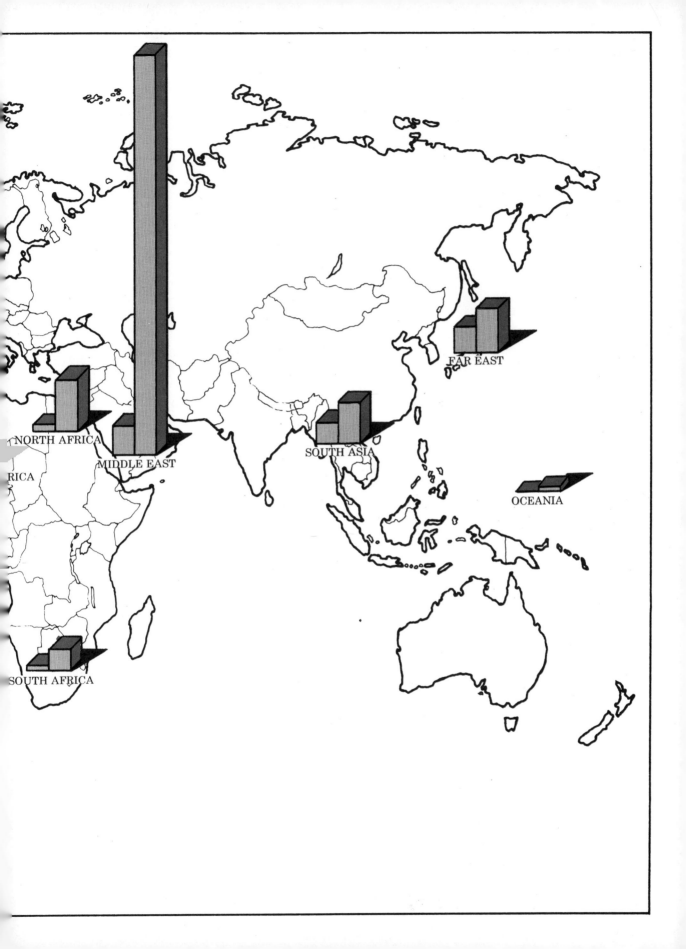

NORTH AFRICA

RICA

MIDDLE EAST

SOUTH ASIA

FAR EAST

OCEANIA

SOUTH AFRICA

Not one single-shot rifle in sight: Angolan UNITA soldiers show off a frightening variety of imported firepower – automatic rifles, mortars, machine-guns and anti-tank missiles

numbers, types, and costs of arms; frequency and intensity of conflict; implications for the superpowers. If conflict is measured by protracted human suffering caused by indiscriminate use of weapons, the American involvement in Vietnam stands alone. This conflict, however, reflects an almost entirely American attempt to defeat regional Communist aggression (or intervention, according to one's point of view.) Two particular characteristics of that conflict put it beyond the scope of the international arms trade and its strategic implications, as considered here. First, although a huge quantity of arms was supplied by the United States to Vietnam, this was part of and usually subordinated to direct American involvement. Second, although the conflict had, and has, many superpower implications – above all, perhaps, the loss of American credibility as a power which knows *how* to fight a limited war – it did not threaten to bring about World War 3.

The Soviet Union's relative caution over Vietnam was doubtless governed by its dispute with China, but may also be seen as an instance of one superpower watching the other dig a pit for itself. The American belief that sheer firepower must produce victory – a legacy of World War 2 – is, however, relevant to the supply of arms for deterrence or use in various Middle East theatres. The accompanying tables show clearly enough how the Middle East dominates the international arms trade, above all, perhaps, in the supply of weapons – including medium-range ballistic missiles, although with conventional warheads – which compare closely with those supplied to NATO and the Warsaw Pact. Arms supplied by the Soviet Union are, relatively, simpler in construction and maintenance terms than those supplied by the United States and others, but they are designed for major war purposes nonetheless.

These have been, and are supplied to

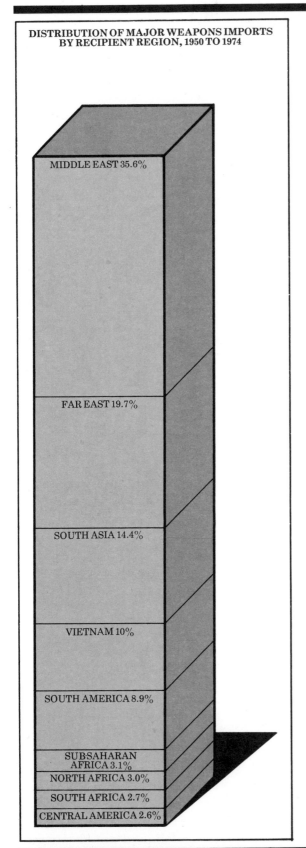

DISTRIBUTION OF MAJOR WEAPONS IMPORTS BY RECIPIENT REGION, 1950 TO 1974

MIDDLE EAST 35.6%

FAR EAST 19.7%

SOUTH ASIA 14.4%

VIETNAM 10%

SOUTH AMERICA 8.9%

SUBSAHARAN AFRICA 3.1%

NORTH AFRICA 3.0%

SOUTH AFRICA 2.7%

CENTRAL AMERICA 2.6%

armed forces whose power to achieve decisive results is limited by political and morale factors, not by geography or climate. The four wars between Israel and Arab states since 1948 show fairly conclusively that the limiting factors have been the relative restraint exercised by Israeli forces when the tactical situation was clearly in their favour, and the inability of Arab forces to operate and maintain modern arms to the required standards. Indeed, these arms have probably weakened the always uncertain morale of Arab forces, except in the early stages of the 1973 war, when victory appeared to be within their grasp. It should be noted, nevertheless, that the regular forces of the Arab states continue to believe in complex arms – arguably, as a reflection of their role in societies which hope to industrialize eventually – whereas Arab guerilla forces have grasped that relatively simple weapons can be effective when the Israelis choose, or are forced, to rely on firepower to an unusual degree for the nature of the conflict in question. The Israeli advance into southern Lebanon in March 1978 demonstrates quite clearly that when the Israelis become especially loth to risk casualties, newfound belief in the effectiveness of sheer firepower is also disproved by events.

The important question for us here, however, is not the nature of the arms supplied to Middle East countries – and specifically in the Arab/Israel context – or how they are used, but whether or not the *suppliers* can, and do, exercise some 'extra-legal' control and also impose some limitation on the conflicts. It is also important to distinguish between control which is, or may, be exercised by refusal to supply or re-supply, and control which may derive from providing weapons or equipments which redress a situation in favour of offensive strategies, tactics, and actual operations – or *vice versa*.

In considering these variations of control, the interests of suppliers and recipients may coincide or diverge. Because of these factors – complicated in themselves, and made more so by their relationship to each other in a dangerously unstable part of the world – the arms supplied have to be considered afresh in terms of their real, or supposed, *deterrent* value. In short, if 'suppliers' control' is to mean anything, the logic of events demands that states which are in actual or potential conflict come to accept a strategic balance. Whatever the *casus belli*, these states must learn to accept each other's existence, as do those in NATO and the Warsaw Pact.

The Arab/Israeli conflicts to date show that negative supplier control, or the *refusal* to do something is a meaningless threat, and certainly does not affect conflicts as such, politically or militarily. The superpowers have too much at stake in the Middle East to allow the countries which they supply to be defeated outright in war. Thus Egypt was rearmed by the Soviet Union in the 1950s, after 1967, and during the 1973 war. Israel was not only resupplied by the United States at a critical moment in the 1973 war, but has been extensively re-equipped since then. These superpower decisions have neither prevented nor limited conflict. What the arms supplied since 1967 have done, however, is to alter the nature of the Arab/Israel conflicts. In this connection, the 1969–70 'war of attrition' across the Suez Canal, the role of quite simple, infantry-operated anti-aircraft and anti-tank missiles, and the electronic and surveillance equipments supplied to the Israelis, have come to assume a growing importance in the *deterrent* sense. It is doubtful whether the United States and Soviet Union have consciously shifted from negative to positive control – or, to define the latter more usefully, positive strategic influence – and even more doubtful if they have done so in tacit understanding. Nevertheless, there is a shift to positive strategic influence, and

this is something to be welcomed not only in connection with the Arab/Israel dispute but for the Middle East as a whole.

There is little doubt that this shift is in the interests of the United States, whose concern for even a semblance of Middle East stability is as painfully obvious as is its dependence on Middle East oil. The shift is in the interests of the Soviet Union to the extent that it seeks superpower detente, and fears the consequences of a Middle East conflict getting entirely out of control. The shift, however, may also suit the interests of the Soviet Union in its role of supporting revolution. A Middle East strategic balance does not preclude revolutionary activity; indeed, it may even encourage it. (The growing similarity to the situation in Europe is worth noting.) The shift, however, will also be in the interests of other suppliers if the superpowers gradually reach understanding on a Middle East strategic balance. The other suppliers, seemingly less aware of the gravity of the issues at stake, will try to provide what the superpowers refuse, or provide only in order to maintain an offensive/defensive balance.

Britain and France, in particular, appear singularly anxious to co-operate with the Arab Industries Organisation for the supply and, subsequently, production in the Arab world of supersonic aircraft, missiles, and other arms. It could be argued that the Arab countries will never accept the concept of balance while the United States provides Israel with the most advanced arms and equipment but hesitates to do the same for Egypt. The superpowers have neither the prerogative of strategic wisdom nor such a domination of arms technology that a role for other industrialized countries in relation to Middle East security is automatically ruled out. But if Britain and France (or any other non-superpower) intend to sell more arms in the Middle East they should understand that they can either contribute to the establishment of or assist with destruction of a strategic balance. If such suppliers pursue merely economic or commercial aims the chances of such a balance being achieved are remote.

The reason why a certain responsibility should always govern arms supplies to the Middle East is the prevailing temptations of or, as Israel has argued, necessities for pre-emptive strategies. It is this factor which makes the establishment of a strategic balance extremely difficult. Surveillance – and UN or other observers – may reduce the temptation or limit the necessity, but neither mechanical ingenuity nor the presence of observers can alter the fact of geography. Israel, small and surrounded, is a prime pre-emptive target, with little possibility of deterring such an attack by the mere possession of second-strike weapons. Egypt has not hitherto pre-empted in this fashion, restricting its air strikes in 1973 to the Bar-Lev Line and its rear. From such restraint it could be argued that it is Egypt's medium-range missiles which are a second-

strike weapon – to deter or to respond to an Israeli pre-emptive strike of unlimited dimensions.

Israel, however, has not been deterred, and although its pre-emptive attacks in 1967, and those in 1969–70 and in 1973 were controlled, the fact is that deep penetration *city* bombing (Cairo, Alexandria, and Damascus) took place. It is in this context, therefore, that the 'ultimate' aspect of supplying arms to the Middle East must be considered. Nuclear weapons are not usually considered as part of the international arms trade, but this is an illogical omission for reasons which apply with particular force to the Middle East. Arab governments seem united in the belief that Israel actually has nuclear weapons, not merely the capacity to make them. Precisely because these governments may come to accept the necessity for a strategic balance – *or* seek a decisive advantage – this nuclear factor must be considered. If an opinion may be offered here, Israel's probable continued strategic advantage in real operational terms would not seem to

Fire-power of the larger variety: US M110 3-inch self-propelled howitzers.
These tracked heavyweights are capable of firing nuclear as well as conventional projectiles

East of Suez, made in Britain: BAC Lightning fighters of the Royal Saudi Air Force

require the maintenance of an ambiguous stance over nuclear weapons. But, by the same token, Britain and France – or any other state with nuclear capacities – should undertake not to supply re-processed nuclear fuels to Arab governments.

The nuclear danger may not be acute in the context of the Arab/Israeli dispute, but it is present. Elsewhere in the Middle East, however, there exists today a dangerous situation which the United States has the major responsibility for alleviating. Specifically, the huge increase in arms supplies from the United States to Iran and Saudi Arabia threatens the establishment, let alone the preservation of a strategic balance in the terms discussed in the preceding five paragraphs, and does so for two reasons: the Arab/Israeli dispute directly or indirectly affects other simmering disputes in the area; the degree of control which can be exercised in order to prevent arms supplied to one Arab country being transferred to another is, in reality, extremely limited. Moreover, there is no standardized legal control imposed by the United States on recipients' use of arms in conflicts. Hence the burden on the United States to be something more than 'even-handed' in relation to specific and simmering disputes is quite extraordinarily heavy.

Unfortunately, it is true that the present American arms and equipments supply practices are characterized by a mixture of commercial opportunism and rather inadequate attempts to impose some some kind of control. Opportunism characterizes the situation in Iran; inadequate control machinery reflects the complexities of the United States' relations with Saudi Arabia. It is important to review the arms situation for and in these potentially hostile Middle East countries, because doing so tells us a good deal about the realities of the international arms trade. The truth of this observation is revealed by recent United States Congressional investigations of arms supply to Iran and Saudi Arabia. The situations which the reports of these investigations describe goes a long way to explain why there should be increasing concern for establishing a superpower balance, not only a strategic one in armaments and systems terms, for the Middle East as a whole and for its component parts.

Since President Sadat cut his ties with the Soviet Union after the 1973 war, we have witnessed not only an American domination of the area so far as arms supplies are concerned (one might say, for Iran and Saudi Arabia, so far as the role of a new 'military society' is concerned), but a virtual, if reluctant domination of the diplomatic scene as well. It is unlikely that the Soviet Union will accept this situation indefinitely, if only because the United States is rapidly reaching the exposed position where pledges of support have been given to all. The odium which eventually but inevitably attaches to policies based on promise and not performance – the essence of the Nixon doctrine – must mean that Middle East societies will remain susceptible to Soviet influence. All other factors apart, there is enough internal dissatisfaction with Arab governments' and the Shah's for the Soviet Union to become again, or more openly, a supporter of revolutionary forces – but with rather more destructive weapons at their disposal, let alone for seizure, than has hitherto been the case.

IRAN: THE FIGHT FOR SALES

If we look at Iran we find a revealing case of understandable American objectives regarding that country (maintenance of good relations and indirect assistance in preserving both internal and external security) distorted by a literal adherence to the Nixon doctrine. Indeed, as the *Congressional Report on Iran* states, 'In May, 1972, President Nixon and the then National Security Advisor Kissinger, agreed for the first time to sell Iran virtually any conventional weapons it wanted . . .' As a result, 'Iran is the largest single purchaser of US military equipment'. The *Report* adds that 'The 1972 sales decision coupled with the increase in Iranian revenues following the quadrupling of oil prices created a situation not unlike that of bees swarming round a pot of honey'. As a further result, American arms manufacturers have supplied Iran's armed forces with weapons and systems they neither needed nor can operate – in some cases did not even seek – to an extent, in fact, that some items are not yet fully operational with US forces but have nevertheless been provided for Iran on a scale which has put strains on

those forces. The strains result, of course, from the fact that American technicians, increasingly in uniform, are needed to maintain the Iranian forces at even a nominal operational state. As has been well said, 'The possession of sophisticated weapons does not necessarily enhance the military capability of a developing country'.

It will be argued by those who defend this flood of material that Iranian dependence ensures American control. But the logic of this argument is that Iran will accept a dependent status *in conflict*, and will allow its pretensions as a 'regional power' to remain at the level of rhetoric. Even supposing this to be so, the type of arms provided for Iran poses a more subtle problem. Inability to handle complex arms weakens Iran against an aggressor who can do so. A pre-emptive strategy, therefore, is imposed on Iran. Yet recourse to such a strategy would be suicidal for Iran in relation to the Soviet Union and pointless regarding Saudi Arabia. The Soviet Union could wreak vengeance; Saudi Arabia is an oilfield, which cannot be destroyed. It will also be said that Iran will not find itself at war with the Soviet Union or Saudi Arabia. In that case, what is the reason for the possession of weapons whose cost has robbed Iran of economic progress? It is surely a question which is part of the United States' responsibilities for the Middle East to answer.

When we turn to the *Congressional Report on Saudi Arabia* (and other sources), a simpler set of relationships is shown as establishing some kind of American control. Nevertheless, this source material is also not particularly reassuring about Middle East stability. It is clear that, unlike Iran, the Saudi Arabian defence budget is not threatening to wreck the economy, and that although the most advanced weapons are being solicited – and, partly, provided – the emphasis is on the defensive variety. Moreover, despite some well publicized arms deal scandals, the control of the United States Government over the *supply* of arms to Saudi Arabia would appear to be much more effective than in the case of Iran. Above all, Saudi Arabia, as represented by the ruling establishment, does not suffer from strategic delusions of grandeur. That factor, together with a degree of dependence on American skills which is accepted, although resented, is probably the best guarantee there is now and for the immediate future of workable US/Saudi relations. *This* relationship could be said to validate the argument that the supplier of arms can meet his own strategic objectives and decide those of the recipient. But US/Saudi relations are by no means static.

Moreover, there are other elements in the US/Saudi relationship which must be considered. Saudi Arabia's rulers may be sensible about regional power status, but they are virtually being forced into the position of a front line state opposing Israel. There is no *guarantee* that the Saudi air force will not be involved in a fifth war. Its aircraft could only operate for a few days, but this factor has pre-emptive dangers. The factor does not mean a firm American hand on the Saudi safety-catch. In the course of intensive exchanges with Congressmen during the investigation into sales to Saudi Arabia, Lieutenant General Fish (Director of the Defense Security Assistance Agency) argued that Saudi Arabia would not engage in conflict, and if it did 'we would cut off support'. That argument simply begs the question, and the exchanges provide plenty of evidence to show that the Saudi Government considers itself free to order its air force to do that which is in the interests of *Arab* countries which are opposing Israel.

General Fish certainly demonstrated that his Government believed that an 'even-handed' arms supply policy for the Middle East was possible. However, such a policy requires co-operation – or abstention – by other arms suppliers. As noted above, Britain and France are planning arms deals which would transfer military technology to Arab countries, and thus render the concept of controlling the *recipient* quite meaningless. Some would argue that it will be many years before an Arab – or any other unindustrialised region's – arms industry is established. Others would say that the real deterrents to unlimited Middle East conflict are diplomatic, economic, and political – overall American leverage, and lack of Arab unity in particular. However, even with these qualifications, it is a fair summary of the issues dealt with to this point to say that supplying complex arms to countries which cannot operate them in sustained – if still limited – conflict increases the risk of their being used to pre-empt an opponent.

We must therefore consider what methods can be devised and enforced for preventing the *use* of very dangerous weapons in the hands of Third World countries, above all in the Middle East. One obvious method, of course, is to supply fewer arms, and confine these to demonstrably limited purposes. It is no rebuttal of this argument to say that if, for example, the United States reduced its arms supplies to Third World countries, other producers would supply the same arms in its place. Arms supplies, their causes and effects are not processes which exist in a vacuum; they reflect a variety of supplier/recipient motives and capacities for achieving changes in national or regional security situations. The facts of the matter are, as we have seen, that the United States, Soviet Union, and European manufacturers supply arms for substantially different purposes, and it is upon this political and strategic reality that a valid case can be made for the United States either to give a lead in the reduction of supplies or to set about this on an international basis – possibly by some extension of SALT for areas where the introduction of nuclear weapons into national armouries is a distinct possibility.

It should also be pointed out that a study of two far from stable Third World areas – Latin America and India/Pakistan – reveals a considerable degree of caution by the United States regarding the former and by that country and the Soviet Union regarding the latter. There are particular historical circumstances which make it relatively easy to the United States to maintain a balance of forces in Latin America. By the same token, the comparable standards of the Indian and Pakistani armed forces (plus some awareness of the wider issues at stake amongst the two countries' leaders) has to date ensured that conflicts have remained at a certain level.

It is very clear that none of these factors applies to the Middle East, bearing in mind the various causes of conflict which have characterized that area for some time. It is even more clear that suppliers' attempts to control recipients' use of arms – whether the latter is direct or by transfer – are unlikely to succeed. The practice of President Carter's administration appears nevertheless to be based on a belief that an 'even-handed' supply within the context of a strategic balance has some kind of deterrent and/or limitation value, and that if such supply is coupled with warnings about the penalties attaching to use in certain conflicts or transfer in certain conditions, the recipients will take heed and act with the desired prudence. The Israeli investment of southern Lebanon in March 1978 illustrates the importance which the Carter administration attaches to this mixture of persuasion and threat. It was in this period that President Carter urged Congress to approve his 'package': F16s to Israel; F15s to Saudi Arabia; F5Es to Egypt. This package reflects an attempt at even-handed supply, but is based essentially on the contradictory supposition that Egypt will be satisfied with a relatively inferior weapon provided Saudi Arabia gets a superior one – but does not use or transfer it in a conflict situation.

During March 1978 it was also reported that the use by Israel of weapons supplied by the United States might inhibit further supplies. This threat has been tried before (in the 1969–70 period of Phantom bombing raids, SAM defences, and electronic countermeasures) and did not work. This threat failed, not because Israeli governments are unaware of or indifferent to pressure from Washington, but because they believe, rightly or wrongly, that their country's security requirements force them to resist it. Here again we have a political reality, one which reflects the role of a superpower towards a state whose security cannot be ignored.

Eventually, therefore, arguments about control must concentrate on the *needs* of the actual or potential recipients. But a critical element in that control argument is the relationship between government and industry in supplying countries, because commercial and strategic definitions of 'need' are somewhat different. Much must be done to improve this relationship in Europe, but, inevitably, it is in the United States where the paramount role of government has to be made absolutely unequivocal. Even assuming 'even-handedness' to be a definable and a feasible policy, it is obvious that it cannot be sustained unless there is complete official knowledge and supervision of all transactions at all times. What has happened in Iran could happen in Saudi Arabia. The assurances given by General Fish and others reflect nothing more than an assumption that the commercial end of the arms business can never upset the strategic balance. There is a long history of conflict to disprove this assumption, and it is an urgent task for a United States government to base arms sales policies solely on a credible foreign policy.

ANTHONY VERRIER

4. NUCLEAR PROLIFERATION

On 18 May 1974, a nuclear device, officially described as 'peaceful' in character, was detonated in the Rajasthan desert in the north-east of India. The blast of 10 to 15 kilotons was just smaller than the size of the blast that destroyed Hiroshima. It was carried out underground to conform with the international prohibition on atmospheric nuclear tests. India has not detonated another device since and her capacity for fully exploiting the military potential of her nuclear energy programme remains unclear. She is still a long way from being classified as a nuclear power, which requires a stockpile of weapons and the means of delivering them to targets as well as the open acknowledgement of this capability.

Whatever the benefits to India's nuclear energy programme or sense of national security and pride, the explosion in Rajasthan made a significant impact on international thinking on a problem which had been suffering from neglect. In 1970 the Non-Proliferation Treaty (NPT) had come into force. The purpose of this Treaty was to halt the spread of nuclear weapons, holding the line at the five acknowledged nuclear powers of the time – America, Britain, China, France and Russia. To persuade the non-nuclear countries to accept continued abstinence they had been offered access to the civil benefits of nuclear technology, guarantees of protection against threats to national security and a vague promise from the nuclear 'haves' that they would take some steps in the future to bring themselves down to the level of the 'have-nots'. An elaborate system of international safeguards had been developed, organised by the International Atomic Energy Agency (IAEA) to check nuclear facilities to ensure that no fissionable materials were being diverted to military purposes.

The NPT system was recognised to be imperfect. China and France, who had developed their own nuclear weapons in opposition to the philosophy of non-proliferation refused to sign and many of the most likely proliferators withheld their signatures, or at least their ratifications. Other flaws were noted in the system: the IAEA safeguards, though efficiently operated, were by no means watertight; even countries that had ratified the Treaty could withdraw after three months notice; the superpowers showed little inclination to make any serious concessions towards the 'cessation of the nuclear arms race at an early date and to nuclear disarmament, and on general and complete disarmament under strict and effective international control' as promised in Article VI of the Treaty. Nevertheless, the prevailing mood was complacent. There was no obvious groundswell of opinion amongst the non-nuclear powers in favour of changing their status, let alone blatant moves in this direction. Early preparations were being made for a conference to review the NPT, scheduled for 1975, in an atmosphere of indifference.

INDIA'S EXPLOSION: THE LESSONS

The Indian explosion of May 1974 came as a rude shock. An international concensus on preserving the nuclear *status quo* could no longer be taken for granted. The Indians had demonstrated key weaknesses in the NPT system. They had used material from a reactor, provided by the Canadians, but which lacked safeguards. The Canadians had not insisted on regular inspections, having been convinced that this was a patronising attitude to take towards a Third World country. In addition, by claiming their explosion to be 'peaceful', the Indians had indicated a strategy which could allow the full development of a nuclear capability while diverting international condemnation. The nation that tested devices with the proclaimed intention of developing a military capability would incur opprobrium. But there was now no need to make intentions so obvious: the same capability could be developed under cover of a peaceful purpose, perhaps for mining or the construction of a canal. Though American specialists had become sceptical as to the practical utility of nuclear explosions for civil engineering, this had not always been the case, and there were still many in the Soviet Union who were not sceptical. So 'peaceful' nuclear explosions (PNEs) could not be dismissed too easily as an excuse for military developments.

Among those concerned about the spread of nuclear weapons the fear grew that India was setting new, low standards. Following this example, other states might resist a safeguards regime and detonate their own devices, while providing reassurance of their peaceful intent. A more specific anxiety was that other states in close proximity to India would sense a deterioration in their security position which could only be remedied by nuclear programmes of their own. In Pakistan, most immediately threatened by any improvement in India's military capabilities, Prime Minister Bhutto insisted that his country now had no option but to take the nuclear road. He promised to 'eat leaves or grass, even go hungry, but we will have to get one of our own. We have no alternative'. There were murmurings in Japan that it was unacceptable to accept a lower status in Asia than India, so less imposing in every other respect, because of the supposed allergy to anything to do with nuclear weapons, a result of the devastating experiences of Hiroshima and Nagasaki.

The Indians created a general awareness that nuclear abstinence could not be taken for granted. In the writings of informed Indians could be found general criticisms of the nuclear monopoly of the major powers and against the inequality of rights and obligations between nuclear and non-nuclear powers contained in the NPT. As France and China had argued before them, the Indians wrote of the dangers of being beholden to the superpowers for military protection and of the national independence that could come from a nuclear programme. One leading proponent of an Indian 'bomb', K. Subrahmanyam, has written of 'the growing view that in the rough and tumble of international power politics, India has been the victim of unfair use of force by other nations'; of the need to prepare 'to live in a possibly hostile and probably unpredictable world by keeping the nuclear-weapons option open'; of the need for any nation–state to 'develop national power commensurate with its size and population'; of the need to develop nuclear power 'to be taken seriously at the international disarmament table'. On reflection, there appeared a number of other states for whom these or similar arguments might prove attractive: Israel, Egypt, South Africa, Brazil, Argentina and Pakistan. All of these remained outside of the NPT system. The mood of complacency turned into one approaching panic, in anticipation of a nuclear epidemic.

It was not solely the Indian explosion that prompted the change of mood. Two other international trends played their part. The first was the increasing importance of nuclear reactors as a means of coping with the energy crisis brought on by the dramatic rise in the price of oil that began in late 1973. In the rush for alternatives to oil, plans were drawn up for nuclear energy programmes which would result in the dispersion of the relevant technology and facilities in large quantities to many parts of the world plus the associated movement of nuclear fuels to and from these facilities. The opportunities to 'go nuclear' would increase. Second, there might well be increasing reason to 'go nuclear' in the future. The débâcle in Vietnam suggested that the United States might not be willing or able to honour its obligations to friendly states in trouble. With pressure to cut down on America's responsibilities abroad growing in Congress and the detente process leading to a close relationship with the Soviet Union, it seemed likely that states which had previously relied upon the United States for nuclear protection might have to look to their own devices and to their own armouries.

'PEACEFUL' NUCLEAR ENERGY: THE DANGERS

The international effort to control the spread of nuclear weapons has been concentrated, in recent years, on capabilities rather than intentions. The preferred method has been to develop a set of technological 'fixes' that would prevent any non-nuclear power from ever achieving a nuclear option. The problem with this method is that it can contradict the deal made in the Non-Proliferation Treaty to ensure that those who renounced the military nuclear way benefited from the peaceful advantages of nuclear technology.

A number of non-nuclear weapon states have ambitious programmes to develop nuclear energy which require facilities beyond simple reactors. States which rely on enriched uranium for their reactors and wish to ensure continued supply may want their own enrichment plant. Those concerned about wasting the plutonium contained in the used fuel rods taken from their reactors may want a reprocessing facility to separate out this plutonium to use again as a fuel. The trouble is that both these processes provide opportunities for the production of weapons-grade nuclear materials denied to those who only possess reactors. Whether because of concern over energy needs in the coming decades or a desire to build nuclear weapons, a number of countries wish to own these sensitive nuclear technologies. And at a time of economic recession it is not surprising that some technologically advanced Western states have been ready to enter into billion-dollar deals to supply the requisite facilities.

Less than a month after the conclusion of the NPT Review Conference a deal was announced in which Germany would provide a complete nuclear fuel cycle to Brazil, a non-signatory to the NPT, in exchange for a guaranteed supply of natural uranium and a large amount of dollars (estimates at the time suggested the deal was worth some $4 billion in export contracts). Meanwhile similar deals were being negotiated by the French with Pakistan and South Korea. This activity caused considerable consternation. The Americans objected vociferously and managed to get the France/South Korea deal, for a plant, called off.

The evidence that the nuclear trade was starting to embrace the transfer of sensitive nuclear technologies gave impetus to a secret group, known as the London Suppliers Group. This group has been meeting since 1975. It originally contained the seven major exporters of nuclear materials and technologies (Canada, France, Japan, Soviet Union, United States, United Kingdom and West Germany). Later membership was widened to include eight more countries. The suppliers have drawn up guidelines involving a 'trigger list' of the most sensitive nuclear materials and technologies plus restrictions on their exports. The guidelines do

MONITORING UNDERGROUND NUCLEAR EXPLOSIONS

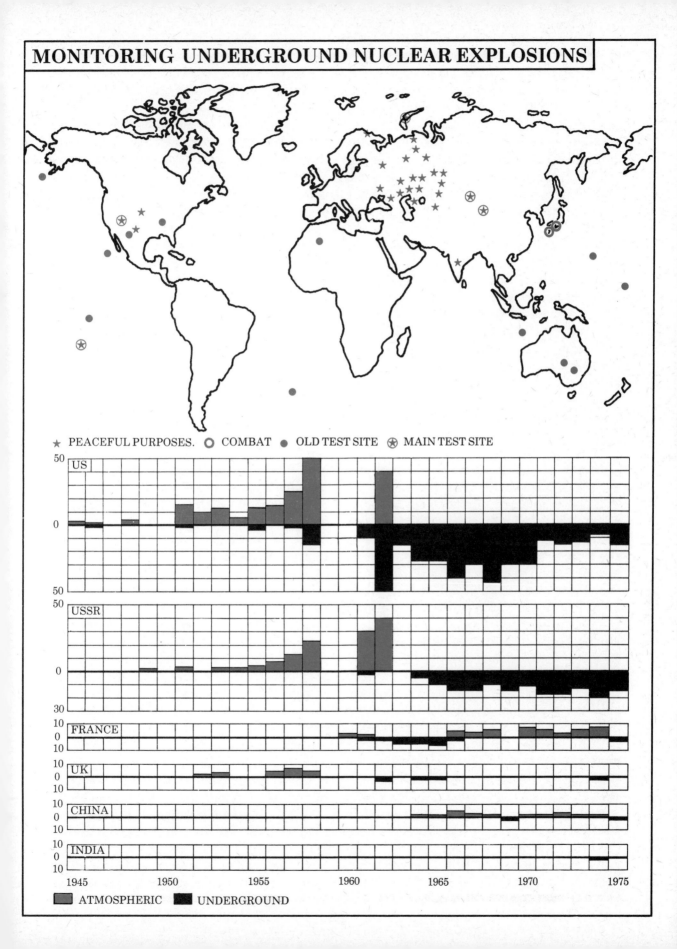

★ PEACEFUL PURPOSES. ○ COMBAT ● OLD TEST SITE ✪ MAIN TEST SITE

▬ ATMOSPHERIC ■ UNDERGROUND

not prohibit exports but establish a strict code of conduct, in which recipients will be placed under a contractual obligation not to divert materials for military purposes and to place all elements of the fuel cycle under the close watch of the International Atomic Energy Agency. In addition, limitations are to be placed on the transfer of technology that might be used in the construction of facilities beyond those covered in a deal. One virtue of the suppliers' agreement is that it should inhibit relaxed safeguards being offered as inducements in competitions for lucrative orders for nuclear facilities.

Under President Carter's administration the United States has been attempting to operate even more restrictive policies. Laws have been passed restricting nuclear assistance to any country which chooses to keep its nuclear projects outside the IAEA safeguards system. Furthermore an attempt has been made to shape international trends in civilian nuclear programmes. The assumption behind the US position is that the current generation of uranium-fuelled nuclear reactors are perfectly adequate to meet energy needs in the future and are also reasonably secure against proliferators. The aim is to prevent the emergence of the so-called Plutonium Economy in which the substance essential to nuclear weapons would also become the key fuel in national energy programmes, through reprocessing facilities and eventually fast-breeder reactors, which have the property of producing more plutonium than they consume. The United States has been attempting to persuade other countries to abandon the Plutonium Economy, as it has done itself. The response to the American call has not been encouraging, though at the London summit of May 1977, it was agreed to establish a two-year study by experts, known as the International Fuel Cycle Evaluation Conference, to explore means of controlling the fuel cycle, perhaps including the development of some

'fixes' to render the materials used in the civilian programmes useless for military purposes.

ANNOYANCE OVER RESTRICTIONS

If the IAEA can keep up with the new demands being placed on it to monitor the production and movement of materials in a growing nuclear trade, which will include the development of sensitive instruments and accounting procedures capable of detecting the slightest violation, then those facilities placed under the safeguards regime may remain geared to peaceful pursuits. The readiness of suppliers to impose stringent conditions on recipients may prevent a rash of new nuclear powers appearing as a spin-off of the rush for new energy sources.

However, there are still difficulties. First, the restrictions being advocated on nuclear exports go against the spirit of the Non-Proliferation Treaty. Many would-be recipients are annoyed at the fact that this new system of supplier controls apparently by-passes the NPT and involves neither consultations with nor concessions to the recipients. They are concerned that interesting civilian nuclear options are being withheld from them, despite pledges during the NPT negotiations that the peaceful benefits of nuclear energy would be fully shared. States that wish to experiment with peaceful nuclear explosions suspect that when the Americans insist, with reason, that PNEs are without value they are paying more regard to a fear of nuclear proliferation than the practical possibilities. There is thus a danger that a tough line by suppliers may weaken the loyalty of the nuclear 'have-nots' to the objectives of non-proliferation.

A more serious danger is that some of the more likely proliferators are not dependent upon the international nuclear market. The problem is not so much one of a renegade supplier but of indigenous capabilities. The relevant knowledge has now been widely spread. The majority of the members of the London Suppliers Group are not themselves nuclear-weapons states, though a few might wish to be in the future. It is also possible for states who can get unimpeded access to some nuclear fuels to construct facilities which though too small to be viable commercially or of much use in a civilian programme, can be used to fabricate a sufficiency of material for a few weapons. The material for India's explosion came from her own reprocessing facility. Israel and South Africa are both known to have developed advanced techniques for uranium enrichment.

It does not seem likely therefore that there is a complete technical answer to the problem of proliferation. Considerable barriers have been created or are being created that will deny many states the opportunity to build nuclear weapons. An ingenious nuclear aspirant may find ways round these barriers, so long as some risk of discovery and the consequent international condemnation and, possibly, sanctions are taken into account. Other, more sophisticated aspirants may feel able to ignore the international barriers altogether because of the level of development already attained by their national nuclear industries.

JOINING THE NUCLEAR CLUB

No country has admitted to either joining or preparing to join the current five members of the nuclear club. To do so would still be considered an anti-social act. Even those who might fully intend to 'go nuclear' do not need to declare their intentions.

Each of the first five nuclear powers gave notice of their aspirations with a test (though the first test of all, in New Mexico in July 1945, was known only to a privileged few). There was no pretence that the tests were for anything other than a military capability. In fact France and China both made these demonstrations a matter of some national pride. India broke this pattern by exploding a device while proclaiming only a peaceful intent. There is no need to go as far as India. Testing is not essential to the development of reliable nuclear bombs. Indeed, the type dropped on Hiroshima had not been tested previously. In the future particular countries may be patently capable of creating a nuclear option for themselves, without there being visible signs of this option being exercised. A country with an advanced civilian nuclear programme can be turned into a nuclear weapons state in a matter of months.

It is, however, important to remember that the ability to achieve nuclear explosions *when* desired is not sufficient to turn a country into a fully-fledged nuclear power. It is also necessary to be able to turn on these explosions *where* desired. Some means of delivering the weapons is required. Crude but effective ways can usually be found to take them to targets within a radius of a hundred miles or so, depending on the state of the enemy defences, using military aircraft. To ensure ranges of any length a missile force needs to be developed, and this can be as expensive or as technically difficult as the construction of the original bombs. Thus India has the scientific know-how to build its own rockets and even has a programme to do so underway, but this is still some way from completion. Those countries anxious to deter established nuclear weapons states have to meet even more stringent requirements. Assured deterrence necessitates a force that can survive an enemy first strike. This cannot be guaranteed when delivery depends on bombers in known bases or fixed land-based missiles. It really requires mobile missiles, preferably based in submarines.

Thus becoming a nuclear power involves much more than the ability to make nuclear explosions. A stockpile of weapons and the means for their delivery have to be developed to a level sufficient to meet military requirements.

THE LURE
OF NUCLEAR PRESTIGE

To appreciate the sources of nuclear proliferation it is necessary to understand the political and strategic factors involved as well as the technical factors. Much of the international activity surrounding the problem has focussed on controlling the spread of facilities, materials and technology, without any serious examination of the motives that cause proliferation, and the non-technical difficulties that can act as disincentives.

One benefit that is thought to accrue from a move to a nuclear-weapons capability is a substantial increment of political power and national prestige. A nuclear weapons capability and great power status are often thought to be synonymous. The five established nuclear-weapons states are those that were victorious in World War 2, have been the permanent members of the UN Security Council and have played pre-eminent roles in the governance of international society since 1945, with obvious variations in the importance of the respective contributions. Furthermore, as drunkards insisting on the abstinence of others, the superpowers have been warning others to stay clear of a nuclear weapons while building up and improving their capabilities at an intensive rate. If they take these weapons to be so essential to national security or as a symbol of national virility, why should not others?

The mere fact of owning nuclear weapons and exhibiting advanced skills in producing them may do wonders for a nation's self-confidence. In France the nuclear programme was seen, in part, as a means of rebuilding national morale after the humiliations of the 1940s and 1950s. In India, the timing of the underground test served to boost the internal political position of the Prime Minister, Mrs Gandhi.

In the long run, however, the benefits have to be judged in terms of improvements to the overall military and political position. In much of everyday international affairs, nuclear weapons are irrelevant. The economic strength of West Germany and Japan and the wealth of oil reserves and revenues of Saudi Arabia and Iran provide more effective forms of political leverage than nuclear weapons, as both Britain and France have come to recognize. To a country poor in general political and economic power resources, outstanding military capabilities may appear to offer the best hope of making a mark, and there are no more outstanding military capabilities than nuclear weapons. Yet here again the value in practice of these weapons does not always match their promise.

Our understanding of the military utility of nuclear weapons is based on inferences derived from their non-use. This thankfully negative experience suggests that while these weapons are efficient when used to deter mortal blows, they are rarely the appropriate response to lesser threats and are unimpressive as instruments of aggression. These limitations stem from the feeling that the detonation of nuclear weapons in anger would have far-reaching and unpredictable consequences. It would involve a departure from the conventions of behaviour that have evolved in international society since 1945. In addition, given that their most plausible role is as an ultimate deterrent, nuclear threats have to be used sparingly. If a bluff is called over a less extreme matter, the credibility of the threat to retaliate after a major attack or as a last resort may be dissipated.

Other arguments for caution before embarking on a nuclear strategy stem from the likely impact on the regional or global strategic environment. The acquisition of a nuclear force by one country acts as an immediate provocation to other states in the vicinity. The general level of tension may be raised or the chances of *rapprochement* with traditional adversaries may be inhibited. Threatened countries may feel that there is no alternative but to develop their own nuclear weapons. This can lead to an arms race and an unstable balance of terror (especially if neither side enjoys a second strike capability) with the potential costs of any conflict rising to unprecedented levels.

When proliferation poses a direct challenge to an established nuclear state more serious dangers can be involved. Those relying on nuclear weapons to maintain a favourable position with another state will not be pleased by any steps taken to neutralize this advantage. There is an incentive to consider a pre-emptive war, before the military balance shifts decisively. The case history which best illustrates this point is that of China. China's nuclear weapons programme was initiated out of a desire to stand up to the United States on her own. The efforts of the Soviet Union to impede this development accentuated the division between the two Communist states. This split forced China to improve relations with the United States. Originally China appears to have planned a balanced force of medium-range and intercontinental missiles. As it became apparent that there were those in Russia who would welcome an opportunity to abort China's embryonic nuclear programme with a pre-emptive strike against her nuclear installations, the effort was concentrated on posing a credible threat against the Soviet Union. Plans for an ICBM, which could threaten the US, were put to one side as the attempt was made to develop missiles capable of reaching far into Russia.

The other strategic problem connected with a move to nuclear weapons is that such a move could be seen as a repudiation of previous security arrangements based on superpower military aid and guarantees. Here the case of Israel is pertinent. There is now considerable circumstantial evidence that Israel has surreptitiously constructed for itself a small stockpile of nuclear weapons and is, in fact, more deserving of the title 'sixth nuclear power' than India. At Dimona, in the Negev, there is a reactor provided by the French free from any safeguards, and capable of producing enough plutonium for at least one nuclear weapon a year.

ISRAEL: THE SIXTH NUCLEAR POWER?

On a number of occasions Arab leaders have indicated that they believe this to be the case, as has the CIA in a 'leaked' estimate. The Israelis have acknowledged their potential, saying only that they will not be the first to introduce nuclear weapons into the Middle East. This putative nuclear capability has been used skilfully to persuade Americans to provide advanced conventional weapons (lest Israel be forced to 'go nuclear') and to add an extra degree of psychological intimidation for the Arabs. However, once this capability was made explicit, perhaps through a test, then Israel's military position would worsen. Some Arab response would be unavoidable, and the Russians would feel obliged to offer some nuclear guarantees. Perhaps more seriously, there would be a major crisis in US-Israeli relations. As Israel depends on America for a large proportion of her conventional military strength, any withdrawal of American military aid could undermine her position.

Thus a move towards a nuclear capability does involve risks of weakening national security, through damaging links with outside sources of military support while exciting suspicious neighbours, in return for the promise of enhanced strength and prestige in the future. The risks vary in nature and intensity from country to

NUCLEAR PROLIFERATION

PRESENT PRODUCERS OF POWER
BY NUCLEAR ENERGY

POTENTIAL PRODUCERS OF POWER
BY NUCLEAR ENERGY

POSSIBLE HOLDERS
OF NUCLEAR WEAPONS

PRESENT HOLDERS
OF NUCLEAR WEAPONS

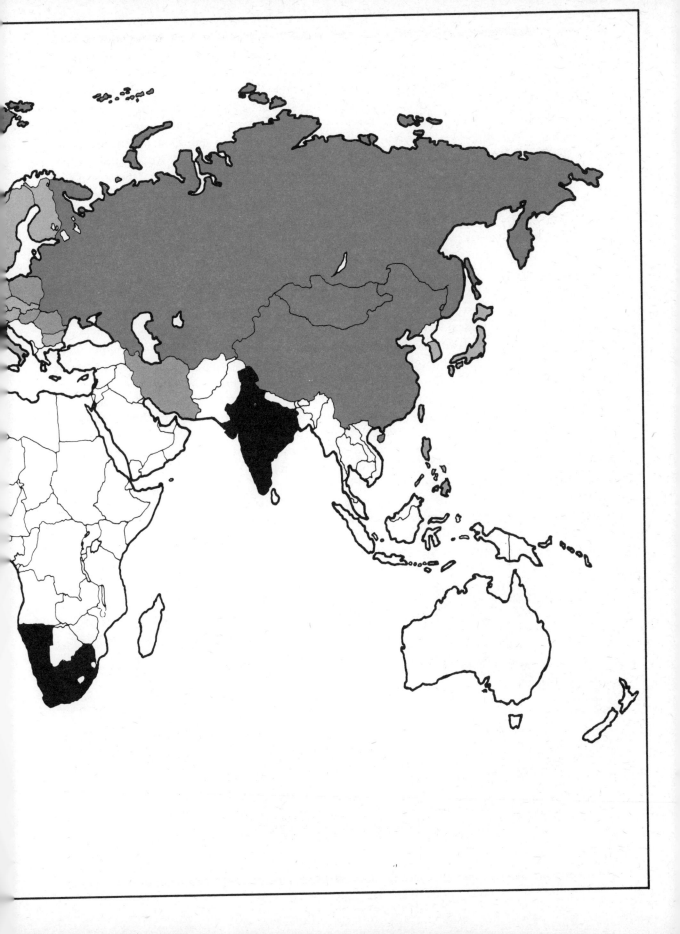

country. At one pole there will be those countries who are more or less independent of outside support and confident of their ability to manage any tensions caused by the transition to nuclear power. At the other pole we will find countries dependent upon the tentative support of a superpower to protect them against their adversaries.

WHEN GUARANTEES
SEEM WORTHLESS

What this suggests is that potential proliferators can be identified through their relations with the superpowers as much as by their current or prospective technical competence and opportunities. Countries already independent of the superpowers may see in nuclear weapons an opportunity to confirm their status as regional powers or as a means of checking a potential enemy without having to turn to a superpower for aid. India's history of non-alignment and regional conflict, plus her disturbing experiences during the Indo-Pakistan war of late 1971 (when the aircraft-carrier *USS Enterprise* was sent by Washington to intimidate her), were important influences in the decision to go ahead with the 'peaceful' nuclear test. In

any nuclear designs of Brazil, Argentine or Iran factors of pride and status, compounded by regional rivalries, will be as significant as strictly military concerns.

Of greater significance are those states who have felt in the past or currently do feel dependent in some ways upon superpowers, but lack confidence that any assistance would be forthcoming in an emergency. Such a lack of confidence has provided the official rationales of proliferation in the past. The French detected a decline in America's nuclear guarantee to Western Europe as the Soviet Union ended the period of overwhelming American nuclear superiority. The Chinese decided on their requirement when it became apparent that their Soviet comrades were inhibited in their dealings with the Americans by the fear of a nuclear war.

Thus if the Israelis ever felt that they could be abandoned by the Americans the temptation would be to make nuclear weapons a central feature of their strategy. The decline in American support for Taiwan has already prompted some talk of a nuclear option, albeit slightly fanciful. The withdrawal of American troops from South Korea has resulted in similar talk in Seoul. The Americans have always insisted that nuclear weapons are essential

Paid for by the Americans before they had to go: the Dalat nuclear research station in South Vietnam

to the defence of South Korea, which provides a good excuse to replace any departing American nuclear weapons with Korean equivalents. Another state feeling isolated at the moment is South Africa. South Africa has ample supplies of uranium and an advanced nuclear technology. In September 1977, the Soviet Union sent a warning to Western leaders that South Africa was about to test a bomb at a site in the Kalahari desert. Whether or not a test was intended, considerable pressure was put on South Africa and no test took place. Nevertheless South Africa's nuclear capability was confirmed and she maintained the right to do what she pleased with this capability.

All this provides the superpowers with plenty of food for thought. The Americans have to recognize that the more certain states are pushed by the international community or left unprotected by the United States, the greater the danger of proliferation becomes. The Soviet Union has to recognize that she or her clients would be in range for many potential proliferators. In the early 1960s, when nuclear proliferation first became an issue, the fear of the superpowers was connected with the danger of allies 'getting the bomb'. The French doctrine, for example, was based on the possibility of triggering a reluctant American nuclear retaliation in the event of a Soviet invasion. This thought did not appeal to the Americans who were anxious to keep close control of any conflict.

Now the problem appears in a different light. It is less a question of who calls the shots within an alliance but a symptom of the deliberate, unavoidable, inadvertent or unintended decline in American responsibilities for the fortunes of other states around the globe. The more America withdraws, the more the likely proliferation becomes. With each new nuclear power the calculations of others with the requisite capability are affected. Nuclear proliferation is not a global epidemic, spread by advanced technology, but possibly a regional epidemic. Thus Latin America, Africa and the Middle East remain, on the surface, nuclear-free, though if Israel or South Africa admitted their capabilities, others would be forced to respond. In Asia the situation is more perilous. The development of Chinese nuclear power helped to stimulate a corresponding development in India. The Indian test provoked the Pakistanis. If South Korea or Taiwan got the bomb for their own purposes, Japan may feel that she has no choice but to follow suit. Australia, Iran and Indonesia might all feel obliged to keep up with the trends.

This may not happen, and in many cases it will take years, considerable financial and technical resources, and some devious international behaviour before it can. Rather than boldly stride down the nuclear road, those so tempted will maintain contingency plans. Under the guise of a civilian programme, the military option can be maintained - only to be exercised if absolutely necessary.

In a world of nuclear powers, the superpowers may want to keep their distance from their former clients and allies lest they get entangled in uncontrollable conflicts. The danger is of a series of regional nuclear balances complicated by asymmetries in capabilities or too many participants, lacking the guiding hands of the superpowers or an appreciation of the conventions that can help to manage crises. An Amin or a Gaddafi (who once tried to buy a 'bomb' on the open market) with nuclear power at their disposal is a frightening thought. But proliferation is not frightening simply because of the quality of the governments who may acquire the bomb. It is frightening because of the demands it will make for restraint in a world where many conflicts are long-standing and bitter, increasing the chances of nuclear weapons being used in anger.
LAWRENCE FREEDMAN

5. WORLD FLASHPOINTS

ince the onset of the Cold War some 30 years ago, international crises involving the two superpowers have occurred at frequent intervals. Over Berlin, Cuba and the Middle East the two have been drawn into dangerous confrontation. They have clashed militarily – at one stage removed – in Korea and Vietnam, where the United States was directly involved in war while the Soviet Union actively supplied arms and assistance to the other side. Their policies in Africa are hostile to each other, with their support being sought by opposing states or factions.

There can be no absolute certainty about deterrence, no complete dependence on rationality prevailing where important national interests touch or armed forces face each other. Crises will come again. If the stakes are sufficiently important, or are thought to be so by either side, the danger of war can never be ruled out.

The NATO versus Warsaw Pact military balance continues to tilt to the East. While NATO forces may still be adequate for deterrence the present position and trend give no comfort. Then there are political uncertainties. The growth of Communism in Italy and France is partly mirrored by emerging nationalism in eastern Europe. Even if this may represent no more than states taking different roads to Communism, the example of Czechoslovakia in 1968 showed clearly Soviet determination to halt unwelcome change with force if need be. Though east European leaders will no doubt be more cautious in future than were those in Prague in 1968, yet there can be no assurance that diversities of view will not breed unrest which could get out of hand. Outside the Warsaw Pact area there is Yugoslavia, with a question mark over its political future when President Tito leaves the scene, as even he must in time.

FRONT-LINE IN EUROPE

The superpowers share no common border to breed disputes as do the Soviet Union and China, but they do have a proxy border in Europe. It is in Europe where their most important outside interests clash, where they have heavily armed forces facing one another across a dividing line. If Europe is not, at this moment, the most dangerous arena of confrontation it is nonetheless the one in which the consequences of any clash would be most serious, where the stakes are highest. For the United States and for her allies these stakes are the political and military security of western Europe; for the Soviet Union, the consolidation of the Communist system and the control of eastern Europe.

BERLIN: A PAWN, NOT A QUEEN

There is tension from time to time, of course. Berlin has often been at the centre of it, as the three Western powers – the United States, Britain and France – have maintained their legal right to be there and the status of West Berlin itself, in the face of hostility from East Germany, encouraged or otherwise by the Soviet Union. Western garrisons in Berlin are very small, hostages to much larger Soviet and East German armies that surround them.

To force the West to give up West Berlin would be an immense political and psychological gain to the East, but one that would make the Cold War dangerously warm. As a step taken in isolation it would not seem to warrant the risks and costs

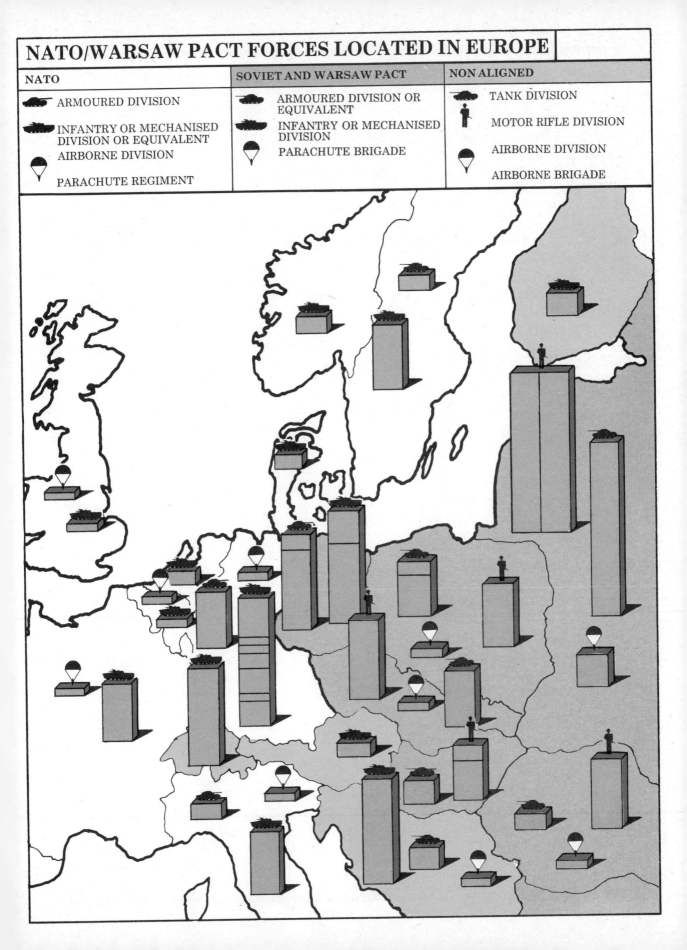

NATO/WARSAW PACT FORCES LOCATED IN EUROPE

NATO

- ARMOURED DIVISION
- INFANTRY OR MECHANISED DIVISION OR EQUIVALENT
- AIRBORNE DIVISION
- PARACHUTE REGIMENT

SOVIET AND WARSAW PACT

- ARMOURED DIVISION OR EQUIVALENT
- INFANTRY OR MECHANISED DIVISION
- PARACHUTE BRIGADE

NON ALIGNED

- TANK DIVISION
- MOTOR RIFLE DIVISION
- AIRBORNE DIVISION
- AIRBORNE BRIGADE

involved. As the opening shot in a war, military action in Berlin divorced from action elsewhere seems improbable. Political pressure is much more likely; the geographical position of West Berlin is enough of an anomaly to put it always at risk.

In the centre of Europe the stakes are much greater but so, for the East, are the military difficulties. The territorial division of Europe is now clear-cut. The *status quo* has hardened into internationally accepted borders that have been confirmed at Helsinki. Tension has been lowered as a result. Any attempt by the East to move these borders or cross them by force would involve a clash not only with substantial West European forces but with those of the United States as well. These forces have nuclear weapons, the use of which could not be ruled out. The Soviet Union has been nothing if not cautious where confrontation with the United States has been concerned. All things are possible but it must be remarked that however little the western European allies or the United States condone Soviet control over eastern Europe they are now most unlikely to go to war, or allow themselves to be drawn into a war, to change it.

THE NORTHERN FLANK

On NATO's northern flank the political and military position is quite different. Both Norway and Denmark, members of the North Atlantic Alliance, follow policies of having no foreign troops and no nuclear weapons on their soil, relying instead on reinforcement by their allies in emergency. There is in the region a delicate Scandinavian political balance with the Soviet Union, in which neutral Finland and non-aligned Sweden play their part, in the context of which Norway and Denmark would hope to be able to regulate at least initially the development of any crisis. There are some points of friction in the North, notably between the Soviet Union and Norway over rights in Svalbard and the Barents Sea, but these have so far been managed by Norway in low key though determined and skilled fashion.

The military equation is regionally very one-sided, with the Soviet Union being able to bring very powerful forces to bear, but membership of NATO gives both Norway and Denmark the political and military strength of the Alliance and – most importantly – of the United States to lean upon. The regional stakes do not seem so high as to warrant the Soviet Union provoking a clash with the United States here.

IN THE MEDITERRANEAN

The southern flank is much less stable. Two Alliance members, Greece and Turkey, have for very many years had a running dispute over Cyprus and more recently a sharpened one over mineral and over-flying rights in the Aegean. The two clashed militarily over Cyprus in 1974, as a direct result of which Greece announced her intention to leave the integrated military organization of the Alliance (though she has in fact not entirely done so) and withdrew access to both NATO and American military facilities in Greece. Turkey also closed American military facilities on her territory as a result of an arms embargo imposed on her by the US Congress after the invasion of Cyprus and has dropped hints that membership of NATO is not the only security arrangement open to her. The Alliance thus has self-inflicted wounds and is in some disarray, as is American policy towards Greece and Turkey. Another war between these two quarrelling states cannot be ruled out.

It would be unlikely to spread, partly since the causes are national in origin, partly because there would be strong international pressure to stop it, not least by the United States. The Soviet Union has tried to make capital out of the dispute by wooing Turkey, to encourage her to loosen her links with the West and with the United States. The damage that would be caused if Turkey, with her strategically immensely important territory, were to leave the Alliance can hardly be overstressed; the NATO position in the eastern Mediterranean would be in ruins. This would be a political crisis of some magnitude, the more so if it resulted from overt action by the Soviet Union, and for that reason alone strong diplomatic and political action would be brought to bear to avert it.

SPAIN AND PORTUGAL

The armed forces of Portugal are not of particular importance to the West at the moment, but Portuguese territory is. If the Soviet Navy were able to operate from there the US and allied navies would be severely handicapped. The Azores also provide the United States with an invaluable staging post and a base for maritime reconnaissance. The United States does, of course, operate naval vessels and aircraft from Spain and has no need of facilities in Portugal; she has ample reason to want to deny them to the Soviet Union. If the Soviet Union took overt steps to influence the direction of Portuguese political alignment away from the West this would undoubtedly create tension and bring political action by the United States and Europe to resist or avert it. Such a Soviet military foothold in Western Europe, and militarily a key part, would be damaging, to say the least.

Spain has a defence treaty with the United States, with some three years still to run, which allows the United States Navy to use a major naval base at Rota, near Cadiz, and affords airfields from which both fighter and maritime reconnaissance aircraft operate. Through this agreement NATO is in effect able to make use of Spanish territory, but many in Spain now feel that Spain should logically become a member of NATO and obtain the full bene-

fits. On military grounds Spanish membership of the Alliance has everything to recommend it; Spanish forces, particularly air and naval, would be a useful increment. It would, however, need to command consensus inside Spain to be practicable and the Soviet Union would undoubtedly use whatever influence was available to prevent it. The issue would be a direct point of friction between the United States and the Soviet Union, but it is hard to see what significant leverage the Soviet Union has beyond encouraging left-wing opposition within Spain.

ITALY: THE COMMUNIST QUESTION-MARK

In Italy any growth in Communist influence in or on government is likely to have adverse effects both for the Western Alliance and for the United States. While Italy has an economic need for close links with Western Europe and the Communist Party has therefore supported both membership of EEC and NATO, there is always the danger of a more conditional attitude to NATO being adopted, akin to that of France, or certainly seen as an option; and there is always, at worst, the possibility of a move towards non-alignment. If such proved to be the case the Alliance would be in great difficulty in the central Mediterranean, with resulting difficulties in being able to provide military support to Greece and Turkey. NATO would be severely weakened and the psychological effect could be felt elsewhere in East-West relations. The American position in the Mediterranean would be directly affected, since the United States has military facilities in Italy which it needs not least for the operations of the Sixth Fleet. Any alteration of alignment by Italy would clearly have its effect on the American attitude to the Alliance as a whole, particularly on the part of Congress. The Soviet Union could, of course, be expected to do whatever was possible to encourage such a development. If things do not go well Italy could be a point of political tension; at worst the cause of a real change in the political balance in Europe.

Yugoslavia is not a member of the Alliance but her status is also important to the future of the political balance, and any change in her present non-aligned status could give rise to major tensions. Here is fertile ground for Soviet political action, or even overt or covert military intervention, to support political or national factions in Yugoslavia that might be sympathetic to Soviet aims. Such intervention would pose few military difficulties for the Soviet Union.

AID FOR YUGOSLAVIA

For the West, however, military action or military aid to Yugoslavia presents problems of political will and military availability. Only the United States and Italy – which country for historical and political reasons might be averse to becoming embroiled in fighting in Yugoslavia – have forces in the area. The other Western allies would undoubtedly look to the United States for a political lead but the extent to which the United States would be willing to offer military help (and the Yugoslavs to ask for it) is unknown. But it is obvious that Yugoslavia is a potential crisis point and one in which military intervention cannot be ruled out.

THE NEAR EAST

Both superpowers are deeply entangled in the Arab-Israeli dispute. Until the war of October 1973, American single-minded support of Israel handed the Arabs to the Soviet Union on a plate, so to speak. The Soviet Union had become the armourer for the Arabs and underwrote their wars just as the United States did for Israel. Neither superpower could allow its own side to lose but neither wanted its own side to win completely, since they themselves would then be drawn directly into confrontation to ensure the survival of their protégé. So each took action to stop the Arab-Israeli wars before they went too far.

The political setting in the Middle East is now a little different, as American policy has changed to one of being more even-handed as between the Arabs and Israel. The Americans are now in a unique position of having some leverage over Israel together with close links with key Arab states. But the situation is still unstable. If negotiations with Israel prove sterile or seem to offer no promise, the Arabs could turn towards war again, accompanied possibly by another oil boycott, as a means of applying pressure. If they did turn to military action they would have to look to the Soviet Union to supply the arms. Emotions run deep in the Middle East and events gather their own momentum. War in the next few years certainly cannot be ruled out.

Could a new Middle East war be stopped quickly, as in the past? Probably, since both superpowers are acutely aware of the dangers. But it is not absolutely certain. The Middle East remains a crisis point involving the United States and the Soviet Union and will do so until such time as a settlement of the Arab-Israel dispute is reached, or is clearly seen to be reachable.

THE PERSIAN GULF

The Persian Gulf is linked with the Arabs and Israel via oil and Saudi Arabia, but is vastly important in its right as the source of oil on which Western economies so heavily depend. Access to this oil is vital and stability in the area is thus a high priority. Both the West generally and the United States therefore give political support to the two Gulf regimes which presently provide this stability, Saudi Arabia and

Iran, whose interest in excluding Soviet and radical influence in the area coincides with their own.

But the Gulf has its own intrinsic problems. There are disputed borders, between states rich with oil: regimes often archaic or autocratic, which may not provide for an equitable division of wealth. Some of these regimes are volatile and unpredictable, like Iraq, or ambitious, like Iran. Modern weapons have flowed into the area in huge quantities, the purchases made possible by new-found wealth, the requirement prompted by local rivalries or fears of the Soviet Union, of Israel or of radically-inspired insurgency. While the Gulf is quiet at the moment it can by no means be regarded as stable. An assassin's bullet, far from unknown in the Middle East, or the overthrow of a government could lead to unrest, to a change of a state's political alignment, perhaps to a threat to the flow of oil. But the flow of oil is vital to the West – the word is not used lightly – and military intervention by the United States to maintain it could not be ruled out, certainly not if the Soviet hand were seen to be at work. This is an extreme scenario and perhaps an unlikely one, but the stakes are such that the Gulf must rank as a potential crisis point where political action could well be backed by military force.

THE HORN OF AFRICA

Just as the Persian Gulf is linked with political problems in the Near East, so it is with the Horn of Africa. Close by the strategically important coasts of the Horn pass oil tankers on their way to Europe via Suez or southwards on the Cape Route. A hostile presence on the Red Sea or Indian Ocean littoral would pose a latent threat to the oil traffic and oil-producing states such as Saudi Arabia and Iran and the oil consuming states of the West have not been slow to notice the dangers of this. The growth of the Soviet naval presence in the Indian Ocean over the last decade has led to the building up of a strong navy by Iran, and to the United States improving her own capacity to operate in the region.

The war between Somalia and Ethiopia has, however, dramatically heightened tension, as the heavy Soviet and Cuban involvement has shown the Soviet Union to be following confident and assertive policies aimed, it seems, at establishing here, as elsewhere in Africa, regimes of Marxist persuasion. Western concern at seeing her political and strategic position thus eroded has not been matched by policies to counter it. The example of a Soviet Union prepared to help militarily and a United States disinclined to do so, could have a psychological impact all over Africa, wherever states or movements within them see military force as a means of furthering political ends.

TROUBLED WATERS IN SOUTH AFRICA

Southern Africa is also providing a fertile ground for Soviet adventurism in support of deeply-felt grievances of black peoples against white minorities, notably against South Africa itself.

The problem is to find a policy that will achieve a settlement between black and white without bloodshed, and that will in doing so also neutralize Soviet influence. The difficulties of finding such a solution to a near-intractable problem are enough in themselves but are compounded by the Soviet willingness to afford military assistance, even to become more directly involved with advisors or through Cuban proxies, while the United States is reluctant to fill a matching role.

Africa is thus an arena in which Soviet policies accompanied by active military intervention are opposed to those of the United States. Again, the stakes are high: the possible spread of Soviet influence in countries possessed of great mineral resources which the West needs, and coast-lines on the Red Sea, Indian and South Atlantic Oceans of great strategic import-ance. Yet it has been an arena in which no one Soviet action has seemed important enough in itself to warrant its being opposed militarily, and one in which the options open to the West so far have not been attractive enough to offer useful policies.

AFTER VIETNAM

Across the Indian Ocean, in South-East Asia, there has been a marked change since 1975 with the collapse of the American security structure there after the fall of Saigon. The United States has now with-drawn from the mainland and has only a maritime strategy. This strategy is ade-quate to the defence of islands or of Ameri-can maritime interests, but cannot affect events on land.

But this altered stance has also re-moved the likelihood of the United States being caught up in a crisis there. The region is now mainly the concern of region-al countries and of China. The Soviet Union has also involved herself through her support of Vietnam – a somewhat un-predictable quantity – and her search for any political position in the region that can be used to oppose the interests of China. For her part, China works to counter or remove Soviet influence wherever it may be; their policies are actively, implacably opposed to each other. The United States can leave the containment of the Soviet Union in South-East Asia to China, turn-ing her own attention further north and to the Pacific.

JAPAN'S SAFEGUARD

In North-East Asia the United States has a military commitment to Japan through a security treaty that is mutually advantage-ous and looks durable. For Japan the US Navy helps keep the freedom of the seas that she needs as a world trading nation. These links with the United States are comforting for Japan, placed as she is near two large Communist countries. She is in no way threatened by the Soviet Union nor fears she will be. There is friction be-tween them from time to time, over such things as fishing and offshore rights, and political coolness over the disputed North-ern Islands and Japan's present leaning towards China, helping build up that country through trade and technical assist-ance. Nonetheless there is no reason to expect Soviet military pressure on Japan. If there were, the United States would be drawn in. The very fact of this is seen by Japan as her safeguard.

KOREA:
A LAND MADE FOR CRISIS

The United States also has a military com-mitment to South Korea and has long had troops in that country. She is planning, however, to withdraw the ground forces over the next five years but leaving the air squadrons and continuing to maintain a security commitment to Seoul. North and South Korea live in an atmosphere of hostility and fear of military action by the North is never far below the surface. US forces have undoubtedly acted as a deter-rent to invasion from the North though not to small-scale infiltration or harrass-ment. The withdrawal of the ground forces will weaken deterrence. Though South Korean forces are to be strengthened there is no question of their providing the degree of deterrence that US forces do by the fact of their presence.

The position will therefore become far less stable as withdrawal proceeds, even though the United States may declare her continued intention to protect the South. The regime in the North is not a wholly rational one. It has been armed by the Soviet Union, as a Communist neighbour that the Soviet Union would like to keep out of the arms of China. Moscow may not want unrest in the Korean Peninsula but if war did break out there she would be forced to support the North and supply weapons, and China would have to do the same out of rivalry at the least, as happened in Vietnam. The United States would be involved directly; the Soviet Union would be in a proxy role as opponent, a replay of the Korean War in the 1950s. The Korean Peninsula must rank as one of the areas of the world with a real question mark over it when US ground forces have gone, perhaps before. Crisis is always lurking in the wings in Korea.

LATIN AMERICA

Cuba is an irritant to the United States, with its Soviet links and its military activity in Africa. It was, of course, once the seat of a major superpower crisis, when Soviet missiles were placed there in 1962. Technology has now removed the need for the Soviet Union to emplace strategic missiles on land outside its own borders, and the lesson of having to face the US Navy near its own bases did not go unlearned. Cuba is likely to generate more political friction but seems unlikely to provoke a major crisis of the 1962 variety again; the ground rules are now accepted, it seems, by both sides.

It is also hard to see major crisis in South America. The region is troubled by constant political and social unrest and inter-state disputes may even lead to armed clashes. The root causes are, however, local and domestic and external intervention has limited utility. This is, though, a region of ideological extremes and great natural resources, and it cannot be ruled out that one superpower or the other will meddle in its politics, even supply arms to one faction or another. The United States would be acutely sensitive to Soviet interference in the Americas but was not able to prevent it in Cuba, close to her own shores. On balance, Latin America seems unlikely to provide the venue for major crisis yet awhile.

CONCLUSIONS

It can be said with fair assurance that nuclear weapons make major war less likely, and that each of the superpowers will do all it can to avoid conflict touching its own territory. This leads to the proposition that such clashes as are likely to occur or may occur will be away from their homelands, around the periphery, and be fought with conventional weapons. Even this proposition cannot be puncture-proof. Events can and do get out of hand.

One last point: the two superpowers are out of phase in their conduct of world affairs. The United States has been through a recent period of active military involvement and global commitment. The dividends proved to be far less than the social and other costs, so she is now in a period of retrenchment. It is as if she had been climbing a mountain, did not much like what she saw on the way up and is now, with a sigh of relief, coming down the other side. The Soviet Union is still going up, liking the view and has so far found the dividends greater than the outlays. This asymmetry between the superpowers gives no comfort but may not necessarily endure. Their vital interests may yet collide. If it is hard to predict where crises may occur, it can be said that there are nonetheless many places where a clash of interests could lead to a clash of arms.

KENNETH HUNT

ABBREVIATIONS, Chs 1–5

ABM Anti-Ballistic Missile
IAEA International Atomic Energy Agency
ICBM Inter-Continental Ballistic Missile
MIRV Multiple Independently-targetable Re-entry Vehicle
NPT Non-Proliferation Treaty
PNE Peaceful Nuclear Explosion
SALT Strategic Arms Limitations Talks
SAM Surface-to-Air Missile

6. THE ELECTRONIC DIMENSION

By 'electronic dimension' we mean those electronic systems and items of equipment used to fulfil what might be called the intellectual requirements of warfare: those needed for command and control (C and C) purposes; the gathering, collating, processing and dissemination of intelligence and operational information; and the automation of many categories of military procedures such as weapon direction. As might be expected, the principal classes of hardware we shall be concerned with in this chapter are digital computers and various kinds of communications equipment.

The electronic element is the mainstay of numerous military systems which are of extreme importance for the best use of the available armament and human resources, and it is thus a prime target for opposing electronic counter-measures (ECM). For this reason, some attention to the subject of electronic warfare (EW) is entailed. Also, certain types of EW equipment are an important source of input data for some of the systems which constitute the electronic element, thereby further justifying their inclusion.

Since computers are central to our subject, it will be convenient to start from these devices and their military roles. There are five main applications of computers in the military context: weapons guidance and control; intelligence; planning; logistics; command, control and communications. The last of these is of most concern to us here, but depending upon circumstances, each of the other applications may assume greater significance at certain times.

The main contribution of the digital computer to each of these roles is its ability to process vast quantities of data very rapidly, and to carry out a variety of sorting and mathematical functions with considerable speed and accuracy. Despite the use of the term 'intellectual' at the beginning of this chapter, it should be noted that computers are not yet widely employed for their reasoning or intuitive capabilities. They are merely extremely hard-working mental labourers.

Examples of the role of computers in weapon control and direction will be found in following chapters, but discussion of one or two applications will be of value now. In certain categories of air defence, the speed and accuracy of the latest aircraft and weapons combine to create a demand for 'autonomous' defensive weapon systems, simply to achieve a sufficiently short reaction time to permit the attacking aircraft to be engaged at all. The extremely short warning time from a low-level, near-supersonic aircraft does not allow for manual target identification and tracking, weapon aiming and firing when an attack may last for a matter of seconds only, and so an automatic response is called for. In such instances, great reliance is placed upon the electronic element.

First, radars are called upon to detect, identify and track the attacking aircraft or missile, supplemented by closed-circuit television (CCTV) or infra-red trackers where radar is not suitable, followed by the automatic launch and guidance of a defensive missile to intercept and destroy the attacker. The best example of such a system is the Royal Navy's Sea Wolf system which has intercepted targets as small as a 4.5-inch shell and as fast as a Petrel research rocket travelling at over Mach 2, and with a reaction time of between five and six seconds from initial target detection. With-

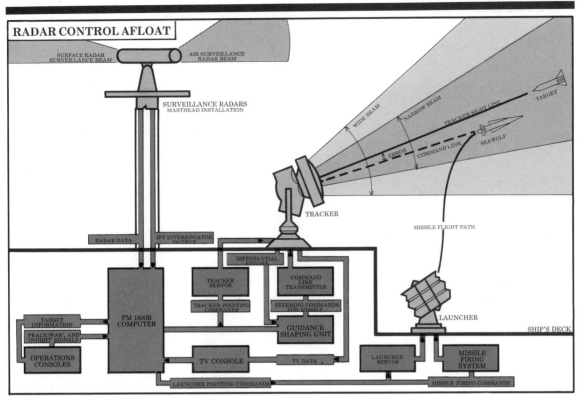

RADAR CONTROL AFLOAT

SURFACE RADAR SURVEILLANCE BEAM

AIR SURVEILLANCE RADAR BEAM

SURVEILLANCE RADARS
MASTHEAD INSTALLATION

WIDE BEAM

NARROW BEAM

TRACKER SIGHT LINE

TARGET

ERROR

COMMAND LINK

SEAWOLF

TRACKER

MISSILE FLIGHT PATH

RADAR DATA

IFF INTERROGATOR OUTPUT

DIFFERENTIAL ERRORS

TRACKER SERVOS

COMMAND LINK TRANSMITTER

LAUNCHER

SHIP'S DECK

TARGET INFORMATION

TRACKER POINTING COMMANDS

STEERING COMMANDS FOR MISSILE

'PEACE/WAR', AND 'INHIBIT' SIGNALS

FM 1600B COMPUTER

GUIDANCE SHAPING UNIT

OPERATIONS CONSOLES

TV CONSOLE

TV DATA

LAUNCHER SERVOS

MISSILE FIRING SYSTEM

LAUNCHER POINTING COMMANDS

MISSILE FIRING COMMANDS

Top: *The cybernetics of Sea Wolf.* Above: *What it looks like on shipboard*

out computers such rapid responses to an attack would not be possible.

This use of computers may be contrasted with their role in a very different weapon system, the US Navy Tomahawk cruise missile. In its submarine-launched, land attack version, Tomahawk will follow a low-level, terrain-following flight path of several hours' duration, under inertial guidance which is periodically updated by the novel Terrain Contour Matching (TERCOM) system. The latter matches the terrain being flown over with a digital map of the area derived from previously obtained intelligence data. A radio altimeter provides information on the height of the ground over which the Tomahawk passes, and these values are compared with a digital contour map stored in the memory of a computer on board the missile, thus enabling corrections to the flight path to ensure that the pre-programmed course is regained and followed.

The target data and all the routes are stored on magnetic tapes aboard the parent submarine, and appropriate sets of route instructions and digital up-dating maps are read in the Tomahawk missile before launch. This process is referred to as 'targeting', and although different guidance techniques are involved, submarine-launched ballistic missiles (SLBMs) and strategic intercontinental ballistic missiles (ICBMs), are now re-targeted in accordance with changing strategic plans by computers, this being very much quicker than by human reprogramming of the individual missile guidance computers. These two examples by no means exhaust the possibilities of computers in weapon guidance and control, but others will be found in the chapters dealing with specific categories of weapons.

Important though they undoubtedly are, two of the military applications of computers mentioned earlier do not differ sufficiently from their civil equivalents to warrant special treatment in this volume. These are logistics and planning, from both of which maximum benefit is derived by the best use of computer techniques in peacetime.

PLANNING AND PREDICTION

For instance, using computers in a planning role the probable outcome of changes made in force levels, weapon deployments, tactics or other factors affecting a given military situation can be assessed by means of computer simulations. Similarly, the computer's ability to predict, or make projections, can be employed to enable commanders to assess which of several possible reactions to a tactical situation offers the best chance of a successful conclusion. Air defence systems and anti-submarine warfare (ASW) computer systems often include facilities of this sort to enable operators to predict future target tracks on the basis of present position and track history, and to assist in such tasks as weapon assignment and threat evaluation.

The remaining computer applications are closely inter-related and are generally regarded as a single combined military element, abbreviated C^3I – for Command, Control, Communications, and Intelligence. This embraces the formulation of operational plans and directives; the issuing of orders to forces to effect the directives specified; provision of all means necessary for the exchange of information and transmission of orders in support of operations; and the collection, processing and dissemination of intelligence data for planning, evaluation and performance of military operations.

All of these activities apply to all levels of military operations, from strategic to tactical, and extend to all command levels. So far as NATO is concerned, the United States of America clearly possesses by far the greatest collection of men and equipment dedicated to these tasks, notwithstanding significant contributions from individual allied states. It should also be noted that integration of C³I services and systems now enjoys a high priority within NATO, bringing with it an increasing degree of standardization and common use of the equipment of several nations.

Less detail is known of Soviet achievements in C³I than the American systems facing those of the Warsaw Pact. The West's strategic objectives are the protection of national territory and interests overseas, and the principal threats are ICBMs and SLBMs, and air attack by bombers. The American ballistic missile warning system plan provides for all potential strategic missile approach corridors to be monitored with at least two different types of warning sensors: early warning satellites using infra-red detectors, and land-based radar systems. The latter, comprising the three BMEWS (Ballistic Missile Early Warning System) radar sites at Thule (Greenland), Clear (Alaska), and Fylingdales Moor (England); two coastal-based radars on the east and west coasts of the USA (codenamed 'Pave Paws'); and a Perimeter Acquisition Radar Attack Characterisation System (PARCS).

Operating together, the satellites and radar systems give reliable and unambiguous confirmation of a Soviet missile attack

ICBM watch: the BMEWS site at Thule in Greenland

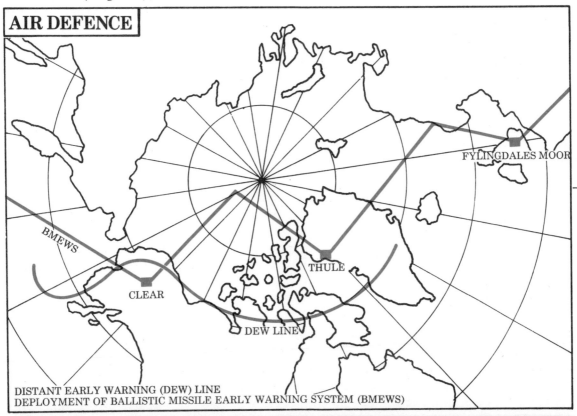

AIR DEFENCE

FYLINGDALES MOOR

THULE

CLEAR

BMEWS

DEW LINE

DISTANT EARLY WARNING (DEW) LINE
DEPLOYMENT OF BALLISTIC MISSILE EARLY WARNING SYSTEM (BMEWS)

within a very short time of launch. The BMEWS radars detect and track objects in space at great ranges, and from the velocity information derived the trajectories, impact points and times can be calculated. Large multiple computer systems are employed at all three sites for control of the radars, processing the radar data, and maintaining a track record of objects orbiting in space, in addition to the main function of missile attack warning. Information of BMEWS targets is transferred by a communications network to the North American Air Defence (NORAD) Combat Operations Centre, and the Fylingdales installation also provides an early warning service to the UK. The 'Pave Paws' radars are provided to give warning of SLBM attacks from Soviet submarines in the Atlantic or Pacific Oceans.

To protect the North American landmass from air attack the main element is the Joint Surveillance System (JSS) which consists of a number of civil/military radar stations in the USA and a smaller number of wholly military radars. Control is exercised from Seven Regional Operations Control Centres (ROCCs), four in the USA, one in Alaska, and three in Canada. Additional sources of target data are a number of Airborne Warning and Control Systems (AWACS) aircraft carrying radar capable of detecting and locating low-flying targets; and by the 1980s, over-the-horizon radars which can detect air targets at any height at ranges of up to 2,000 miles, and a number of unmanned radar stations in Canada will provide for the improved detection of bomber targets.

In Europe, the manned aircraft is seen as the principal air threat, and the multinational NADGE (NATO Air Defence Ground Environment) project, later complemented by a number of AWACS and Nimrod Airborne Early Warning airborne radar aircraft, constitutes the main element of warning and control. NADGE was set up to improve existing air defence systems within NATO and to integrate them operationally. It was started in the 1960s and has been subsequently updated, and there are provisions for working with the air defence networks of other friendly nations in the event of hostilities.

Air defences of the Warsaw Pact countries are organized under the Soviet National Air Defence Command (*PVO Strany*), which has its headquarters underground at a site about 50km from Moscow. This central command centre co-ordinates the operations in 16 air defence districts, ten of which are in the USSR and the other six in other Warsaw Pact states. Each air defence district is usually divided into two air defence areas, themselves further subdivided into air defence sectors (two at most). Districts are commanded by air force generals with special command staffs and command posts. There is a combat command post in each air defence area and a fighter control command post for each air defence sector. Soviet frontal aviation units have constructed additional fighter control command posts in the forward areas.

Operational control of the air defence system rests with the headquarters of each air defence sector, and tactical employment of air defence resources is the responsibility of the supreme commander of the SAM (surface-to-air-missile) units and the commanders of air divisions. The command and control system to effect this is based upon what has been described as a layered system of secure telephones, direction finding, and radio networks. Work on a semi-automatic command system has already been initiated, so that by the 1980s a much greater degree of automation can safely be assumed.

The present strength of the Soviet National Air Defence Command is estimated at 6,500 surveillance radars, with such types as the 'Tall King' and 'Hen House' providing long-range early warning facilities; and an operational force of about ten Tu-20 ('Moss') airborne early warning radar aircraft, which may also have a command and control capability; about 10,000 surface-to-air missiles; and 2,600 interceptor aircraft. Surrounding Moscow there is also the world's only operational anti-ballistic missile system for strategic defence, the Americans having dismantled their equivalent Safeguard ABM system in early 1976.

COMPUTERS AT THE TOP

Overall control of the US armed forces is exercised by the National Command Authorities (NCA) by means of the National Military Command System (NMCS) which in turn consists of a National Military Command Centre (NMCC), and Alternate (or standby) National Military Command Centre (ANMCC), and the National Emergency Airborne Command Post (NEACP), together with the relevant interconnecting telecommunications and automatic data processing support facilities. These elements receive, evaluate, and display intelligence, warning, and force status information, and direct and control the forces carrying out national tasks. In 1977 construction of an expanded NMCC and a new National Military Intelligence Centre was completed; in November 1977 the first phase of an Improved Emergency Message Automatic Transmission System became operational. This provides for more efficient composition, reception and acknowledgement of emergency action messages. Communications to the forces were also improved by providing access to Air Force Satellite Communications System (AFSATCOM) for both NMCC and ANMCC.

An alternative means of rapidly and reliably passing SIOP (Single Integrated Operational Plan) orders – authorization for a nuclear response – from the NCA to strategic forces is imperative. Because of their mobility, airborne command posts offer a greater chance of survival than do the more vulnerable surface and underground command centres, and the E-4B Advanced Airborne Command Post (AABNCP) will take over from three interim E-4A aircraft which have fulfilled this function since 1975. The E-4B model (of which six are planned) differs in having UHF and SHF (Ultra High Frequency and Super High Frequency) satellite communications terminals, a high-power LF/VLF (Low Frequency/Very Low Frequency) airborne terminal and improved secure voice and communications processing capabilities.

For communication between airborne command posts and submerged strategic nuclear submarines a VLF radio link is used called 'Tacamo', the use of very long wavelength signals necessitating a trailing wire antenna some 5 miles long, and special EC-130Q aircraft are employed to carry the VLF transmission equipment and radio links for the reception of orders from other elements of the NMCS. The E-4A/B airborne command posts themselves are installed in a military version of the civil Boeing 747 'jumbo-jet' airliner which has an operational crew of more than 90.

For the command, control and communications for American strategic forces, the President and his staffs need a reliable, flexible and survivable C and C system to serve the National Command Authorities in all types of military operations, and this is provided by the World-Wide Military Command and Control System (WWMCCS), which incorporates a number of unique and independent C^3 systems to ensure effective communications with particular elements of the strategic forces.

One way or another, every operational order for all US forces anywhere in the world reaches its destination via one or more of the 30 or so computer complexes located at major service headquarters that form the WWMCCS, and one or more of the varied communications systems connected to it. Some of the latter will be mentioned briefly later. WWMCCS is in a constant state of growth and improvement to en-

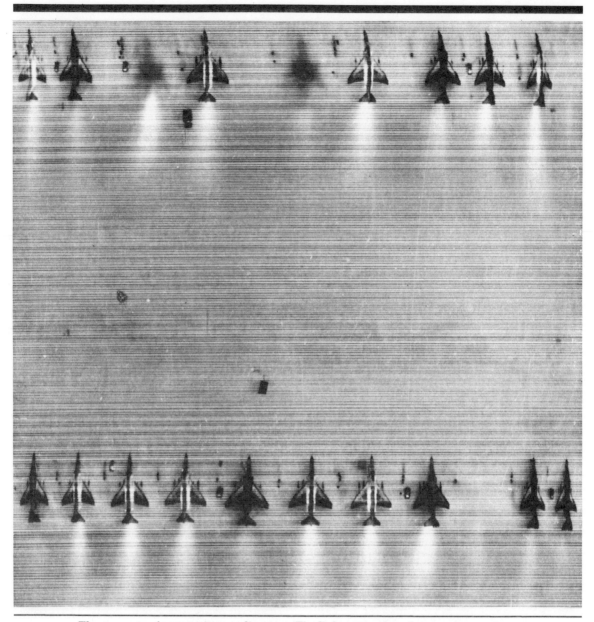

*The accuracy of reconnaissance linescan. The light areas show hot running engines,
or still-warm areas of ground left by departed aircraft;
cool areas and aircraft show up dark on the scan*

hance its performance and to enable it to meet the evolving threat of the Warsaw Pact. Recent developments of this sort initiated include provision for linking Minuteman and Titan ICBM launch control centres to WWMCCS nodes; for coupling of the Defence Satellite Communications System (DSCS) to Simplified Processing Stations of the early warning satellite system.

Within the WWMCCS lies the Minimum Essential Emergency Communications Network (MEECN), a system which employs the entire radio frequency spectrum from ELF (Extremely Low Frequency) to SHF (Super High Frequency) in an effort to ensure that vital strategic command and control messages reach strategic bomber, nuclear submarine, and ballistic missile forces. Major components of the

MEECN are communication satellites and a variety of land-based and airborne communications systems. In the former category, AFSATCOM (Air Force Satellite Communications System) supports worldwide strategic communications needs, and two other systems, the Defence Satellite Communications System (DSCS) and Fleet Satellite Communications System (FLT-SATCOM) are also employed. These systems also support other defence C³ requirements mentioned later. A successor, the Strategic Satellite System (SSS), is planned to take over from AFSATCOM in providing communications for the transmission of nuclear strike authorization messages. The SSS will have greater survivability and resistance to counter-measures. The operational characteristics of strategic bombers and the missile force allow the use of HF, UHF and SHF communications systems, including land, airborne and satellite systems, such as AABNCP, AFS-ATCOM. and landlines.

In the case of strategic submarines the most urgent communications requirement is one-way shore-to-ship transmission. At present this is accomplished by means of VLF and LF shore-based transmitters on US soil and at a number of other locations provided by friendly nations around the world, as well as the Tacamo airborne relay aircraft, and to a lesser extent by HF radio and satellite communications. However, more advanced submarines coming into service have greater operating ranges and are capable of cruising at greater depths, and so something better is being sought. While LF and VLF signals can penetrate sea water to a certain extent, the aim is to provide a system that will allow submarines to receive signals while operating at depths of several hundred feet. To do this, it is proposed to use ELF signals and a system based on this has been proposed under the code name of 'Seafarer'. Environmental objections concerning the siting of the land transmitter has so far held up implementation of this plan, but another, somewhat less capable system using ELF is now under consideration.

FRONT-LINE RECONNAISSANCE

In considering tactical C³I it will be convenient to treat land, or battlefield, operational requirements and the associated air support operations as one aspect, and the naval requirements as a separate topic.

Inevitably, the increasing use of electronic surveillance systems to increase the efficiency of ground forces also provides the opposing forces with an excellent source of target information. Army battlefield reconnaissance systems are mostly concerned with achieving the most effective detection, identification, and monitoring the movements of opposing forces near the front lines, and also in the support areas for a distance of about 50 km beyond the Forward Edge of Battle Area (FEBA). This information is required in near real-time, and on a continuous basis, for target designation and engagement purposes, as well as for tactical planning.

By the 1980s the US Army will have a force of about 90 OV-1 Mohawk twin-engined aircraft and a number of specially-equipped helicopters for roles of this kind. The former can carry cameras and other conventional reconnaissance equipment as well as side-looking airborne radar (SLAR) which enables the aircraft to fly parallel to the front, on its own side of the lines, while surveying enemy territory up to 70 km beyond the FEBA. This system produces two permanent photo-radar maps of targets, on which both fixed and moving targets are plotted. The maps are available almost immediately in the aircraft and can also be transmitted simultaneously via a data link to a ground recording terminal up to 100 nautical miles away. Some aircraft of the Mohawk force are equipped with an Elint (Electronic Intelligence) system code-named 'Quick Look', and these aircraft

SURVEYING THE ENEMY: ELECTRONICS AT WORK

TO WASHINGTON

FORWARD C^{3}I COMPUTERS RECEIVE INPUT DATA PASS IT ON AND RELAY INFORMATION TO FORWARD TROOPS

SLAR FLIGHT LOCATES NEW ARMOURED UNITS AND V/STOLS CAMOUFLAGED IN WOODLAND

PERMANENT RADAR REPORTS MASSED HELICOPTER FLIGHTS INTO FEBA (PRESUMABLY SUPPLY AIRCRAFT)

MICROPHONES

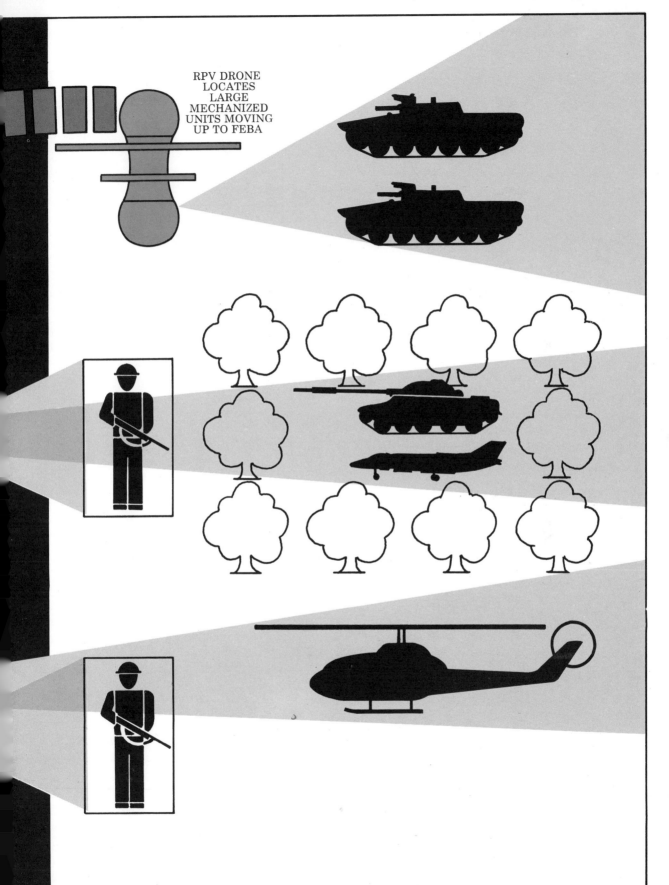

RPV DRONE
LOCATES
LARGE
MECHANIZED
UNITS MOVING
UP TO FEBA

have as part of their mission patrols carried out flying on a course parallel to the NATO/Warsaw Pact boundary line to gather data on radar activity within the Warsaw Pact territory. The system provides for accurate identification and location of such emitters, and for the relay of intercepted signals back to a ground base.

By the early 1980s the SOTAS (Stand-Off Target Acquisition System) will be operational, artillery with a day/night, all-weather capability of detecting moving targets with sufficient accuracy for indirect engagement, using a helicopter flying between 15 and 20km on the friendly side of the FEBA as a spotter aircraft. Target detection and location will be by means of an advanced type of radar, with the target information being relayed direct to a ground station for analysis and display. The tactical air forces will also provide special aircraft to gather electronic reconnaissance information using systems such as TEREC (Tactical Electronic Reconnaissance) and equipment similar or the same as that carried by the Army's Mohawk aircraft to locate enemy non-communications ground-based emitters, and providing data on these emitters to ground stations by data link or in recorded form.

A force of about 20 to 30 special RF-4C Phantom aircraft will be employed by the USAF in this role to provide ESM (Electronic Support Measures) information to the theatre commanders. These aircraft will also carry additional sensors such as side-looking airborne radar, and infra-red target detection devices. Under the UPD-X programme, in which West Germany and the USA are collaborating, a new advanced SLAR is being developed for use in the European theatre. Other European NATO nations have their own individual or co-operative programmes for the use of helicopter and conventional drones and RPVs (Remotely-Piloted Vehicles) for reconnaissance purposes.

The American forces have had considerable experience in the use of drones, particularly in South-East Asia, and are building on this experience in the evolution of new systems for wider application. 'Compass Cope', for example, is a high-flying, long-endurance, high-reliability RPV intended to fulfil a variety of missions, among them those of serving as an airborne relay station for electronic intelligence (Elint) and other reconnaissance data, and also for the actual gathering of such information. Other types are under development for shorter duration missions of the same sort and also for possible battlefield use to attack certain categories of target (eg radars).

Many of these developments will be combined in the USAF PLSS (Precision Location Strike System) which has as its main objective the provision of an integrated system that will accurately locate emitters and non-radiating targets, and will have near real-time capabilities. It will provide all-weather precision guidance for stand-off weapons, and accurate aircraft positioning for all-weather delivery of free-fall weapons also. Separate means are provided for the location of radiating and non-radiating targets. PLSS comprises these basic elements: airborne platforms which carry the emitter and target locating equipment; a ground processing system which processes location and strike data; and strike aircraft armed with guided weapons that utilize distance measuring equipment (DME) guidance.

Two new US Army ground-based systems now nearing entry into service, and which will complement the airborne systems just described, are the Tactical Communications Emitter Location and Identification System (TACELIS) and the Automated Ground Tactical Emitter Location Intercept System (AGTELIS). Both are vehicle-mounted. A number of the latter will be deployed with US Army Corps formations, and in operation, sites on high ground will be sought and the location of

AGTELIS units will be arranged to provide the maximum possible baseline between adjacent reception sites to permit triangulation on emitters within mutual detection range. TACELIS can be used at corps level and may also supplement divisional collection and airborne collection and direction-finding systems.

Tactical command, control and communications systems must operate with sensor and intelligence systems like those described above (and with others, such as those of allies) to provide adequate warning, responsive control of forces and assessment of operations. Strenuous efforts are being made to achieve this, involving more widespread use of automation, increasing the resistance of communications and data links to jamming and/or interception, improved means of target identification, and integration of battlefield command and control systems. AWACS radar aircraft will give airborne early warning of aircraft or cruise missile attack, including low-level threats, and will be linked to ground-based command centres for airborne surveillance purposes and for the control of both offensive and defensive missions by 'own' aircraft operations. The US Army's Tactical Operations System is now being modernized by the adoption of improved automatic data processing and display techniques to make it more responsive to battlefield needs at divisional and corps level. One aspect of this affects the USAF Tactical Air Control System (485L), and another is the USAF automated air command and control in Europe.

Steps are being made to bring about better use of reconnaissance and intelligence information gathered by different branches of the armed forces under the programme known as project BETA (Battlefield Exploitation and Target Acquisition). This envisages the setting-up of sensor information fusion centres for use at army corps and division centres and air force tactical air control centres. The fusion centres are fully standardized and exchange sensor-derived data (from ground and airborne systems) obtained in near real-time.

BETA mobile fusion centres will provide target information, develop the battlefield intelligence picture and provide for battlefield sensor management. It is also planned to extend the scope of existing techniques to make the Tactical Air Control Systems and Tactical Air Defence Systems (Joint TAC/TADS) inter-operable. Thus the air control and air defence systems of all US forces will be able to communicate directly with each other without the need for external co-ordination. The later programme, JINTACCS (Joint Inter-operability of Tactical Command and Control Systems) will extend the principle to other types of tactical command and control centres.

TACTICAL COMMUNICATIONS

If full advantage is to be derived from improvements of the kind outlined above, tactical communications have a vital part to play; and the present period is seeing the implementation of advanced plans that have been the subject of considerable efforts by the defence experts of many nations for 10 or 20 years.

America has a joint tactical communications programme (TRI-TAC) which provides for common multi-channel communications equipment for all arms of the US forces. It features mobile, protected hardware using automatic switching for the rapid dissemination of data messages and voice communications. The general use of TRI-TAC common equipment throughout the theatre of operations will also link single-channel tactical users with other theatre systems, and US systems with the systems of allied nations.

Close to the FEBA, command and control is exercised primarily through the use of combat net radio sets, and a new range of hardware is being developed for

NATO use by units of land and air forces. The new family of radios will include man-pack, vehicle-mounted and airborne sets to provide single-channel VHF, jamming-resistant sets. The combat net radio programme involves contributions from the USA and a number of European NATO member states, but field hardware is not likely to appear in sufficient quantities to achieve the ultimate objective – close battlefield integration of multi-national forces – before the mid 1980s.

The same applies to another advanced programme now under way, the Joint Tactical Information Distribution System (JTIDS). This is intended to provide a jamming-resistant, secure integrated communications, navigation and identification system for tactical forces. It has been designed to permit real-time distribution of critical combat data to large numbers of fighting units. It will provide AWACS with a link to ground command and control centres and tactical aircraft, and this is expected to be the first operational application, some time in the 1980s. Other uses are as an integrated communications, navigation and identification system for the US Navy, replacing older data and voice communications equipment. Land-based applications are under study by the US Army and Marine Corps, and the possibility of its use for mid-course guidance of cruise missiles is also under consideration.

SYSTEMS FOR THE FLEETS

Naval command, control, communications and intelligence requirements, as appropriate to the US Navy, comprise major systems ashore and afloat for dealing with both surface targets and submarines. Systems exist or are planned which will provide ships at sea with information on the location and activities of Soviet surface warships, submarines, and other ships of interest, as well as those of other nations. This information is also required at shore establishments, in particular the Fleet Command Centre (FCC) located within the US Navy Command and Control System.

The FCC's objectives are to process and display information for the Fleet Commander-in-Chief, to provide the National Command Authorities and the Navy Department with operational and resource information on request, and to exchange information between tactical commanders at sea and ashore. It is also intended to provide facilities by which enemy targets beyond the surveillance horizon of individual ships can be detected, located, identified and attacked while remaining outside the range of enemy weapons. Tactical commanders at sea are to be provided with Tactical Flag Command Centres (TFCCs), each one an integrated shipboard command centre providing the tactical flag commander with a situation display to enable him to plan, monitor, and direct operations. The provision of intelligence and surveillance information in support of these operational facilities is the function of the Ocean Surveillance Information System (OSIS).

Sources of input data for OSIS include reconnaissance satellites (and later special-purpose ocean surveillance satellites similar to those used by the Soviet Union), aircraft, surface ships, shore sensors, and underwater detection systems, plus data from any other sources. A number of Orion maritime aircraft have been modified for electronic surveillance duties, in which role they are designated EP-3E, and these play an important part in ocean surveillance.

Their equipment has been the subject of continuous modification and improvement, the latest example of which includes better systems for the correlation of emitter signals received to specific ships (or class of ship). This is achieved by computer techniques coupled with recorded 'libraries' of the characteristics of Soviet and other warships' radars and other electronic equipment. Automatic computer comparison of intercepted signals with the recorded radar signature enables rapid identifications to be made in near real-time.

Due to take over this function is the Tactical Airborne Signal Exploitation System (TASES) which will employ the latest S-3A twin-jet maritime aircraft airframe, equipped with radar, IFF, Elint and Communications Intelligence (Comint) receivers, infra-red surveillance and optical sub-systems. Information obtained from these carrier-borne aircraft will be transmitted directly into the tactical commander's command and control systems. Three data links will be available: one linking the aircraft and the ship's Command Information Centre, an ESM link between aircraft and the shipboard TASES control system, and a computer-to-computer data link which will allow for secure transmission of eight channels of raw data back to the ship. Operators aboard the parent ship will be able to control the electronic intelligence sub-systems on the aircraft by remote control if required.

For underwater target surveillance the latest system is the US Navy's Anti-Submarine Warfare Centre Command and Control System (ASWCCCS). This is a world-wide network giving ASW force commanders and their area or sector commanders facilities for decision-making and control of their respective forces. Sources of target data include the Sound Surveillance System (SOSUS) consisting of fixed undersea acoustic networks of passive hydrophone detector arrays around the USA, and to which major improvements to the signal and data processing elements of the system have been implemented. The other main source will consist of SURTASS (Surveillance Towed Array) systems. These are replacing the earlier Towed Array Surveillance System (TASS), and are long arrays of passive sonar sensors towed at slow speed over designated patrol lines. Data obtained from these sensors will be relayed in real-time to shore analysis and correlation data processing centres (probably the same ones as those set up on the east and west coasts of the USA to process SOSUS data). Funding for the first three SURTASS ships, 217 ft long, 11 knot twin-screw diesel-powered vessels designated T-AGOS, was included in the US defence budget of 1978.

The American Defence Advanced Research Projects Agency (DARPA) has hopes of a largely secret Undersea Surveillance programme which apparently relies heavily upon tremendous concentrations of computer power to make sense of extremely weak acoustic sounds emitted by submarine targets at long ranges. In conjunction with linear acoustic arrays up to ten times longer than hitherto thought possible, satellite links for real-time data transmission from a number of such arrays to an Acoustic Research Centre (ARC) in California, and no less than 20 computers of eight different types, DARPA employed what has been claimed as the world's most powerful computer, ILIAC IV, to demonstrate the technique. The satellite link was used to transmit data from towed arrays to the ARC, and three inter-array processing techniques were used to track both co-operative and non co-operative targets. It is expected that an operational system could be handed over to the US Navy in 1981.

BETTER AND BETTER NETWORKS

Huge computer networks of this scale are an accepted feature of the United States' military machine. We have already described the WWMCCS, but in parallel with this global network there are others which are available for other military communications purposes. The bulk of the day-to-day routine DoD telecommunications traffic is handled by the Defence Communications System (DCS) which provides US forces throughout the world with long-haul, common-user voice, data, and teletype services. The principal elements of this service are the Automatic Voice Network (AUTOVON); AUTOSEVCOM II, a global secure voice network; and AUTODIN II, which is the main switched data communications network and provides for interactive computer communications. AUTODIN II is a development of the ARPANET, which as its title suggests was developed by the Defence Advanced Research Projects Agency and consists of a computer network stretching from Europe across the USA to Hawaii. About 60 computers of 26 types are employed, and the net is used by more than 1,000 establishments, ranging from defence laboratories to military installations, and including a subsidiary network that processes ASW information.

A feature of modern networks of this kind is known as 'packet-switching', which enables messages to be broken down into digital 'packets' of, say, 1,000 bits each of which contains a coded address of the intended recipient. These packets are then automatically routed by the computer switch over any free route through the network, the packets are reassembled at their destination and an acknowledgement sent back to the originator. In the event of an error, the sender automatically repeats the message packet. To enable computers of different types to 'talk' to each other, small computers are used as go-betweens, automatically making any necessary conversions in signal or programming formats.

In this chapter it has been possible only to outline the more significant instances of the electronic element of modern warfare, but other chapters in this volume offer excellent grounds for the study of the other, more detailed, examples of what has been called 'mechanical intelligence' at work. There can be little doubt of the present and growing importance of this element of modern warfare, or of the enormous power that such techniques add to the inherent potential of current weapons.
RON PRETTY

ABBREVIATIONS, Chr 6

AABNCP Advanced Airborne Command Post
AEW Airborne Early Warning
AFSATCOM Air Force Satellite Communications System
AGTELIS Automated Ground Tactical Emitter Location System
ANMCC Alternate National Military Command Centre
ARC Acoustic Research Centre
ASW Anti-Submarine Warfare
ASWCCCS Anti-Submarine Warfare Centre Command and Control System
AUTOVON Automatic Voice Network
AWACS Airborne Warning and Control System
BETA Battlefield Exploitation and Target Acquisition
BMEWS Ballistic Missile Early Warning System
C and C Command and Control
C^3I Command, Control, Communications and Intelligence
DARPA Defence Advanced Research Projects Agency
DCS Defence Communications System
DME Distance Measuring Equipment
DSCS Defence Satellite Communications System
ECM Electronic Counter-Measures
ELF Extra Low Frequency
ESM Electronic Support Measures
EW Electronic Warfare
FCC Fleet Command Centre
FEBA Forward Edge of Battle Area
FLTSATCOMS Fleet Satellite Communications System
IEMATS Improved Emergency Message Automatic Transmission System
JINTACCS Joint Interoperability of Tactical Command and Control Systems
Joint TAC/TADS Tactical Air Control Systems + Tactical Air Defence Systems
JTIDS Joint Tactical Information Distribution System
LF/VLF Low Frequency/Very Low Frequency
MEECN Minimum Essential Emergency Communications Network
NADGE NATO Air Defence Ground Environment
NCA National Command Authorities
NEACP National Emergency Airborne Command Post
NMCC National Military Command Centre
NMCS National Military Command System
NMI National Military Intelligence
NORAD North American Air Defence
OSIS Ocean Surveillance Information System
PARCS Perimeter Acquisition Radar Attached Characterisation System
PLSS Precision Location Strike System
ROCC Regional Operations Control Centre
SAM Surface-to-Air Missile
SHF Super High Frequency
SIOP Single Integrated Operational Plan
SLBM Submarine-Launched Ballistic Missile
SOSUS Sound Surveillance System
SOTAS Stand-off Target Acquisition System
SSS Strategic Satellite System
SURTASS Surveillance Towed Array System
TACELIS Tactical Emitter Location Intercept System
TASS Towed Array Surveillance System
TERCOM Terrain Counter Matching
TEREC Tactical Electronic Reconnaissance
TFCC Tactical Flag Command Centre
TOS Tactical Operations System
UHF Ultra High Frequency
WWMCCS World Wide Military Command and Control

7. LAND WEAPONS

f we confine this discussion to war on land, in Europe, between the central forces of NATO on one side and the forces of the Warsaw Pact on the other, we can begin by dismissing the classical principles of war. This is not because they are no longer valid, for that is not so, but because one side – NATO – is prevented by self-imposed constraints from applying them in planning its own defence against aggression.

These principles, so-called, are no more than the lessons of past conflicts and are accepted by the Free World and the Marxist world alike. They argue that the outcome of protracted war is decided by the total resources the belligerents have at their disposal: populations, natural resources of energy and minerals, the size of the industrial bases and degree to which they have developed science and technology. This principle of war is also firmly imprinted on the Soviet military mind. Soviet strategists believe that armed conflicts are decided by offensive action pressed to the point of destroying the enemy's armed forces, liquidating its government and physically occupying its territory. These were the lessons of the 'Great Patriotic War of 1941–45', as the Russians call their struggle in World War 2.

In the Soviet view there is a sound working principle not found in the Western textbooks: *never fight in your own country*.

The whole Soviet view of national defence is coloured by the catastrophe which befell the USSR when the German armies overran the country from the Polish frontier to the gates of Moscow. The invaders were ejected, but only at vast cost in human life and material, and by

the use of all the national resources in *mass*. *Mass*, the concentration of all effort, and *offensive action* are therefore Soviet watchwords. But there is another consideration. The Soviet forces in being must be strong enough to preserve the territorial integrity of the Soviet Union *and* her westward-facing belt of Soviet-aligned Marxist states.

THE WARSAW PACT: POISED FOR SMASHING VICTORY

The consequences are clearly to be seen in the present military posture of the Soviet Union, including the Warsaw Pact forces which are under firm Soviet control. Russia's armed forces are many times larger than is required for her territorial defence, bearing in mind that by any analysis her NATO opponent, at whom these preparations are directed, is in no way capable of offensive action on land in Europe.

It cannot be certain that the Soviet forces would never be used to extend the area of territory under Russia's control. Soviet strategy is fundamentally *defensive in principle* but *offensive in practice*: if threatened, the best defence is to attack and crush the aggressor. There are good reasons for this, endorsed by both classical strategy and the newer theories of nuclear war. The offensive confers all the advantages of timing, choice of points of attack, surprise and, when attacking an alliance, the inevitable delays among its members in deciding on concerted action. If the NATO front can be broken quickly, Soviet armoured columns can be sent crashing into the exposed command system and infrastructure of the defence and, vitally important, the airfields and missile sites from which nuclear weapons might be brought to bear.

SOVIET DOCTRINE: USE HEAVIEST FORCES AT MAXIMUM SPEED

Soviet military doctrine does not believe in any *gradual* application of force. Once committed to war, every weapon will be used and maximum force brought to bear to secure a swift and total victory. The only limiting factors might be expediency. Although the Soviet land forces possess nuclear weapon systems and also the resources for chemical and biological warfare, the precise moment of their deployment (and, in the case of chemical weapons, their use at all) would vary. The Soviet planners might conceivably decide to avoid the use of nuclear weapons altogether, bearing in mind the openly expressed Western desire to delay using them for as long as possible. Part of the Soviet operational philosophy is the use of *desant* forces, for attack on the enemy strategic rear; and the Russians might think it possible to take out NATO's sources of nuclear firepower by direct attack before they could take effect.

NATO: RESTRICTIONS OF THE ENFORCED DEFENSIVE

The problem of defending NATO's European frontiers from aggression, launched for whatever reason, looks very different indeed.

In the wars of the pre-nuclear era the universally-accepted strategy for repelling an invasion could take the form of a preemptive offensive to disrupt the preparations of the aggressor, or of deploying a defensive shield behind which a counter-offensive could be prepared. A rigid, linear frontier defence was regarded as a formula for certain defeat. Experience taught that a determined attacker was bound to penetrate any defensive system to some degree. Accordingly defensive systems have always been organised in *depth*. In practice this means that the defence is elastic, with the forward troops free to give ground, sometimes for many miles to the rear rather than offering a rigid and therefore easily ruptured front; that there are sufficient troops to prepare and occupy one or more lines arranged in depth behind the other; and that behind these fixed but elastic positions are positioned ample mobile, armoured reserves, ready to make local counterattacks to preserve the integrity of the defensive system as a whole until the main counter-offensive can be mounted. For a practical example of this we need to go no further back in history than to Sinai in 1973.

For NATO such a strategy is completely banned, for three reasons.

The first is that the whole ethic on which the Atlantic Alliance is based is deterrence and the avoidance of war. The jingoism of the Soviet leaders ('we don't want to fight/but by Jingo if we do/we have the tanks/we have the guns/and nuclear weapons too') is denied to the NATO planners, because the climate of Western opinion demands that not only must the Alliance's intentions be devoid of aggression in any form, but that this be manifest from its war plans and the way NATO defences are organized.

The second is that economic forces limit the size of the NATO armies. The Supreme Allied Commander lacks the resources to mount a restorative counterattack, let alone a counter-offensive or anything so extravagant as a pre-emptive counterstroke.

The third is that elastic defence in depth, trading territory for time, means sacrificing a large part of the most prosperous and powerful of the European states to enemy occupation and to use it later as the scene of a mobile, armoured and possibly nuclear battle.

In consequence NATO's defence is necessarily linear, rigid, without depth or massive reserve armies and as far to the east as possible. At first sight it seems to any military student brought up on the classical principles of war a formula for rapid defeat, and in fact it is.

The aim, however, is different from the now obsolete patterns of war of the 19th and early 20th centuries. Faced with these constraints, the NATO aim is to use its weapons to inflict the maximum amount of attrition and delay on an aggressor, using, if conventional weapons fail, nuclear weapon systems designed for battlefield use. The NATO use of force is not so much to impose any political solution, but to use firepower to hurt the aggressor so much that he may conclude that his aggression is unprofitable. The NATO use of armed force is, in short, designed as a deterrent to aggression, and not as a means of eliminating the aggressor's powers of mischief. For this there are no precedents in military history. It may be a valid strategy. It certainly rests on super-abundant firepower.

With sharply restricted numbers and severe restrictions on the permissible methods of use, the Atlantic Alliance must therefore rely on superior military technology; and this has already caused a radical change in the nature of land forces.

In historical perspective, this change was clearly visible as early as 1918, when the first tanks, the first ground-attack aircraft, the first means of acquiring target intelligence by electronic devices and the camera, and the first radio networks for command and control were being used in battle. In World War 2 there were two more innovations (excluding nuclear weapons) which were to make up the family of weapons of the new technology dominating land warfare today. These were radar and the experimental use by the Germans of guided missiles, especially surface-to-air missiles (SAMs). These were all remarkable but it was the improved tank which stole the scene, despite the fact that in the Russian theatre, where the biggest and bloodiest battles were fought, the two decisive weapons remained the rifle-carrying infantryman and the simple field artillery piece used in divisions numbered by the hundred. This, broadly speaking, was true of all armies, including that of the United States, by 1945 the most advanced in the world.

TECHNOLOGY VERSUS THE BIG BATTALLIONS

The armies of World War 2 were in fact, in the language of economics, *'labour-intensive'*, exploiting muscle-power eked out by machinery. Navies and air forces were already *'capital-intensive'*, using men to operate very expensive weapon-systems. The radical change which gives hope to any advanced power wondering how to cope with aggression based on massed forces is the parallel but delayed evolution of armies into capital-intensive organisations. In modern warfare 'attrition', the baneful policy of World War 1 trench warfare, no longer concentrates on killing human beings (although this is still a consideration) but on the elimination of weapon-systems. (The term *weapon-system* distinguishes between a simple *weapon*, like an anti-tank gun, and a *system*, like a SAM, with its early warning and fire-control radars and computers all linked by an electronic command and control system.)

A very simple model exists in the shape of the Israeli defence forces. Because of a shortage of manpower and in order to exploit quick Israeli wits and Israeli aptitude for mechanical engineering, the strike force of *Zahal* is a combination of tanks and fighter/ground-attack aircraft. An ordinary infantry company may consist of 150 men, a tank company of 45; but a strike force of ten or so tanks in terms of firepower and mobility is altogether of a different order. Armoured shielding also has the advantage of protecting the crews from the lethal effects of nuclear weapons by a factor of ten. As a result the combat element of modern armies is all-armoured and based on the tank. Infantry and forward air defence – SAMs and anti-aircraft artillery (AAA) – are all in tracked, armoured vehicles.

The 1970s have seen the dominance of the tank/aircraft combination but there has inevitably been a parallel development of counter-weapons. The tank, formidable as it is, is now the most hunted quarry on the battlefield. No single weapon can be completely effective against it: a family or spectrum is needed, extending all the way from guns and hand-held missile dischargers to anti-tank guided weapons (ATGW) of increasing sophistication. At the same time, by a sort of homeopathic process, the poison itself has proved the best antidote. The most effective anti-tank defence is by guns mounted in tanks.

Modern tanks are far less inflammable than those of 30 years ago. Protected with composite armour, equipped with a huge gun, assisted by laser or other advanced fire-control instruments and used from prepared defences (dodging, as the Israeli tanks did on the Golan plateau in 1973, from one tankpit on an elevated ramp to another, exposing nothing but the turret), the tank is the most effective counter-weapon on land. Tanks also have the advantage, as compared with aircraft, of being very cheap at a time when the financial burden of maintaining up-to-date stocks of weapons in adequate numbers is too much for even the advanced countries.

The factor of cost and the abandon-ment of labour-intensive weapons has led to solutions to the problem of defence involving volumes of misdirected fire being discarded in favour of expensive but accu-

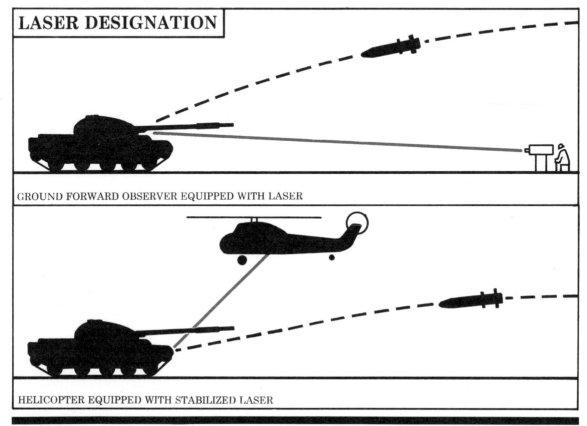

LASER DESIGNATION

GROUND FORWARD OBSERVER EQUIPPED WITH LASER

HELICOPTER EQUIPPED WITH STABILIZED LASER

rate missiles with a high probability of a first-time hit. Despite their high cost, the exchange value is overwhelmingly in their favour. The alternative threat to the tank comes from a family of ATGW, some for the self-protection of the infantry, some for direct attack on tanks. The majority are manually guided by the operator by electrical impulses transmitted along a thin filament or wire. Examples are the Russian *Sagger*, the British *Swingfire*, the American *TOW* and the radio-controlled Russian *Swatter*. Under development is quite a different sort of missile in the shape of a long-range artillery projectile with terminal guidance by a remote observer.

The most radical counter-weapon, and in the opinion of some the most effective, is the combination of an ATGW with the fast attack helicopter. This is a system pioneered by the Americans as one of a family of weapon-carrying helicopters. It must be seen not as another form of aircraft, shooting downwards on targets selected in the process of aerial patrol, and so an easy prey for fighter aircraft from above and air-defence systems from below, but as a special sort of gun-platform, used to concentrate the fire of many ATGW in a sector threatened by armoured attack. Helicopter tactics are to operate from cover, flying close to the ground, climbing briefly to obtain a line of sight and fire before ducking down again. It is, in a sense, a sort of tank, except that the main battle tank is relatively very slow but heavily protected, while the attack helicopter has only the slightest or no armour to protect its crew but mobility in three dimensions and speeds of 100–150 knots. It is one of the most promising responses to massed tank attack, but it is a rich man's solution. The quality of manpower required is high and the time required for training long compared with that of tank crews.

DEFENCE AGAINST AIRCRAFT

The air-tank confrontation is a perfect example of how weapon-systems continually produce counter-weapons and counter-counter weapons, and so on. Tank encounters are decided in advance by which side has control of the air, as we shall see in the following chapter. The power and versatility of the air arm is such that defence against it has to be, literally, in *depth*: organised in layers or concentric zones from the ground up.

This has resulted in the development of a range of SAMs to counter high-performance ground attack aircraft and weapon-carrying helicopters in the 0–1,000 metres band up to 35,000 metres effective altitude and 70,000 metres 'slant range'. In the combat zone there will be no 'fronts' or 'flanks' or 'secure areas', only the shifting tank battle with aircraft intervening at low level. The air defence units must be able to accompany the tanks and armoured infantry and survive. The slant range of the more vulnerable and less mobile high-altitude systems is to enable them to reach forward to cover the combat

ARMOURED BALANCE: TANK STRENGTH 1978						
	Northern and Central Europe			Southern Europe		
	NATO	Warsaw Pact	(of which USSR)	NATO	Warsaw Pact	(of which USSR)
Main battle tanks in operational service*	7,000	20,500	13,500	4,000	6,700	2,500
*Included here are four Category 1 divisions in Hungary and a number of divisions that might reinforce Southern Europe rather than the central sector. Soviet naval infantry are not included.						

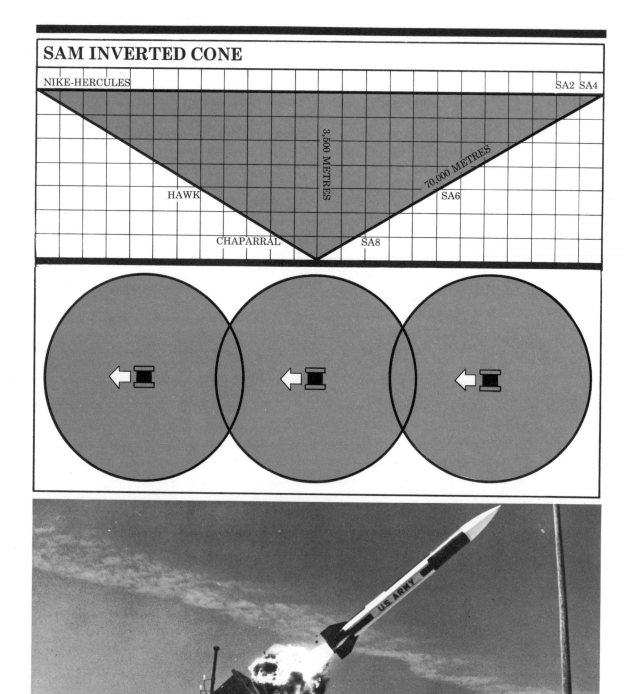

SAM INVERTED CONE

NIKE-HERCULES

SA2 SA4

3,500 METRES

70,000 METRES

HAWK

SA6

CHAPARRAL

SA8

Top: *The inverted cone of air cover provided by SAMs of different altitudes
and slant ranges. Also: Overlapping zones of protection from a trio of mobile SAM batteries.*
Above: *America's SAM-D ('Patriot')*

troops from positions in the rear. At the very bottom, low-level self-defence is provided by hand-held SAMs such as the Russian SA-7 and the American *Redeye*, both heat-seeking and homing automatically on the jet exhaust, and the British optically-controlled radio-command *Blowpipe*. Tank columns are protected by the highly sophisticated and very costly descendents of the AA-tanks of World War 2: armoured tracked vehicles carrying pairs of small-calibre guns with a high cyclic rate of fire or guided missile launchers with on-carriage fire-control instruments and target-acquisition radar, such as the West German 35mm gun *Gepard*, the American Vulcan 20mm-M113 and the Soviet ZSU 57-2.

Among the SAM equivalents are the Russian SA-8, the American *Chaparral* and

With the West German forces: a triple-rack 'Hawk' SAM launcher being checked by Luftwaffe *technicians*

the French *Roland*, which has a slant range of 6,500 metres; next the American *Hawk* and the Russian SA-6, going up another step, for cover of the combat area up to 20–25,000 metres slant range and mounted on tracks; and at the top, *SA-2, SA-4* and *Nike-Hercules*. *SAM-D* is under development to supersede *Hawk* and *Nike-Hercules*. All these, with their associated radars for early warning of attack and for target acquisition, illumination and fire control

in each SAM battery and the command and control communication network, make up one extensive surface-to-air weapon system of great cost and complexity. Its real costs are difficult to determine, but apart from the capital expenditure involved in establishing the systems, the cost only of missiles shot away in Egypt and Syria in a few days in 1973 may have run into tens of millions of dollars. Bearing in mind that the NATO concept of defence is based on attrition, its prospects of success depend not only on numbers of systems but on having ready for use sufficient missiles – which may mean thousands of missiles – of all natures.

CONSTANT SEARCH FOR ADVANTAGE

The evolutionary process does not end at this point. Implicit in it is the natural law demanding a penalty in return for each new advantage. The more sophisticated a new system may be, the more vulnerable it becomes to attack from two opposed directions. The high-technology counter is the assault on their 'nervous systems' by electronic counter-measures or ECM, requiring in turn defence by counter-counter measures (ECCM). This electromagnetic battle is accompanied by more direct attack, such as by guided missiles using 'passive' guidance homing down radar beams to destroy their source, which demands in turn rapid frequency changes to baffle them, and so on. More economical and more brutal is reversion to primitive methods: ground attack by commando-type troops to kill the operators and capture or disable the equipment. The Russian armed forces include airborne and air transported troops in large numbers trained in *desant* tactics: attack on the rear areas where all this vulnerable equipment may be located.

It will be seen, therefore, that any hope that one side or the other can maintain a permanent technological advantage over the other is illusory. This is not a prediction of the future: it is the position at the moment. Almost every weapons system on one side is matched by an equally sophisticated weapon on the other, and the search for improvement is continuous. The only limitation is the cost of research and development and the subsequent capital cost of production in sufficient quantity to influence the military balance.

NATO'S PROSPECTS: BLACK IN THE LONG RUN

We are back therefore to the principle of mass, and the question of the relationship, if any, between numbers and the relative efficiency of weapons. The answer is that there can be no certain forecast of the outcome of an armed clash, great or small, simple or complex, but that 'models', mathematical in their nature and based on probability theory, can offer insights, if not predictions, into the way a combat develops.

Such theoretical analysis allows some sort of parity between the two sides in terms of leadership, determination, command skills and the efficiency of the command and control structure in cybernetic terms. In *protracted* combat, however, the advantage lies markedly on the side with the margin of superiority, and that this margin increases like compound interest until the defence collapses as the combat proceeds. This forecast, gloomy for the Western defence concept, unfortunately corresponds closely to experience.

It might reasonably be asked that if this is so, how did the Germans in their early *blitzkriegs*, and the Israelis in 1967 and again in 1973, so crushingly defeat such superior numbers? The answer is that the *blitzkrieg* only works when the victim is mentally and physically unprepared. In the last of the October 1973 armoured battles which prepared the way for the Israeli crossing of the Suez Canal (a crossing which 'took out' a number of SAMs supplied by the Soviet Union and so breached the air-defence screen under which the Egyptians were operating with relative safety) the Israelis eliminated an Egyptian armoured division (about 97% total loss) for the loss of three tanks. This happened because when the Israelis shot at the Egyptians they scored hits, while the Egyptians missed. Immediately after this an Israeli spearhead forced open a corridor, in places only a mere few hundred yards wide, through the densest of the Egyptian defences to the point chosen for the crossing. No NATO planner in his senses could hope for such a disparity in battle-craft and leadership between the Russians on the one side and the Americans, British and Germans on the other. They are all as good, if not better, than the Israelis, and therefore numbers will prevail.

Let us adapt the model, which is really a model of attrition, to a linear defence attacked by a force enjoying 3:1 superiority in, say, three equal successive waves, bearing in mind that the defenders have no reserves and may not withdraw, except locally. (There is no point in withdrawal, because in the absence of reserves it is useless to trade space for time to mount the counter-offensive.) The simplest form of the model postulates an attack distributed evenly along the front – an unreal situation – and even this eventually erodes the defence to a point at which it cannot be sustained. Assume that the first wave is eliminated altogether, while the defender remains in being but reduced in numbers. The second wave therefore starts at an advantage, and the attrition suffered by the defence is a percentage of the remainder. These survivors in turn have to face yet another wave of fresh attackers at an even greater disadvantage, and the ratio of attrition is beginning to run strongly in the attacker's favour. Unless the defender has ample reserves to throw into the fight he is doomed.

BLUEPRINT FOR DISASTER

This particular model is unreal because no aggressor is likely to be so obliging: the reality will be a good deal worse. He will direct his columns as his knowledge of the terrain and of his opponent's dispositions indicate. The attacker's best chance of success is to seek for the soft spots, concentrate fire and numbers on them, penetrate as deeply as possible, probing for the vulnerable artillery and headquarters areas, and the airfields and supply dumps behind them, pouring his reserves into the gaps so created and using them for a series of internal envelopments and even deeper penetrations, to break up the rigid cordon into segments and eliminate them piecemeal.

THE NUCLEAR NIGHTMARE

The next question is, can the defence be sustained long enough to act as a protective screen for the various nuclear weapon systems which form the next stage of NATO's territorial defence? At first sight nuclear weapons seem to free the defence from the tyranny of numbers, as no weapon before has ever held out the promise of annihilating targets. A tactical theory has been developed and altered as the strength and limitations of the weapon became better known to military planners. It remains, of course, a theory: fortunately there has been no precedent. Unlike conventional tactics which are fundamentally concerned with manoeuvre, nuclear tactics are based on calculable weapon effects and probability theory. The likely effects of a warhead of given size were known from experimental physics and the practical application to a given target from the numerical probability of inflicting a desired level of damage or, in the case of troops, of percentage casualties. These can be combined with the delivery error of weapons systems. The statistics of former conventional combat showed that roughly 25–$33\frac{1}{3}\%$ casualties inflicted in a short space of time rendered a unit incapable of further effort. It is tacitly agreed, outside of paper exercises, that after an exchange of some 50 or 60 weapons (let alone the 700-odd believed to exist for the defence of the NATO side alone) with all the attendant horrors, the troops would either bolt or go to ground in panic.

The early tactical solutions were ingenious, but unsound. The first combined classical defence with nuclear counter-attack. For this, conventional tank/infantry forces took up conventional positions, the infantry dug in and the tanks in packets ready for local counter attack or blocking operations. The idea was to force the attacker to concentrate in sufficient strength for him to attempt a breakthrough and so offer a profitable nuclear target. If a breakthrough was achieved, then the mobile reserve, such as it was, was to seal it off while the attacker pressed blindly on into the sack or bulge so formed, again to be eliminated at the right moment by nuclear weapons. Apart from the fact that this credited the attacker with little sense ('the fallacy of the passive enemy') certain impractabilities were revealed by analysis.

Nuclear weapons may be immensely destructive but also almost intolerably difficult to use on a battlefield. The tactically useful effect is circular in shape and intensely concentrated, but falls off rapidly from the point of burst. These diminished effects, only marginally useful against targets, constitute a grave danger to friendly troops who may be injured by blast, scorched *and* blinded. In addition the soil near the point of burst may become dangerously radioactive, and should the fireball touch the ground soil might be sucked up, irradiated and deposited as dangerous 'fallout' over a large area on friend and foe alike.

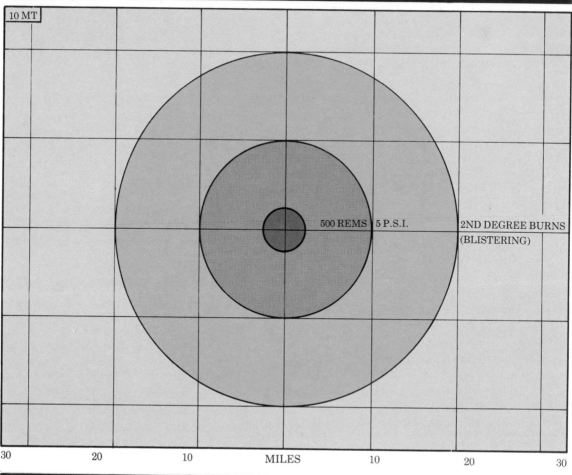

10 MT

500 REMS 5 P.S.I.   2ND DEGREE BURNS
(BLISTERING)

30   20   10   MILES   10   20   30

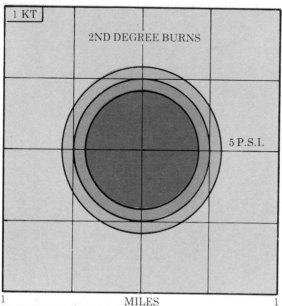

1 KT

2ND DEGREE BURNS

5 P.S.I.

1   MILES   1

To give some idea of the distances involved, the safe distance for gamma-radiation from a 1KT (equivalent 1,000

Destruction charts for 10-megaton (above) and one-kiloton bursts. '5 p.s.i.' represents the circle in which nearly all conventional houses will be irreparably damaged; '500 REMS' the circle within which nearly all persons outdoors or indoors (not in shelters) will die of exposure to initial nuclear radiation – chiefly neutrons and gamma rays

tons of conventional high explosive) is 1.1 km (0.6 miles) and 2.1 km (1.3 miles) for a 100KT, but for first-degree flash burns 1.1 km and 8.5 (5.3 miles) respectively. If the attacker had the good sense and courage to use his armoured troops, whose steel protection reduces these effects by a factor of up to ten, to press as close to the defender as possible or, better still, take every risk and thrust into his positions to create as confused a situation as possible, nuclear weapons become almost impossible to use as a quick-reaction close-in weapon.

And what good is a *slow* reaction in the fluid and rapidly changing circumstances of an armoured battle?

An alternative scheme accepted this and reversed the roles of the conventional and nuclear forces. Small armoured battle groups, widely dispersed so as to avoid attracting hostile nuclear attack, would act as the scouts and protectors of mobile nuclear batteries, seeking to find and briefly fix targets which would be duly eliminated by nuclear fire. This postulated the free use of nuclear weapons for fleeting targets of opportunity and offered no protection against armoured forces sufficiently powerful to brush aside these little battle groups, attack the force from mobile nuclear delivery systems and race on to disrupt the defence by attacking it in depth. This scheme was also discarded.

There obviously had to be much research into how the weapon effects could be tamed. Quite apart from the question of safety of friendly troops, these notional battles were to take place in the most prosperous and densely populated and urbanised part of the territories they were supposed to defend, and the object would hardly be achieved by reducing it to a smoking and radioactive desert.

The trouble with the whole concept lay in the strategic, not the tactical sphere. (The British in particular, who for economic reasons urgently wanted to reduce the size of their conventional armed forces, allowed hope to lead analysis.) The strategic plan was to meet *any* aggression by 'massive retaliation', meaning that if the tenuous Allied conventional defence cordon was breached, it was to be interpreted as aggression and the whole panoply of nuclear deterrence would immediately be used. This was known as the 'trip-wire' strategy. The disadvantages of so desperate a remedy hardly need to be discussed. When saner counsels prevailed the doctrine of 'graduated response' to aggression was formulated. This is simple and can be expressed in simple terms. Aggression, defined as or at least assumed to be an invasion in strength of the NATO central sector, would be met as far forward as possible with only as much force as required to halt it. This is an over-hopeful assumption, and really only an expression of injured virtue or pacific intentions necessary to NATO's political posture, as all available evidence indicates that Soviet military doctrine does not believe in half-measures and that once the die is cast the maximum available forces will be committed to the offensive. The first defensive measure would be conventional defence which without doubt would take initially a heavy toll of the leading armoured echelons, as would air interdiction of those following in the rear, and conventional air attacks on the Warsaw Pact airfields.

It is assumed – unwarrantably – that the Warsaw Pact will not choose to use nuclear weapons first. The next defensive step would be to use NATO's tactical weapons, beginning with the smallest, on carefully selected targets to relieve a dangerous situation. This is a declaration of determination not to submit to aggression, whatever the risks involved. This would be followed, gradually stepping up the nuclear bombardment in intensity and size of weapon and extending it to targets, still military in nature, at increasing ranges to the eastwards. The basic difference between this policy and the 'trip-wire' is that the moment at which the final, suicidal stage of nuclear attack and counterattack by intercontinental missiles with warheads in the megaton (1 million tons of equivalent high explosive) is at least deferred.

This is the ultimate doomsday event. What is of greater concern to the land and air commanders concerned with the early stages of the combat is the moment of applying nuclear fire-power and the means of doing it. There are two promising developments. One is the improvement of guidance systems already used in aircraft bombs and adaptable to artillery shells with a zero or insignificant dispersion around the point of aim. The second is advances in the designs of warheads which suppress or obviate undesirable effects and retain or enhance the useful military, anti-weapon effects. One variant is the so-called 'neutron bomb' which exploits the ability of the flux of these deadly but short range particles to penetrate armour but produces little blast and heat. The combination of a totally accurate delivery system with warheads whose lethal effect may be contained in a circle of 0.5 km not only could permit targets to be engaged even in the confusion of an armoured battle, but also obviates what is euphemistically known as 'collateral damage': the destruction of property and civilian casualties on a vast scale.

The mere prospect of such small weapons has aroused alarm: on the Soviet side because it improves the credibility of the graduated response and the strength of the defence, and among Western strategists because a 'lowering of the nuclear threshold', or in plainer language offering the defenders the prospect of using nuclear weapons earlier in the initial stage of the battle with less rigid controls, might result in a premature escalation to unrestricted strategic nuclear bombardment. If this point of view prevails in NATO it will add yet another self-imposed constraint on its defensive land strategy.

A WARSAW PACT BLITZKRIEG?

There is, however, one further consideration which knocks the underpinning from all novel strategies based on a passive defence and attrition whether by nuclear or conventional means. The Warsaw Pact must be credited with having analysed the prospects of offensive action with as much care as the defender. It might choose to risk all in a modern version of the *blitzkrieg*. Appreciating the difficulties lying in the way of rapid concerted action by

any alliance, and aware of the location of every single NATO unit and the time requited to deploy to battle stations, the Soviet planners may conclude that a headlong advance over the frontiers without any previous mobilisation or preliminary deployments may have the best chances of success. Faced with such a prospect, NATO is in the same position as Israel was in October 1973. The mere fact of preliminary mobilization on NATO's part may be regarded as provocative (not necessarily by the Soviet leaders, but by NATO.) Any permanent alteration towards greater readiness would be too great a burden economically. Political rather than military factors will decide whether this is the correct reaction.

The other considerations are purely military and even grimmer. What if the aggressor, instead of gambling on overrunning the NATO defences using conventional weapons only (by no means impossible), decides to use nuclear weapons from the beginning of his offensive? He too can acquire neutron bombs and precision delivery systems, if he has not already done so. There is absolutely no reason to believe that a *weak* force with nuclear weapons can prevail over a *strong* force with nuclear weapons. An attacker, in addition to all the conventional advantages conferred by possessing the initiative, is favoured by first using nuclear weapons, as he can choose the targets and warn his conventional troops well in advance, and can also employ the tactics of bombarding what he perceives to be the key points in the opposing defensive system and then manoeuvring his armoured forces round them. The only possible counter is to reply in kind and risk the escalation of nuclear response, which is what the defenders have been trying to avoid from the first.

Such are the problems, dilemmas and paradoxes of Western Europe's defence.

SHELFORD BIDWELL

8. AIR WEAPONS

hough some traditional air missions are irrelevant to a World War 3 scenario, it is scarcely possible to discuss the future of air warfare without briefly looking back at the past.

Before 1914 the only task for which flying machines appeared to be suitable was reconnaissance over the battlefield. But as early as 1911 Italian pilots were dropping bombs in anger, during Italy's conquest of Tripoli, and the following year the obvious desirability of interfering with enemy aircraft has led to proposals for what we today call fighters. By 1918 military aviation included three basic categories: reconnaissance (including 'spotting' for artillery), bomber and fighter aircraft, plus sea patrol and anti-submarine, close-support and trench straffing, and carrier-based naval aircraft. The only roles yet to be refined were assault by airborne forces, and AEW (airborne early warning), which has today developed into the AWACS (airborne warning and control system).

Today there is no place for the large strategic bomber over or near the land battle (though it may play a vital deterrent role in peacetime). The task of hitting enemy ground forces now devolves upon several classes of aircraft, and these are increasingly becoming mere platforms for 'systems' which both help them survive and enable them to place their weapons accurately.

The core of a tactical air force used to be the fighter-bomber, which was simply a fighter that carried bombs (or air-to-ground rockets). This blurred the distinction between the fighter and the bomber, but, as will shortly be explained, tactical attack aircraft of today may look like fighters but

cannot be made to behave like them. Today there are several other classes of tactical attack aircraft.

One group comprises relatively light STOL (short take-off and landing) fixed-wing machines which also serve as 'casevac' (casualty-evacuation) transports, front-line supply transports, 'psy-war' (psychological-warfare) platforms, FAC (forward air control) platforms, and even as trainers. Originally created to participate in so-called 'brushfire' or limited wars, they persist because of low price and general utility. Another group are helicopters, with special relevance to anti-tank defence. Yet another are purpose-designed anti-tank aircraft in which all pretentions to fighter-like quantities are abandoned in favour of hitting-power and self-protection. Yet another class are the jet V/STOLs like the Harrier 'jump-jet', with the ability to do without airfields.

Basic advances in technology have been reflected in fundamental changes in combat aircraft and in their methods. Some 30 years ago it became possible to build a fighter carrying powerful radar linked by a computer to its flight-control system and armament, so that it became possible to detect, track and destroy hostile aircraft without the pilot even seeing them. As air-to-air missiles increased in effective range, so the role of the interceptor shifted. From being a fighter in the traditional sense it became a mere carrier of radar and missiles to a place in the sky where they could 'see' their target. Today the most powerful fighter radars and missiles can be used over ranges exceeding 130 miles.

Thus, in theory, the all-weather defence against aircraft or cruise missiles could be left to long-endurance aircraft such as the AWACS itself, or purpose-designed machines based on existing relatively cheap or low-performance aircraft. Indeed, the parallel development of clever systems for sensing and weapon guidance have likewise taken some of the pressure off the design of tactical attack aircraft. These in theory no longer need to approach within many miles of their targets but can operate from a distance which at least keeps them away from the worst of the defences.

The period 1979-85 is one characterized by the entry to service of many important types of aerial weapon or related system which, though visible for decades and subjected to protracted refinement, have not in the past made a tangible contribution to warfare. The following is an overview split into major categories.

RECONNAISSANCE

As the first duty of aircraft in war, and to some degree the first duty of every military commander, finding out about the enemy is going through more change than any other branch of tactical air power.

Air reconnaissance used to be limited to manned aircraft equipped with cameras, and even observers with notepads and radios; but by 1944 electronic reconnaissance was already a fine art, the aim being to come back with a hard-copy record of every enemy electromagnetic emission. Today 'Elint' (electronic intelligence) aircraft can detect all emissions from radars, infra-red equipment, communications radios, lasers and any other emitting devices, put it all on precise record and send the information back to a friendly base, literally as it happens. Not entirely jokingly, it has been said that an enemy using an electric typewriter or shaver could be told immediately if there was any fault in his equipment. In such an environment the act of switching on a radar at all looks foolhardy in the extreme; for example, hundreds of RAF bombers in 1943–45 would not have been shot down if they had not switched on their radar (which was often a tail-warning radar intended to protect them).

Until the late 1950s there was an obstinate belief that aircraft could evade defences by flying faster and higher. The Lockheed U-2 was a classic example of the high-fliers, while its successor, the SR-71A, combines extreme speed with even greater altitude. But this policy is no longer viable

Technicians service a reconnaissance pod slung beneath a Jaguar of the RAF in Germany

in the face of improved surface-to-air missile (SAM) defences. For 15 years, where reconnaissance of land battles is concerned, the emphasis has been on three quite different methods.

The most obvious is to package all the required equipment into the smallest possible streamlined pod and attach this under a modern tactical aircraft. The term 'tactical aircraft' is in this context meant to include fighters and bombers, but, above all else, aircraft specially designed to survive in a hostile environment.

Generally speaking, survival no longer involves flying high but as low as is safely possible, in order to make it more difficult for the defences to get a good radar lock and guide missiles to bring the aircraft down. There is no problem in making a modern tactical aircraft fly at about Mach 1 (760 mph) at a height of around 100 feet, though fuel consumption is extremely high so range at this altitude is severely limited. Fixed-wing aircraft generally reach speeds between Mach 0.9 and 0.95, while swing-wing machines at maximum sweep reach 1.0 to 1.2, provided nothing is being carried but a reconnaissance pod.

The pod normally contains forward-looking, vertical and oblique cameras, SLAR (side-looking airborne radar) and an IR (infra-red) linescan to give multi-spectral coverage capable of defeating all known camouflage and showing virtually everything detectable with e.m., or electromagnetic radiation. Almost certainly there are other parts of the e.m. spectrum that could convey additional information, but the technology does not exist to use them.

A second reconnaissance method is the stealthy, ultra-quiet aircraft. Though useful in South-East Asia, it is doubtful that such aircraft could survive in a European World War 3 environment. The problem of making light aircraft so quiet that they cannot be heard by the human ear at close range, except as an unobtrusive rustling like leaves, was solved in the 1960s, and

with only slightly less success has even been applied by Hughes to helicopters, an infinitely more difficult task. Lockheed was the pioneer of stealthy fixed-wingers, and on a dark night could guarantee to fly over hostile forces encamped in the open at very low level, bringing back detailed pictorial and electronic information without the presence of an aircraft being suspected. But this would be impossible with sophisticated troops maintaining ceaseless radar surveillance, especially once they were used to such intruders. The perennial dream of building structures transparent to radar has yet to be realised.

The third battlefield reconnaissance technique is to use unmanned platforms. These can assume many forms, from a tethered balloon to a supersonic missile, but in each case the objective is to gather information with a sensing platform whose loss or destruction is acceptable, even on a large scale. One very prolific family of vehicles, known as RPVs (remotely piloted vehicles), comprises what are really free-flying model aeroplanes. The US and British armies have experimented with many, but though they are extremely cheap and simple they carry little and cannot go far afield. Some, such as the British RCS Heron, have control radii as little as 3 miles, while most others demand line-of-sight control by the human operator (of course, the latter can be on a hill or even in another aircraft, but the latter negates the main advantage of having nobody in the sensing platform).

No fewer than 48 distinct families of small reconnaissance RPV have recently been developed in Western countries, of which 42 are American. Some are hovering platforms, and one of the best-known of these is Britain's Skyspy which has obviously made enough progress for it to be security-sensitive. Shorts, the manufacturer, states merely that work is now in hand on Skyspy systems for operational roles. Skyspy is a small vertical ducted fan, with control surfaces across the exit duct, driven by a self-contained engine of sufficient power to lift the required payload of sensors. A type broadly similar to a motorcycle in size, mass and power can lift a 44 lb load for 90 minutes to speeds exceeding 100 mph at all heights up to 6,000 feet. It has been proved to be by no means easy to shoot down. A related family of reconnaissance vehicles are the RPH (remotely piloted helicopter) family. Again a British product, the Westland Wideye, is especially promising. Marconi-Elliott Avionic Systems is helping provide the all-weather surveillance sensors for this 200 lb device, which follows the 66 lb Wisp delivered to the British army since 1977.

But most unmanned RPV platforms look like miniature aeroplanes. Here again there is a vast range of options, some small enough to be carried by a man and others with wing-spans as great as 90 ft.

This was the span of Boeing's YQM-94A Compass Cope B, one of two participants in a valuable programme terminated by President Carter in 1978 after a decade of research. Called the 'B-Gull', YQM-94A, weighed 17,220 lb, was powered by a turbofan engine (that used to power the twin-engined A-10A tank-busting aircraft) and could carry 1,200 lb of equipment at over 60,000 ft for 27 hours. The YQM-94A could also perform SLAR surveillance, communications relay, 'sigint' (signature intelligence), photo-reconnaissance, atmospheric sampling and (for the US Navy) various forms of ocean surveillance: an impressive and versatile heavyweight.

As a contrast, two NATO members, Belgium and Canada (indeed almost all technically advanced countries) have developed small battlefield reconnaissance RPVs. Belgium's, the Epervier, has a delta wing a little under 6 ft in span and flies at over 300 mph on the thrust of a small Lucas turbojet. Carrying day/night cameras (with photoflashes), and IR linescan and low-light TV, both with real-time transmission to the ground station, Epervier ranges out to a distance up to 47 miles and is back for re-use in about 25 minutes; recovery is by parachute. Canadair's CL-89, called USD-501 by armies, is rather longer, heavier and faster, cruising at 460 mph and presenting an extremely difficult target. Packed with photographic and IR linescan equipment, CL-89 provides several NATO armies with all-weather surveillance and target-acquisition.

GROUND ATTACK

In modern tactical aircraft the former diverse roles of the strategic bomber and fighter-bomber have come together. The bomb load of even quite small attack aircraft, such as the Jaguar, is similar to that of the largest bombers of World War 2, and modern means of precision delivery make it possible to entrust single aircraft with the destruction of difficult targets. In general the Soviet Frontal Aviation is still not quite up to the level of technology of Western tactical aircraft, but they have made fantastic progress and virtually closed a gap that was once enormous. Recently a Russian officer said: 'If it is there, we can see it. If we can see it, we can destroy it. And we expect to do it with one weapon.' This is worth quoting, because that is what modern 'tac-air' is all about. Nobody can hide from it, and, except by shooting down the oncoming (not the departing) aircraft, nobody can escape destruction. This is a basic fact of life all too often overlooked, simply because it is easier to remember the past than look into the future.

Another telling quotation is ascribed to an officer of the US Air Force on the occasion of the second overseas deployment of the F-111 swing-wing bomber to South-East Asia in 1973. Asked 'Do you people have smart bombs?' he replied 'No, but we've got smart aircraft'. The slick adjective 'smart' was applied to describe traditional 'iron bombs' to which had been added some form of precision guidance system, usually either using radar wavelengths or an EO (electro-optical) system, but today also based on IR, IIR (imaging infra-red) and laser light.

The first ASMs (air-to-surface missiles) of the *Luftwaffe* in World War 2 were steered into the target by an operator aboard the launch aircraft who watched bright flares on the missile and worked a miniature control column to steer it by radio command link. A few small ASMs even used guidance signals sent via trailing wires, as in the case of most early anti-tank missiles. Today the airspace over an enemy army would be too hostile for such methods. Tactical missiles have to be of the 'fire and forget' type; they have to know their target before launch and home on to it, while the aircraft makes good its escape. Even then, the missile may not penetrate far into the defenses of a modern army – especially a modern Soviet army.

There are two main reasons for the revolution in ASM technology and the decline of the 'iron' bomb. One is the increased strength of anti-aircraft defences, which make it virtually suicidal to try to fly over a modern army, even at night or in foul weather. The other is the difficulty of aiming free-fall weapons with sufficient accuracy to hit pinpoint targets such as a bridge, a tank or other blast-resistant structure. With modern technology it is possible to make a small and preferably supersonic missile carry a warhead right up to the assigned target and detonate it against it, or at whatever stand-off distance is best.

It is worth noting several major advances in warheads and bomb types, some of which have given a breath of new life to the inaccurate free-fall bomb.

Cluster munitions scatter large numbers of 'bomblets' over considerable areas, thereby in most cases achieving much greater lethality, even against hardened structures and armoured vehicles, than a single bomb of the same aggregate mass. A

A huge nose gun and ungainly rear engines identify America's A-10 ground-attack aircraft

typical cluster bomb, the BL 755, weighs 600 lb and distributes 147 bomblets evenly over an area whose dimensions depend on horizontal speed and, it is claimed, launch error. Complex *rod-type* and *multiple-hollow charge* warheads are available for specific use against designated battlefield targets. *FAE* (fuel/air explosive) *munitions* have revolutionized effectiveness against large structures such as buildings, radars and ships, even quite small FAEs being able to wipe many targets clean off the face of the earth. They function by ejecting a large cloud of finely divided fuel, usually in the form of powder or, more often, microscopic liquid droplets, which is then detonated. Air delivery of FAEs is a highly refined technique; it is also possible with some missiles and rockets, but has not yet been announced as applicable to artillery shells.

DETECTION OF TARGET, AIMING OF WEAPON

Methods of detecting and hitting surface targets are almost without number. Ships at sea are simplicity itself; there are several ways in which a missile can home on them automatically, by using semi-active or fully-active radar illumination, laser designation, magnetic-anomaly effects, IR radiation, EO homing or various kinds of TV guidance. Homing is essential because ships move about, and if the ship is foolish enough to switch on any kind of emitter, such as a radar, the homing should become even easier. But battlefield targets generally do not stand out so well, and the fact that most World War 3 scenarios envisage rapid movement over considerable distances rules out anything involving known geographical co-ordinates.

Any major fixed target, once constructed – such as a transport depot, fixed-base missile emplacement, pontoon bridge or airfield – immediately becomes attackable not only by tac-air but also by army weapons fired from a distance on the repor-

ted location. One supposes that such targets would be few indeed, and that virtually every air strike would be against mobile hostile forces extremely well provided with Triple-A (anti-aircraft artillery) and SAM defences.

SWARMS OF SYSTEMS

There is simply no practical way even of listing the hundreds of existing target sensing, designation and weapon-guidance systems already partly or completely developed. They make use of almost every part of the e.m. spectrum, as well as inertial guidance, which is wholly self-contained but steers towards a pre-selected location. Then there are MAD (magnetic-anomaly detection) around AFVs; diesel and similar exhaust detection (originally pioneered in ASW, anti-submarine warfare); and such outlandish methods as steering towards the source of Triple-A projectiles which is entirely practical and at least could make field armies site their anti-aircraft defences several miles from whatever they are protecting. One guidance method first used 25 years ago and now important for cruise missiles is TERCOM (terrain-comparison); this now seems irrelevant to tactical operations where details of the terrain change minute by minute. Another method that is important in strategic missions involves various kinds of satellite, either oribiting or hovering over a fixed point, but these again cannot be used to steer weapons over the fluid situation in a land war.

A fundamental point is that, like ECM, EW equipment and other ancillary devices discussed in Chapter 6, 'The Electronic Dimension' airborne sensing, target designation and weapon-aiming equipment may be part of the aircraft; or hung on it; or even part of the weapon. The variety of systems is enormous; eight years ago, the number of separate tac-air designation, detection and aiming projects under the aegis of the Department of Defense exceeded 300.

AIR COMBAT

Any invader has to take his air-superiority forces with him, in the form of air-combat fighters and highly mobile (preferably amphibious) Triple-A and SAMs. This is precisely what the Soviet Union can do. The NATO countries, on the other hand, are extremely short of modern air defences. How can they best clear the skies of swarms of MiGs and Sukhois? Obviously, by the large-scale use of tactical SAMs. These are the ideal weapon, and the invader must risk them or stay at home. Use of fighters merely gives the enemy an easily destroyed defence system, the Achilles' heel being the air-strips. If fighters get into the air, trading them on a one-for-one basis merely helps whichever side has the greater number, both in the squadrons and in reserve, and the answer here is self-evident.

One of NATO's greatest collaborative achievements was the NADGE (NATO Air Defence Ground Environment) defence network, which links into one organic whole radars, computers, displays, communications and data links from the North Cape to eastern Turkey. But there could hardly be a more immovable infrastructure, and its vulnerability to air attack, sabotage

The only NATO aircraft able to operate from a woodland clearing,
a Harrier taxies out from its camouflaged shelter.
Each Matra launcher slung under the wings carries 19 68mm rockets

and enemy investment has in recent years thrown greater attention on AWACS-type aircraft for the direction not only of the air situation but of virtually the entire war in a theatre. Just as Watson Watt's radar chain more than doubled the effective size of Fighter Command in the Battle of Britain, so do AWACS-type aircraft more than double the effectiveness of modern fighter forces. Even extremely sophisticated fighters such as the USAF F-15 and US Navy F-14 can benefit greatly from integration into a complete electronic environment, and in the next decade it is probably going to become apparent that the environment ought not to be based upon fixed ground installations.

Regarding fighter aircraft themselves, there were, 20 years ago, several mistaken beliefs which it took time to correct. One, prevalent only in Britain, was that they were obsolete as a class. Another, stemming from the vague definition of fighter-bombers in World War 2, was that a fighter was a tactical aircraft that could carry bombs and rockets, and this led to a succession of so-called fighters which were poor air-combat performers and so were hardly ever used in that role. The earlier development of semi-automatic all-weather interceptors had the effect of making the eyeball-confrontation dogfight appear *passé*, so such excellent weapon platforms as the F-4 Phantom were developed with little thought for in-flight manoeuvrability or armament for use in close air-to-air combat. It took the difficult conditions of Vietnam to rectify that situation, partly by putting a slatted high-lift wing on the Phantom, together with an internal gun, and partly by spurring the development of a new generation of out-and-out dogfighters.

Fighters have to be designed to meet requirements totally unlike those that rule attack aircraft, even though to the laymen the two may look alike. Wing loading – the weight supported by unit area of wing – needs to be as high as possible in an attack aircraft, the limiting factor being the length of runway needed for safe operation. Too big a wing means drag in cruising flight, reduced speed in the attack and, most important, such severe buffeting through low-level air turbulence that the crew cannot function efficiently and the structure soon fails through fatigue. A typical wing loading for an attack aircraft is 120–130 lb/sq ft. A fighter, in contrast, needs the largest possible wing in order to pull the tightest turns compatible with the limits of the structure and the pilot, even at extreme altitude (where attack aircraft almost never go). Typical wing loading for a fighter is 70 lb/sq ft.

Again, the attack aircraft needs the smallest engines possible to minimize fuel consumption and either carry more weapons or fly further. The biggest limiting factor is the thrust needed to get off the ground, and a typical thrust loading (engine thrust at sea level divided by gross weight) is 0.35. In contrast, a fighter needs SEP (specific excess power, the thrust left over from propelling the aircraft which is available for climbing and manoeuvres) in the most abundant possible measure, even if this cuts the range or increases the fuel load. Modern fighters have thrust loadings higher than unity; in other words, engine thrust at sea level is greater than the gross weight in dogfight trim. There are many other points where the two types are shown in stark disparity; for example, the radar, weapon subsystems and the weapons themselves are bound to be totally different.

Despite this, attack aircraft such as the A-7 and Jaguar are (at least in the opinion of their pilots) fully capable of taking care of themselves in an air battle, while many fighters such as the F-14, F-15 and F-16 are to some degree able to serve in the surface-attack role. There is no reason to scorn either aircraft operating in the 'other' role, but it must be recognized that – even in the case of impressive all-rounders such as the F-14 and F-15 – the

FAIRCHILD REPUBLIC A-10A (GROUND ATTACK).

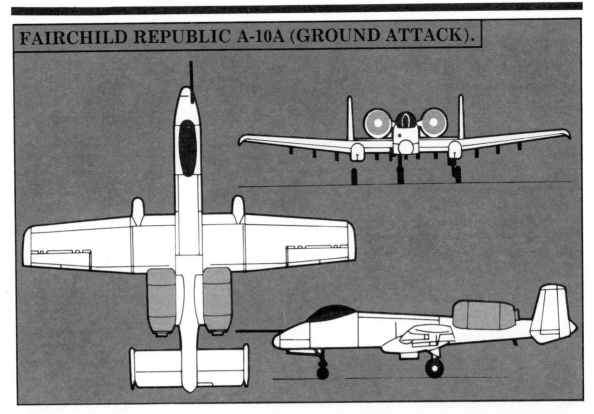

MIKOYAN MIG 21 (FIGHTER).

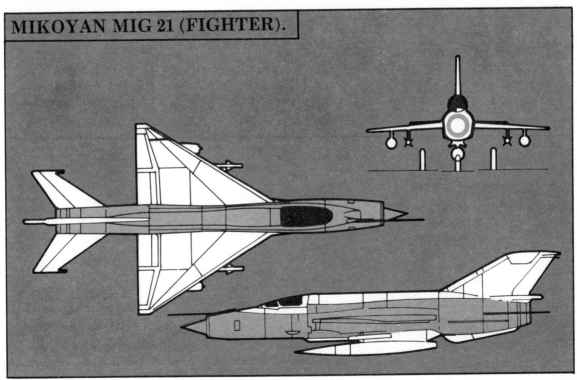

The deep-rooted differences between modern fighters and ground-attack aircraft,
with engine areas for these two examples shaded in grey.
Note also the modest wing of the A-10

result is always inferior in some respects, if not in all, to that achieved by a purpose-designed aircraft.

(It is unfortunate that three of today's most important fighters should have confusingly similar designations. The US Navy's F-14 (Tomcat) has two crew, two engines, swing wings and extreme versatility – at high cost. The US Air Force's F-15 (Eagle) has one seat, two engines, a fixed wing and excellent performance, but it is still expensive. The F-16 is smaller and simpler, and some consider that it will prove more cost-effective.)

One of the imponderables is the extent to which such formidably expensive aircraft as the fighters just mentioned are justified. Some 25 years ago the RAF bought the Hunter but refused the much cheaper Gnat, claiming that pilots cost more than aircraft and that it was pointless to cheesepare with 'inferior' aircraft. Yet today India not only still uses the Gnat but still has the latest version in full production. The American F-16 was specifically created to see how far it would be possible to fly the required missions with a fighter much cheaper than an F-15. Commercial pressures soon turned a technology-demonstration programme into a massive production programme for the USAF inventory, and an increasing queue of other air forces. What does it lack, in comparison with the F-15? In addition to the trite answer 'a second engine' one cannot yet reply, pending assessment of the brand-new Westinghouse multi-mode radar, but the F-15 sets a standard of such effortless capability that at present it appears worth the money.

Incidentally, while the F-14 uses its 130-mile range radar and IR sensor to lock-on six 130-mile AIM-54 Phoenix missiles one by one, picking off individual aircraft from a close formation even at that great distance and killing each with an individually locked-on missile, the F-15 follows the rather less demanding 'look-shoot-look-shoot' technique. The pilot watches his bright display, from which everything is erased except the few items vital to his mission at that moment, studies the target (which might be one aircraft or a close formation, say 25 miles away) and fires an AIM-7 Sparrow missile. If a target remains visible, he fires a second. After a few seconds, if it is still there, he fires a third. This assumes that each missile reduces the enemy formation by one aircraft.

In the 1980s France and Britain expect to have two rather different kinds of fighter from those just described. The Mirage 2000 is a small but agile dogfighter that superficially looks like an old-fashioned delta Mirage III. Compared with its predecessor the 2000 will have a more powerful engine and, among other improvements, a later wing with hinged leading and trailing edges which will work together to give exceptional manoeuvrability (according to Dassault, 'far superior to the F-16'). It will not be able to defend France, except on a local basis, and despite Dassault's assertions to the contrary will have a wing loading more appropriate to air combat than to the attack mission. The RAF's long-range hard-hitting Tornado will also emerge as an interceptor, chosen for the air-to-air role in the ADV (air-defence version). Unlike the Mirage 2000 and the F-15 or F-16, this is not a dogfighter but a 'stand-off' all-weather interceptor, intended to defend British airspace by killing hostile aircraft from a distance. Long range is achieved by using small and efficient engines, and both the radar and British Skyflash missiles are likely to be unsurpassed in the early 1980s for lethality over medium ranges in the 20/30-mile bracket. An F-15 could do the same job, but at greater cost in aircraft and fuel. And it is significant that all the new tactical aircraft, for both offensive and defensive missions, all carry at least one gun as well as missiles.

BILL GUNSTON

9. SEA WEAPONS

The defence requirements of any country are to protect its own land and people and, in the event of war, to add to this the destruction of the enemy's power to wage that war. So far as sea power enters into this equation, there must be certain prerequisites in peacetime and certain basic actions in war.

The overall aim is to be able to use the sea for one's own purposes and to deny that use to the opposition, the peacetime preparations being such that a potential enemy may be deterred from any ultimate trial of strength. At the same time consideration has to be given to other aspects of national policy, for at no time is there likely to be a sea war without it being part of an overall struggle or, at least, have certain repercussions on the land and in the air. Nor can the maritime business be divorced from the overall economic and industrial state and requirements of the country concerned.

There has rarely, if ever, been a time when some powerful nation's policies did not ultimately rest on war or the threat of war. Thus other governments, in pursuance of their role as guardians of their land and people, were forced to make preparations for their own defence. Those that failed, either through inertia, financial problems, or a combination of both, frequently failed in their duty. From the naval point of view in peacetime, a careful consideration of what threatens their vital interest - geographically, quantitively and qualitatively - is essential if adequate arguments are to be advanced for the necessary financial allowance.

A fleet needs many things which vary in quantity and type according to the tasks it is likely to be called on to perform. Because it takes longer to plan and build a warship than any other weapon, first must come the ordering of adequate numbers of hulls. Then must come the recruiting and training of sufficient people to man and support that fleet. The question of bases may be vital - support afloat is commonplace today, but it can never replace the advantages of an alongside berth where vital maintenance can be carried out. Such bases need adequate defences against all forms of assault and need not necessarily be on land belonging to the country concerned. In the past, alliances have frequently provided the important centre. Finally (although this is not the province of any navy, which is merely the tool of policy) comes the political will to resist infringements of international legal requirements and, if necessary, to deploy force in their support.

At this point it is worth considering how such infringements can occur because, if not resisted, they can eventually achieve the ends of the transgressor without that government having to resort to war. On the open oceans harassment can be achieved in many forms. Interference with fisheries or their destruction by fishing over the legal limits, and interference with shipping routes by the declaration of huge danger areas are just two of them. Encouragement of terrorist attacks on shipping with missiles or mines is a further extension into the more violent forms and, in these days of surrogate forces, not unlikely; mining is among the most anonymous forms of attack. Closer inshore we find the threat of force being used to unseat a hostile regime and, as an eventual corollary, the use of force to support a failing government whose continued existence is necessary to national policies.

Many have argued that the arrival of

nuclear and thermonuclear weapons has so changed the probable course of any future war that conventional armaments are outmoded and, therefore, a waste of money. This is certainly not the view of the directing forces of NATO. Should the current stalemate be broken and a full-scale nuclear exchange take place it certainly would seem unlikely that life and activities as we know them could continue. The misery and destruction of such a catastrophe would be so immense that we can only hope it is unlikely. If so, the classic requirements of sea power to transport one's own men and commerce in safe and timely fashion while denying that capacity to the enemy remain as true today as they have over the centuries.

What has changed out of all recognition is the means of conducting such a war at sea. In all three aspects, below, on and above the water, present equipment has made the tactics of 30 years ago totally outmoded. The same is true, in a rather more subtle way, of maritime strategy and this is reflected in the command and control field where communications have achieved an even greater importance than ever before. This is true also in the field of intelligence, where satellite information must be passed swiftly to the forces involved and where long-range aircraft sightings must be relayed to dived submarines.

THE SUBMARINE: CHANGED OUT OF RECOGNITION

Submarines have developed to a startling degree in the last 70 years. In 1910 their potential was little understood, a condition which had changed radically by 1918. So violent had been the impact of the German U-boats in World War 1 that several nations suggested their abolition. This pious hope had little chance of realization and it was to this form of vessel that the Soviet Union turned first when in 1926–28 she was planning her first naval building programme

after the Revolution. So keenly did the Russians pursue this policy that by September 1939 they had 185 boats built, a number which rose to 218 by the time of the German invasion of June 1941. Despite this formidable array the Soviet submariners achieved little during the ensuing four years. The hulls were available but their equipment was poor and their knowledge of the use of what there was, embryonic. Stalin's purge had made gaping inroads into the ranks of the more senior officers and this resulted in faulty use of this large fleet. On patrol Soviet submariners were resourceful and courageous, but a lot more was needed to bring their service up to the standard of Western underwater forces.

The chance to improve their material condition came with the end of the war when the USSR captured not only German plans but also the finished articles of sonar sets, radar, new weapons, new propulsion machinery and the most advanced hull forms in the world. With the assistance of German scientists and technicians, the Russians began the largest submarine building programme ever known. In 1950 they began to build at the rate of 78 hulls a year, a programme of such size and momentum that by 1965 the total was due to stand at 1,200 – 200 were to be long-range boats, 900 of medium-range and 100 coastal submarines. This apportionment was in line with the Soviet theory of national defence in depth based on three zones – the outer warning zone, the central combat zone and the coastal defence zone which was to be reinforced by aircraft, fast attack craft and coast artillery.

Of this ambitious design, only a third of the forecast numbers was achieved. The death of Stalin brought adjustments to naval policy, and the advent of nuclear propulsion changed the whole scene.

In 1953 the first Russian submarine reactor was put in hand and five years later the first nuclear propelled submarine of the *November* class was commissioned. This

THE SUBMARINE RACE 1967–1976													
Submarines		1957–66	1967	1968	1969	1970	1971	1972	1973	1974	1975	1976	Total
Ballistic missile, nuclear	WP	9	2	4	6	8	6	6	6	6	6	6	65
	NATO	40	2	2	1	—	1	—	1	1	—	1	49
Ballistic missile, diesel	WP	29	—	—	—	—	—	—	—	—	—	—	29
	NATO	—	—	—	—	—	—	—	—	—	—	—	—
Cruise missile, nuclear	WP	31	4	2	2	3	2	2	1	—	1	—	48
	NATO	1	—	—	—	—	—	—	—	—	—	—	1
Cruise missile, diesel	WP	23	2	2	—	—	—	—	—	—	—	—	27
	NATO	1	—	—	—	—	—	—	—	—	—	—	1
Torpedo attack, nuclear	WP	14	2	2	2	2	3	3	2	2	2	2	36
	NATO	25	8	5	9	4	9	4	3	4	2	3	76
Torpedo attack, diesel	WP	91	5	5	3	2	1	—	1	1	1	1	111
	NATO	61	8	6	4	3	1	5	7	5	8	2	110

was only a few months after the United States Navy had commissioned *Nautilus*, the forerunner of today's huge fleets. By 1963 the USN and the Soviet Navy were numerically little different in this type of vessel and in the next four years neither navy built many more attack submarines. This was due to the concentration of US building yards on the production of ballistic-missile submarines, a factor which also influenced Soviet planning at the same time as the design of a completely new hull form and more modern propulsion equipment was in hand.

The result of this last was the arrival of the *Victor* and *Charlie* classes in 1967–68, the former torpedo-armed and the latter fitted, in addition to torpedo tubes, with eight launchers for 25-mile cruise missiles. This design was to remain the basis of future programmes although in 1972 the first *Victor II* appeared, some 20 feet longer than *Victor* and apparently fitted for firing the 25-mile range SS-N-15, an air-flight weapon capable of carrying a nuclear warhead or a homing torpedo. This missile is probably also carried by the *Tango* class of diesel submarines, the first of which was seen in 1973, three years after the first of what may be a prototype or trials submarine of the nuclear-propelled *Alfa* class.

Thus by the end of the 1970s the Soviet submarine fleet had become numerically very strong, although of the total of about 440 hulls, two-thirds were still diesel-propelled. Out of this number, over 100 could be ignored, probably being in reserve and in no fit state for patrol. Of the remainder, about 90 carried ballistic missiles, 22 of them being diesel-propelled; 72 were cruise-missile carrying, 26 of these being diesel boats. Finally, there were 42 torpedo-firing nuclears and about 150 diesel boats for the same task. Of the nuclear submarines, therefore, over 40% were devoted to a possible strategic exchange, the remainder being evenly divided between cruise missile and torpedo submarines.

This concentration on ballistic-missile craft is the reflection of a long programme which began when in 1945 the USSR became aware of German experiments in this direction. Within ten years (1955) the Russians launched their first 300-mile missile from a converted diesel-submarine of the *Zulu* class. From then on the tempo mounted – the nuclear *Hotels* and the diesel *Golfs* were eventually able to strike at 700 miles range and in 1967 came the first of 34 submarines of the *Yankee* class. With 16 launchers for the 1,300 mile SS-N-6 missile they were a notable advance, which was continued by improvements to the range and head capability of the SS-N-6 and, from

SUBMARINE DETECTION AND SURVEILLANCE

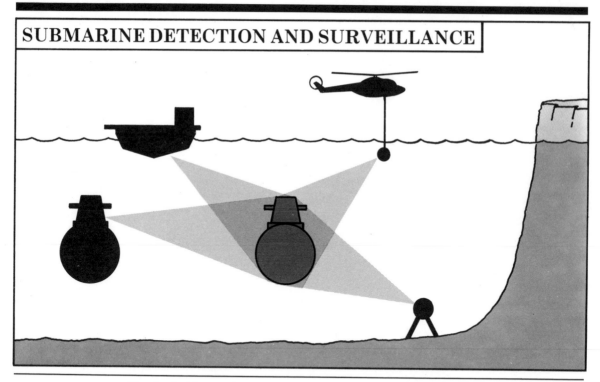

How both sides monitor enemy submarines. Helicopter 'dunking',
shipboard sonar, hunter-killer submarines and detection-posts
positioned on the sea bed make a formidable quartet of detectives

the mid-1970s, by the embarkation of the 1,800 mile SS-N-17. But these were only improvements. In 1972 the first *Delta* class were commissioned, carrying 12 SS-N-8 missiles with a range of over 4,000 miles, to be followed by the *Delta II* and, four years later, by the *Delta III* whose 5,200 mile SS-N-18 missiles can reach any part of the northern hemisphere from Soviet-controlled waters.

With this great variation of firing ranges the Soviet Navy had enormously aggravated the anti-submarine problem facing any adversary. The same was true of the family of cruise-missile firing submarines which originated in an attempt to counter the Western aircraft-carriers' ability to strike at the Soviet homeland. From 1958 various conversions were commissioned, all carrying the surface-launched SS-N-3 missiles with a maximum range of 400 miles but which, even at the optimum range of 150 miles, needed external guidance from ship or aircraft. The

advent of the *Charlie* class in 1968 brought a new dimension into this field. Faster than their predecessors, this class carried eight of the new SS-N-7 missiles with a range of only 25 miles but with the tremendous advantage of dived launch. Even though the acquisition of target data may cause problems, these submarines have added further to the problems of any opposing surface-force commander.

The originality shown in the design of Soviet submarines has been equally clear in the numerous classes of surface ship built in the last thirty years. By 1958 ships were appearing with surface-to-surface missile (SSM) launchers, followed in 1962 by the first of many equipped with surface-to-air missiles (SAM). In the later cruisers of the *Kara* and *Kresta II* classes the largest launchers are devoted to the SS-N-14 missiles which are apparently anti-submarine weapons. As it is hardly likely that these large ships would be abroad with only 57 mm or 76 mm guns as their primary

108

surface armament, it seems not unlikely that the SS-N-14 has a secondary anti-surface capability. This view is reinforced by the fact that in all other aspects (A/S helicopters, SAMs and point-defence systems) these ships are quite capable of operating on their own.

1967 was a year of great change: it was then that the first A/S cruiser *Moskva* appeared. She was the first 'flat-top' of any kind in any Russian fleet and, carrying 18 helicopters as well as the new SUWN-1 missile launcher and variable depth sonar, clearly had a primary anti-submarine role. Only two of the class (*Moskva* and *Leningrad*) were completed. The anticipated success of the new Soviet Vertical/Short Take-Off and Landing (V/STOL) aircraft may have caused the cancellation of as many as six more ships of the type.

Kiev, *the Soviet navy's first carrier, showing Yak-36 V/STOL aircraft and patrol helicopters*

Whatever the reason, this decision must have been taken some time before *Moskva* appeared because in 1973 the first of several Soviet aircraft-carriers, *Kiev*, was launched. She has subsequently appeared with both helicopters and V/STOL aircraft, the result of a change of plan in the early 1960s. But her design owes nothing to Western ideas. Using steam turbines she has a speed of over 30 knots which is comparable to Western practice, but there the similarity ends. *Kiev* is an aggressive ship in her own right rather than a vast floating airfield relying on her aircraft. Armed with eight long-range SSM launchers, short and long-range SAM launchers, an A/S missile launcher, guns, twin sonars and all forms of radar and electronic warfare equipment, she is fully capable of being the centre of a task force bent on surface, subsurface or air warfare. With a very comprehensive communications organization she is an ideal centre for command and control in any theatre of operations.

Behind the major warships are very strong light forces. In 1962 the first attack craft with missiles were introduced into the Soviet fleet – a world 'first', in fact. These, with torpedo craft, patrol craft, mine warfare forces and a growing strength of hovercraft and hydrofoils provide a backing in the third defence zone. The naval infantry is well provided with amphibious ships and craft while the entire fleet is supported by an increasing force of depot, maintenance and repair ships, as well as fleet support ships and tankers.

All in all, this is a remarkably impressive navy in its ships and weapon systems. Whether the officers and men who run them are equally impressive is a debatable point but it must be remembered that a conscript force, particularly one with recruits taken up at the age of 18, is always suspect when compared with a long-term volunteer force. Nevertheless, the physical capabilities are present: capability for an enormously destructive nuclear strike, sufficient SSBNs for some to be held back for a second assault, capability for violent submarine assaults on both naval and merchant shipping, an increasing capability for anti-submarine operations, amphibious operations and mine-warfare. The Soviet Naval Air Force is strong and missile-armed, and behind all this strength lies the third zone of defence. Quite what part that is planned to play in a war for which none of the Western powers is fitted for any form of direct assault *en masse* it is hard to understand. But one last point is clear to any who have watched the Soviet navy operating: command from the top is all-embracing and could well inhibit initiative. If communications were disrupted, confusion could result.

NATO: THE LEAN YEARS

In the immediate aftermath of the Korean War the United States Navy numbered the largest force of aircraft-carriers ever known in active service in peacetime and beside them were ranged the 17 carriers of the Royal Navy. In the USN trials had been going on from 1947 until in 1950 the first squadron of Savage aircraft, capable of carrier-based operations carrying nuclear bombs, was embarked. The Soviet Navy reacted by producing missile-carrying ships and submarines with an anti-carrier role.

In 1964 there were numerous significant events. As the United Nations' force withdrew from the Congo the first brushes between North Vietnam forces and those of the USA took place while, further north, the first Chinese nuclear device was detonated. Looking back, this was a sinister triad of events which was to lead to further failure of international action, the failure of the USA to keep pace with modern military requirements, and the entry into major reckoning of the Peoples' Republic of China. The field was open for more superpower rivalry with little to interfere from without and the usual postwar reactions were taking place in other NATO nations.

By 1966 it had become clear that the British Labour government was retreating

to its own island perimeters with consequent reductions in naval and air power.

Other NATO countries were clearly as unwilling as Great Britain to provide more than minimal defence expenditure. At the same time, national interests continued to inhibit any form of standardization policy within NATO, resulting in up to 40% wastage of available funds. In the background, political and industrial turmoil resulted in crippling delays to those programmes which had been authorized.

The problems of the USA, some would say self-inflicted, came at a critical juncture. As the building programmes of the Soviet Navy came to full flower, so the available funds of the USA were expended in the current expenses of Vietnam, a fruitless war which embroiled more men and caused more casualties than the hostilities in Korea during the previous decade. Up till the final cease-fire agreement of January 1973, ships had been kept running beyond their hull-lives and the money needed for this purpose had been deflected from necessary new construction. During the period when Admiral Zumwalt was Chief of Naval Operations, USN, this situation was grasped with determination and foresight – the old were to be deleted, the elderly put into reserve (and there were few of them), while new construction was to be pressed forward.

As a result, the number of major warships in the USN has dropped from 900 in 1964, 976 at the peak of the Vietnam War, to 460 today. In the last ten years, though – in the same way that has been seen in the Soviet Navy – weapon capabilities have improved so much that these 460 are being armed to a far higher standard than their predecessors and the latest aircraft-carriers, including the three nuclear-propelled ships, have embarked a new generation of aircraft. The Viking S-3A anti-submarine aircraft, the Tomcat F-14 fighter, advanced V/STOL aircraft and helicopters have increased the performance of the naval air-wings while new short-range defence by Phalanx gun-systems and missile armament has improved the carrier's ability to survive.

In cruisers, destroyers and frigates considerable strides have been taken to remedy the situation which had developed by 1970, when the Soviet Navy's armaments were way ahead of the best that NATO could offer. For anti-aircraft defence the latest Standard missiles are as good as and, in later versions, probably better than Soviet weapons. The Standard missiles share launchers with the well-entrenched Asroc anti-submarine missile, which can operate as a nuclear depth-bomb or a launcher for a homing torpedo to a range of 6 miles. To engage other surface forces a great effort has been put into re-arming the USN with Harpoon, a missile with a 60-mile range. At the same time Tomahawk, a cruise missile ranging up to 275 miles in the tactical form, has been put under trial. In the underwater world a somewhat similar pattern has developed with both Harpoon and Tomahawk being capable of launching from a torpedo tube in a similar way to Subroc, which is a nuclear-headed weapon with a range out to 30 miles.

FEWER AND BETTER

The main debate in the USA has been whether the USN needs more hulls at the expense of large and costly ships or the reverse. This fundamental argument appeared to be partially resolved in the mid-1970s as new frigates began to take their place alongside large modern destroyers. The propulsion for both types was gas-turbine with nuclear power being used in the new cruisers, enabling the latter to operate for long periods with the nuclear carriers.

Submarine building was concentrated on two classes in the late 1970s, both nuclear propelled. For normal patrols the *Los Angeles* class of much the same size as the Soviet *Victor II* was planned at the rate of about 4–5 each year. The strategic missile task, with 41 older submarines already available, is to be undertaken by the *Ohio* class, monsters of nearly 19,000 tons (dived displacement) and armed with 29 tubes for the Trident I missile. These missiles in their original form are being fitted with MIRV (Multiple Independent Re-entry Vehicle) heads with a range of about 4,000 miles and are to be retro-fitted in the ten most modern of the earlier and smaller SSBNs. Further range improvement to 6,000 miles is planned for the Trident II missile. But once again the USN has been beaten to the punch by the Soviet Navy. By 1980 when the first *Ohio* class is likely to be on patrol the USSR will have some 25 of the *Delta* classes available, all armed with missiles with a longer range than Trident I but each having only single or triple heads compared with the 12 or more separate vehicles carried by Trident.

Parallel with the Trident development, the production of a strategic form of Tomahawk has been in hand. This cruise missile has a range of some 1,500 miles and, in one form, can be launched from submarine torpedo tubes. It is subsonic but has a terrain-hugging flight path, increasing its chances of being undetected. This weapon's development means that any submarine or ship fitted with the surface-launched variant can have a strategic role. While defence against Tomahawk is easier than against a ballistic missile, its availability would certainly increase the options open to its owners whilst materially increasing the problems of the defenders.

The lack of any notable policy of NATO standardization has meant that the various members of the alliance have gone their own national ways so far as ship design is concerned. Some measure of compatibility has been achieved in such areas as communications and certain aspects of logistics, but the rising cost of weaponry and the research and development required is forcing NATO into using more and more of the available systems rather than developing individual hardware. Such items as the Exocet surface-to-surface missile, the OTO-Melara 76 mm Compact gun, Rolls-Royce gas turbines and Harpoon missiles are cases in point. But, proportionally speaking, no country has produced as much material support for a war at sea as the USA, although several have taken considerable steps towards such support for their own areas. What is clear, though, is that the major burden of deep-water operations will be taken by the USA with assistance from the United Kingdom, the Netherlands, Canada and, if she becomes involved, France. In the Mediterranean the main surface forces would be those of the US Sixth Fleet, Italy, Turkey, and possibly France. It also seems unlikely that the increasingly strong Greek fleet would be held back.

ESCALATION:
MORE LIKELY AT SEA

The forms of maritime conflict are so varied that the chances of an escalatory process are probably higher at sea than elsewhere. No problems of frontiers exist to provide a cut and dried moment of aggression; no civilian populations are placed at risk when forces engage in battle. Cover, except for submarines, is provided only by storms or cloud, generally penetrable by radar, while underwater a sufficient knowledge of water conditions can provide an indication of the chances of submarine detection. But all ships make a noise above a certain speed and this provides a means of localization which has been exploited in the American Sound Surveillance System (SOSUS), a far-ranging acoustic system designed primarily for detection of submarines. Allied with aerial and satellite reconnaissance, a picture of the deployment of potentially hostile forces can thus be built up with inputs from such varied sources as merchant-ship sight-

ings, the Surface Towed Array Systems (SURTASS), Airborne Early Warning (AEW) aircraft and shore reports. With the use of massive computer effort this intelligence is processed for dissemination by the USN's Ocean Surveillance Information System. It is only by such constant vigilance that the various indicators of possibly hostile deployments can be made available to the various command centres and ships at sea.

At this point, secure communications become of the utmost importance. With surface ships this is a great deal easier than with submarines, whose depth below the surface has an immediate effect on reception. Huge aerial arrays are required to handle the great power needed to transmit Very Low Frequency (VLF) and Extremely Low Frequency (ELF) transmissions which are the only forms capable of dived reception below periscope depth without the use of buoys or floating wires. These antenna sites ashore are therefore vital links which, because of their size, are vulnerable to direct attack or sabotage. Their importance has become even more fundamental in the last 20 years because they are needed not only for routine traffic but also to order strategic nuclear missile strikes. For all steps of escalation good, secure and continuous communications are a prime need.

Modern weapons and methods have made other forms of electronic emissions and their handling in both tactical and strategical situations matters of the highest importance. The interception of wireless, radar and sonar transmissions from a ship not only serve to provide location data but, very often, identification of her type, class and, sometimes, her name. This is achieved as a result of endless intelligence work in peacetime and points the need for adequate forces for surveillance long before hostilities are at hand.

Not only do these transmissions provide a bearing and a range, if more than one is obtained, but also a homing-point for certain missiles tuned to react to the frequencies used. Such considerations are essential to the safe conduct of any naval force, and the development of electronic warfare over the last 30 years has meant a totally new approach by all tactical commanders, at every level. Intercept equipment, jammers, analysis equipment and homing heads have all combined to ring the knell for the old, freewheeling days of endless chatter, active sonar and radar flooding of an area. Any ship keeping a regular active sonar watch is providing an enemy submarine captain with a perfect beacon signal to be avoided or attacked as circumstances require.

HOW WILL IT START?

The problem that confronts the commander of any naval force or unit from the Supreme Allied Commander down to the most junior submarine commanding officer is what form hostilities will take. It has already been said that maritime operations allow what is probably the most flexible area of choice and it must be remembered that naval forces with their long range and endurance are in the strongest position of any military grouping to apply pressure in a general sense in peacetime. Their habit of carrying their own food supplies, munitions and fuel for an extended period of operations makes them less dependent on 'lines of communication' than most. But the time must come, and the smaller the ship the sooner, when all three will run out and reliance must be placed on fleet support or a shore base or haven. Even nuclear-propelled ships, although they can manufacture vast quantities of fresh water, have to rely on external sources for their food and their armament supplies. Thus when two navies, evenly matched in experience, morale and fighting value come to conflict, the one with the best logistic support must overcome in the end. This is equally true of the long periods of vigilance before conflict as it is when

hostilities exist. Among the many factors to be considered in the evaluation of the form and outcome of a future war this is, therefore, of great importance.

In any clash between the Warsaw Pact countries and those of NATO there are many considerations which have to be taken into account and it is impossible to make any sensible appraisal without taking all factors into account. History has shown that very rarely has any war been resolved by maritime operations alone. The possession of overwhelming superiority or skill at sea has frequently weighted the balance but today, as in the days of Elizabeth I of England, the possession of certain abnormal capabilities and the continental side of the equation must have at least equal relevance.

A submarine war on trade very nearly upset the balance twice in this century despite an apparently overpowering preponderance of surface ships on the side of Great Britain and her allies. On each occasion the entry of the USA came barely in time to redress the balance both on land and sea, as merchant ships were demolished at an increasing rate in the North Atlantic. Had the European mainland been totally occupied by the Germans in 1917, as it was in 1940–41, the story could well have been very different. The change in capabilities of A/S defence were altering in 1940–41 but there are few who would care to estimate what the eventual result of the Battle of the Atlantic would have been if the Germans had been given time to deploy their new classes of submarines into that struggle in 1945–46. Today the equivalent of one modern submarine compared to the German Type XXI is as immeasurably greater as the capability of that type was to that of the previous classes of U-boat. Numbers mean nothing, unless overall capability is evaluated with the greatest care. Great hearts will never conquer if totally outnumbered, yet superior forces may be routed by carefully managed, well-trained and fully experienced fleets, even if the latter are in the minority.

Skill in maritime affairs depends on training, experience, mutual trust and the morale which stems from these essentials. Today the Soviet navy is lacking in long-term junior sailors. As a result of their system of conscription, insufficient time is available to produce the able- or leading-seaman who is fully at one with his allotted weapon system. As a result, greater strain is thrown upon the senior ratings and officers who must wonder how their juniors, who are all 21 or less, will react to a major crisis. This is a problem which does not exercise their opposite numbers in the major Western navies to nearly so great an extent, who command ratings of a younger age-group than before but who through comparatively long-term voluntary service attain the experience which a three-year conscript period cannot give.

At the same time, too rigid control from the centre must affect the ability of officers at all stages to exercise initiative and independence. This has been illustrated on several occasions and can only succeed in inhibiting the resourceful approach so frequently required in a difficult situation. When this form of control exists, the need to prevent the enemy's high command taking a hand in local decision-making is therefore paramount: communications must be disrupted.

THE SOVIET ROAD TO ALL-OUT WAR

These communications will control the approach to any period of hostilities. Soviet ships will be sailed under all-embracing orders to carry out activities which may be on an exercise pretext or to sustain some political activity. The whereabouts of many of them will most probably be known to Western commands because of the Soviet Union's geographical limitations and the resultant need to deploy through narrow maritime defiles. Lurking behind in the sanctuary of home waters, well covered by local naval and air forces, will be the ballistic-missile submarines under the overall command of the strategic rocket forces and charged with the execution of their part of any nuclear strike plan. With the warning element resulting from the decision to attack coming from the Kremlin, up to 20 of the *Delta* class could be in readiness, a total of 600 to 700 warheads depending on the quantity of MIRVs employed. At the same time, the *Yankee* class could well have at least half its strength deployed – a minimum of 280 warheads. Thus some 1,000 warheads of varying megatonnage or kilotonnage would be at sea covering the whole world, the greatest proportion covering the Northern Hemisphere from virtually inviolate patrol areas in Soviet-controlled waters.

At the same time as this menace lurks in the deep or well-protected waters the remainder of the navy, probably two aircraft-carriers, two helicopter ships, 25 cruisers, 40 or more missile destroyers and over 100 destroyers and frigates could be on the move. Some would be in the Norwegian Sea and Pacific approaches to the USSR and others in the Black and Baltic Seas, but the greatest percentage could be expected in the North Atlantic and Mediterranean, opposing the Allied fleets on the aircraft perimeter, protecting their own submarines' deployments and searching for NATO ballistic missile submarines. Thus the defence of the USSR would be a major preoccupation and both aircraft and shore-based nuclear missiles could be expected to be involved, targetted on both task forces and patrolling SSBNs.

On the assumption that the USSR had achieved some measure of surprise, if not in intent at least in timing, their leaders could reasonably expect delay in reaction because of the complex workings of NATO and the resultant slow transition to war schedules in the Alliance countries. Thus

The old and the new in naval fire-power. Top: Iowa, *one of the last four*
American battleships in commission (nine 16-inch guns);
Above: *Soviet 'Osa' fast attack craft (four 'Styx' missiles). Totally different*
in concept and operation, the 'broadsides' of the two vessels are compatible

the flow of support across the Atlantic would be some time in achieving momentum, time which could be used in the surface ships and aircraft clearing paths into the Atlantic for the submarines detailed to assault the convoys with missiles and torpedoes.

The subjugation of Europe being a primary aim, after which the more distant areas of Africa and Asia could be simply reduced by steady attrition, the Pacific would be an area for a holding campaign and the main thrust should be expected in the North Atlantic. At this point it must be made clear that the deployment of the USN in peacetime is, except for submarines, fairly evenly divided between the Pacific

and the Atlantic and any ship transferred through the Panama Canal must face a passage of over 4,500 miles from San Diego, California, to Norfolk, Virginia. For the great majority of present US carriers the passage of the Canal is impossible due to their beam and flight-deck width, and the rounding of Cape Horn would mean an extra distance of over 7,500 miles to be covered. Under these circumstances maximum warning time is needed to carry out any redeployment, and this is a problematical area.

Deployments of large numbers of Soviet ships do take place and these have, so far, been associated with major exercises. Because of the problems of political acquiescence and the high cost factor it seems unlikely that NATO commands would be authorized to assume a war footing because of major Soviet naval deployments for an already advertised world-wide exercise. Thus the advantage of warning time from maritime operations would be lost. But army and air force reinforcements could provide a more telling argument to politicians because land operations are far more irreversible than those at sea. Unfortunately for NATO, however, such a warning need not be given.

With a few days of calculated assault on world shipping lanes the economies of all the NATO countries could be reduced to a most parlous condition. The rupture of North Sea oil pipelines, the sinking of a quantity of large tankers and selected ships carrying vital cargoes could result in a deplorable, if not disastrous, situation for all concerned. The USA is considered as a more self-sufficient entity than any other in NATO, yet 99% of the volume of her trade is seaborne and this volume will increase by over 200% in the next ten years. About half her petroleum requirements and more than half of 20 out of 30 critical raw materials come by ship. These figures are a subject of concern in Washington, though little heeded by the average citizen in the country at large. While these figures cause worry in the Pentagon other NATO countries are considerably more dependent on external sources of raw materials, and concern should be even more deeply rooted in the considerations of their governments.

The USSR's situation is very different. Although there are now signs of problems in her extraction of oil and her agricultural policies are frequently less productive than forecast, the USSR is far less dependent on supplies from abroad than are the Western countries. Her very large merchant fleet, which is now used not only as a source of hard currency but also as a means of undercutting and debilitating Western mercantile traffic, can therefore be annihilated

without undue repercussions at home.

FOUR STEPS TO DISASTER

From all the foregoing a possible pattern of hostilities emerges, and escalation is its main theme. Attempts to dislocate Western maritime interests through direct action or by the manipulation of allied foreign forces of all kinds are actions which could readily be halted or, in some cases, disavowed. They must therefore be attractive to any country which, bent on victory, sees grave disadvantage in a precipitate resort to major violence resulting in the exchange of nuclear weapons. So 'Stage One' would be limited operations at sea.

Once the Western powers' will to resist had been tested, the next decision would be needed. On the very real assumption that United Nations action would be too late, too feeble or, possibly, even vetoed, the reaction of Western governments would be crucial. If the current spate of weak-willed vacillation were predominant 'Stage Two', a land and air offensive in Europe, would probably follow. It seems unlikely that China would intervene at this point, particularly if threats of Soviet action in the Far East were backed up by both land and sea deployments. Should 'Stage Two' result in an exchange of tactical nuclear weapons, it must be assumed that a similar activity would follow at sea.

This would be the lead-in to 'Stage Three', an all-out assault on both naval and mercantile shipping concurrent with the shepherding of submarines into focal areas by both surface and air forces. In the event of this campaign being unsuccessful the options open to the USSR would be further reduced. The battle could prove to be a long and sanguinary affair. It could well develop into the violent nuclear interchange in whose aftermath the destruction of large portions of the human race, their animals and crops would be inevitable.
JOHN E. MOORE

10. STRATEGIC NUCLEAR WEAPONS

The most economical way to think about strategic nuclear weapons is to concentrate upon the notion of deterrence.

For a first-class nuclear power – and the United States and the Soviet Union are the only current examples – strategic nuclear deterrence operates at three levels. The first and most obvious level is the deterrence of large-scale nuclear attacks on cities and other centres of industry and population by the threat that such an attack will lead to retaliation in kind. The second, which does not altogether follow naturally from the first, is the deterrence of deliberately limited attacks on targets insufficiently crucial to justify the sort of retaliation which will itself provoke a massive population-destroying counter-blow, but important enough to merit avoidance through the deterrent effect of threatening retaliation on a similarly limited scale.

The third, the least widely appreciated and the last to develop historically, has relatively little to do with war but plays an important part in persuading the first-class nuclear powers to keep the rate at which they innovate and deploy new strategic nuclear weapons reasonably well regulated.

Acceleration is deterred by two factors. Experience teaches that an attempt to obtain a substantial margin of superiority either in numbers of weapons or in their design will be quickly detected and almost as quickly offset by compensating procurements of appropriate weaponry by the other first-class power. There is also the suspicion that if for some reason compensatory procurement was impossible the disadvantaged state might feel constrained to run dangerous risks, even to attack its rival, preferring mutual near destruction to waiting for the day when its rival's new weapons were fully operational and its own inferiority clearly marked.

In the beginning, from 1945 until the late 1950s, the United States was the only first-class nuclear power. Nuclear deterrence operated only at the first level, and solely to the benefit of the United States. Important allies of the United States could be reasonably confident that for as long as the Soviet Union could not, even with surprise on its side, launch a substantial nuclear attack on the United States itself (simply because of the short range of Soviet bombers and missiles, and the crudeness of their few nuclear warheads), there would be almost nothing to prevent the United States responding to Soviet attacks on American allies with massive nuclear blows on Soviet cities. Assuming a Soviet appreciation that this was how things stood, the threat of massive destruction *and* an American victory would be enough to deter the Soviets from even the most limited warlike move against American interests. Although things were never quite as simple – for instance, there were always uncertainties about how far and how fast Soviet nuclear technology had developed – this sort of calculation originally persuaded many states, including those of Western Europe, to look for security and assistance to the United States.

As Soviet advances in nuclear and long-range missile technology became apparent and the USSR itself became able to operate first-level deterrence against the United States, the United States gradually responded by developing the capability for second-level deterrence – expanding its conventional (non-nuclear) forces and modifying or rearranging its nuclear forces to permit their use against isolated targets either of civilian or military kinds.

And it is upon second-level conventional deterrence that the security of its European allies has come to depend – that, and the indispensable link to first-level of the Soviet Union's not daring to inflict a crushing defeat upon the United States and its allies in a European war (even if it were militarily capable of doing so), for as long as the United States looked as though it might well prefer the mutual near destruction of a strategic nuclear war to defeat and discredit in Europe at Soviet hands.

Third-level deterrence was the last to evolve. (Some commentators even today might deny its existence, feeling that an 'arms race' is a better description of how the superpowers go about making additions and alterations to their strategic nuclear forces, but this view is surely hopelessly old-fashioned in an era of near static levels of missile launchers and bombers, and of well established and virtually continuous arms control negotations.)

The first reaction of the United States to the Soviet advances in long-range bomber and missile technology of the late 1950s was to channel more resources into developing and enlarging its own strategic nuclear forces, somewhat heedless both of Soviet capabilities ultimately to match this expansion and the dangers of desperate Soviet reaction if they could not. In the event the Soviets did react desperately by attempting to place nuclear armed missiles on Cuba, and in the longer term did build up their own nuclear forces to match those of the United States; both these facts of course contributing to the subsequent appreciation of the nature of third-level deterrence. The arms control discussions between the United States and the Soviet Union today, the so-called SALT, reflect a joint awareness that vigorous striving for a margin of superiority is probably dangerous, probably pointless, and certainly extremely costly.

First-level deterrence is the easiest to understand and probably the easiest to achieve and maintain in practice. It is at least a defensible proposition that the nuclear forces of Britain and France, small though they are, put each of these countries in a position to deter the Soviet Union from launching an unrestricted nuclear attack on their cities. The reason for this is that the physical means of retaliation are probably adequate, in that the Soviet Union could not hope to destroy them completely in the course of its attack, and the psychology of West European decision-makers does not give the Soviets much hope that when the means to retaliate are available the will to do so will be lacking.

Assuming that the will to retaliate is present, and the technical means to translate this will into action are secure from attack, first-level deterrence strengthens in proportion to the size of the retaliatory force surviving after the enemy has done his worst to eradicate it. At first sight this is an argument for large forces, and to some degree it is. But it is also an argument for protecting these forces from attack either by concealment in, for instance, submarines, or by placing them in armoured containers – the so-called silos of the land-based missiles of the Minuteman type – or by keeping them mobile or capable of mobility at short notice, as in an alertable bomber fleet. It is also an argument for preferring a variety of methods of protection to a single method, which an ingenious opponent might be able to circumvent. And it is an argument for defending the retaliatory forces directly, at least where this is practicable.

The operation of third-level deterrence between the Soviet Union and the United States has a consequence that there can be no substantial difference in the size and character of their forces, or, if there is, that it will not be tolerated for long. This means that first-level deterrence between them must always be first-level deterrence

On the pad: an American 'Minuteman' ICBM awaits a test firing

Both countries developed missiles for silo emplacement and for putting to sea in submarines partly because, even if as new technologies they were at first more costly than bombers, they could be better relied on to ride out or evade any attack (and to penetrate defences) and therefore made good sense as retaliatory (sometimes called second-strike) weapons.

So far each country has deliberately avoided giving its cities and other centres of population and industry much protection from nuclear attack – either by the *passive* means of shelters for population and dispersion for industry or the *active* means of anti-aircraft and anti-missile defences. This is chiefly because third-level deterrence means the other side can quickly and cheaply, in comparison, nullify such precautions by modifying the density and pattern of its attack. Moreover, both sides have – for the time being at least – converged on the idea that the maintenance of first-level deterrence comes first. Serious attempts to defend population and industrial centres from nuclear attack would weaken first-level deterrence through depriving the retaliator not of the means or the will to retaliate, but of the assurance that, once launched, his retaliatory blow would be devastating.

The United States (and here it becomes much harder to speak for the Soviet Union) has a great respect for the robustness of first-level deterrence, and the clearest sign of this is its dogged pursuit of the means, and methods to employ them, of second-level deterrence. The United States, in other words, has at no time since the mid-1960s acted as though it could rely on a massive nuclear strike on the Soviet Union to deter the Soviets from lesser forms of aggression against the United States or its allies. Quite the contrary, the United States has acted as though the Soviet Union would be unimpressed by such a threat, because the consequence of its execution would be a Soviet retaliation of

between equals. No doubt the United States would think her first-level deterrence *vis à vis* the Soviet Union nearer to perfection if she possessed much larger forces than her rival. The reason for this is that the threat of *defeat* (which implies victory for your opponent) can be a surer deterrent than the threat of *near destruction* (which implies equivalent destruction for him). A moment's thought shows that two equals cannot deter each other from attack by threatening defeat, for they would not then be equal: the maximum threat possible is the stalemate of mutual near destruction.

The good quality of even British first-level deterrence *vis à vis* the Soviet Union does not mean that the superpowers have always acted as though the maintenance of high-confidence first-level deterrence (sometimes called a 'stable balance of deterrence') was an easy matter. When the Soviets first developed long-range land-based missiles (ICBMs) the Americans became anxious lest their bombers would be caught on the ground and destroyed before they could be used in retaliation.

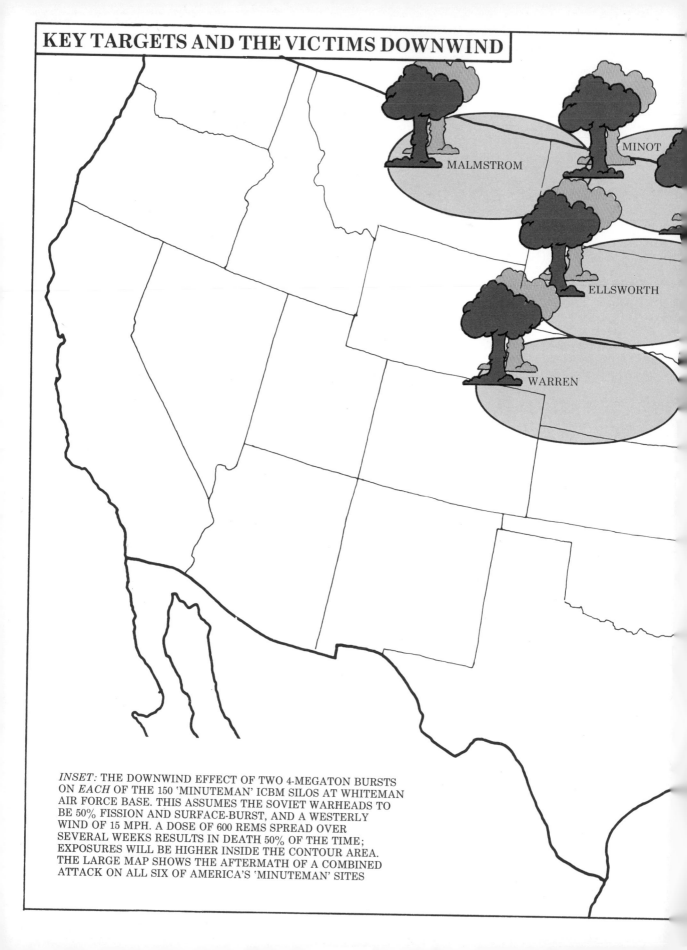

KEY TARGETS AND THE VICTIMS DOWNWIND

MALMSTROM

MINOT

ELLSWORTH

WARREN

INSET: THE DOWNWIND EFFECT OF TWO 4-MEGATON BURSTS ON *EACH* OF THE 150 'MINUTEMAN' ICBM SILOS AT WHITEMAN AIR FORCE BASE. THIS ASSUMES THE SOVIET WARHEADS TO BE 50% FISSION AND SURFACE-BURST, AND A WESTERLY WIND OF 15 MPH. A DOSE OF 600 REMS SPREAD OVER SEVERAL WEEKS RESULTS IN DEATH 50% OF THE TIME; EXPOSURES WILL BE HIGHER INSIDE THE CONTOUR AREA. THE LARGE MAP SHOWS THE AFTERMATH OF A COMBINED ATTACK ON ALL SIX OF AMERICA'S 'MINUTEMAN' SITES

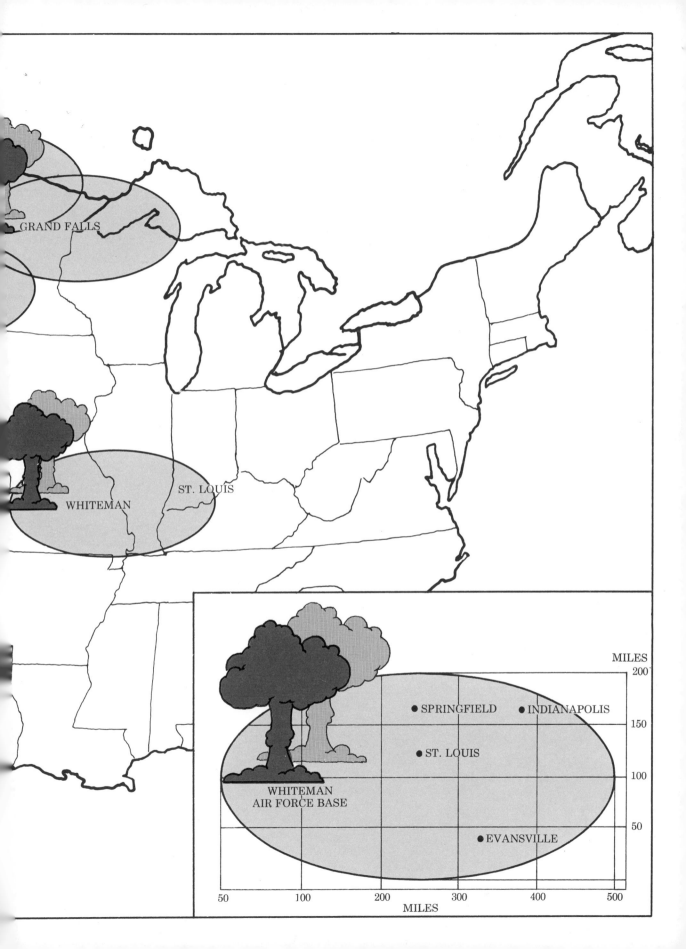

GRAND FALLS

ST. LOUIS

WHITEMAN

MILES
200

● SPRINGFIELD   ● INDIANAPOLIS

150

● ST. LOUIS

100

WHITEMAN
AIR FORCE BASE

50

● EVANSVILLE

50   100   200   300   400   500
MILES

Removing one of the old 'Polaris' missile tubes from USS James Madison
during her conversion to the MIRVed 'Poseidon' SLBM.
Madison *was the first SSBM to be so converted*

at least comparable destructiveness on the United States *irrespective of how the United States executed its threat.*

Second-level deterrence has two separate jobs to perform. The first is the deterrence of attacks resembling in kind the massive nuclear blows first-level deterrence looks after, but very much smaller in scale. An obvious example is a deliberate attack, probably using small nuclear warheads, on *one* bomber airfield or on *one* small outcrop of population or industry. It is no good hoping the threat of a massive nuclear counterblow will deter this kind of attack, because it will simply not be believed. A much better deterrent would be the threat of retaliation in kind. But to be able to execute this threat it is necessary to possess nuclear weapons not only in *sufficient numbers* to prevent a limited ret-

aliation itself from significantly reducing the ultimate capacity for a massive retaliatory blow, but also of a type that allows for *maximum selectivity* as to the targets attacked and the damage done. All this will usually call for highly accurate means of delivery combined with small-yield warheads designed to produce very little radioactive fallout.

The possession of the means to implement second-level deterrence of this kind is the surest mark of a first-class nuclear power. Britain, and to a lesser extent France, is highly vulnerable to a deliberately limited nuclear attack. What could the Cabinet do if one of Britain's Polaris submarines went 'missing'?

It will be immediately evident that second-level deterrence of limited strikes by or against strategic nuclear forces has its awkward features. Foremost among them is its tendency to weaken first-level deterrence. A capacity to respond with precise counterblows to a similarly carefully-restricted attack can be put at the services of quite a different policy. These same highly accurate forces, if sufficiently extensive, could be used in a surprise attack on the widest possible scale against the forces that constitute the other side's means of retaliation; his cities meanwhile being carefully avoided to give him an incentive not to strike back (with whatever he has left) against the attacker's cities, for fear of retaliation in kind.

What has so far prevented second-level deterrence of limited strikes on retaliatory forces compromising first-level deterrence is third-level deterrence: simply the probability that further counter-measures of dispersal, camouflage, mobility, armoured protection and diversification will be the reaction to any improvements in the accuracy and number of the other side's warheads, as it has nearly always been in the past; and where counter-measures cannot be found, there is the risk that the disadvantaged party will prefer in desperation to take the initiative and to make his attack sooner rather than later, before this inferiority becomes fully felt.

Second-level deterrence of limited attacks neither using nor aimed at strategic nuclear weapons directly is a far more complicated matter, but of consuming interest to all allies of the United States. It is perfectly clear that the United States has concluded that first-level deterrence can do little more than prevent an unrestrained Soviet nuclear attack on American territory (and any similar attacks by a third country). And it is becoming clear that second-level deterrence of small-scale nuclear attacks on United States' (and probably Soviet) territory works reasonably well. What remains obscure is how second-level deterrence operates to prevent Soviet attacks on United States' allies.

In an ideal Atlantic Alliance we might postulate that a Soviet invasion of NATO territory, using conventional forces only, is deterred by the existence of NATO conventional forces (together with NATO resources for wartime mobilization) sufficiently large and well equipped at best to halt and stalemate the Soviet move, and at worst involving enough of an American political and moral investment for their defeat to represent something no United States government could take lightly (leaving ominously vague the question of how the United States would actually react). One difficulty with this arrangement is that it is highly sensitive to the level of the United States' contribution. The smaller the US commitment to NATO conventional forces becomes, the weaker the conventional deterrent *and* the smaller and more tolerable the affront a Soviet victory would represent – or so it might appear to the Soviets.

All NATO countries including the United States have found it increasingly difficult to follow the obvious route of matching Soviet increases and improvements in its conventional forces by expanding their own conventional forces. The reason for this, ultimately, is widespread disbelief among NATO electorates that the economic and personal sacrifices needed to build larger and better equipped conventional forces are justified. The United States, after urging the European NATO members to provide more of their own defence – something they have fairly successfully avoided doing, and possibly rightly, if the ideal Atlantic Alliance is correctly described above – has been unable to increase her own conventional contribution much, but has been more willing to make available to her own and allied forces in Europe new and more effective types of nuclear weapons specifically designed for use on the battlefield. These are usually called tactical nuclear weapons or theatre nuclear weapons (TNW).

To the extent that a willingness by the United States to put new battlefield nuclear weapons at the disposal of NATO is a re-affirmation that the defence of Western Europe matters to the United States, second-level deterrence is being upheld. What precisely the TNW are meant to contribute in their own right is more prob-lematical. Keeping our ears and eyes open teaches us that what are generally held in the West to constitute improvements in battlefield nuclear weapons are new de-signs that incorporate smaller nuclear war-heads (smaller in yield, but more especially in physical size), or more accurate means of delivery, or 'cleaner' warheads that more tightly restrict radioactive after-effects in space and time. In other words, what NATO planners tend to see as a better TNW is one that, lethal area of destruction per pound weight apart, more closely resembles a conventional weapon.

THE 'NEUTRON' WEAPON

An example of a modern NATO TNW is the so-called 'neutron' bomb or warhead. For all low-yield nuclear devices (one kiloton TNT equivalent or less), it has been known for years that the lethal effects of the nuclear radiation associated with an ex-plosion (neutrons and gamma rays, chiefly) extend to a greater range than those associated with the blast and the heat of the explosion, even though the latter con-stitute usually over 90% of the energy released. The lethal effect of nuclear radiation is purely biological and the occu-pants of tanks will be vulnerable to neu-trons from a one-kiloton explosion (in the sense that the dose will be fatal within days at the most) up to a quarter of a mile from the point of the explosion, *even when sitting behind 12 inches of armour plate,* which will keep out blast and heat and even gamma rays quite effectively. (This, of course, relates only to tanks. The many other armoured vehicles essential to their

support will have far less protection and so be vulnerable at greater distances.)

Presumably the key feature of the neutron bomb is a design that keeps blast and heat, as well as long lived radioactive fallout at a very low level, and the neutron burst at maximum intensity by designing the bomb casing to be as free as possible of neutron-absorbing material. In other words, it is reliably believed to be a miniature hydrogen bomb. The intense burst of neutrons will automatically induce high levels of radioactivity in the im-mediate region of the explosion, in the soil and in buildings, but this will decline to insignificant levels within a few hours. The neutron warhead mimicks a conven-tional warhead, then, in that the destruc-tion, though intensive, is localized, and not persistent to any great extent. Yet in its method of operation it is more like a gas attack than anything else.

If the Soviets accepted modern TNW as honorary conventional weapons, there would be no difficulty. The greater numbers of TNW (and their superior quality) in NATO hands would – at least until the Soviets developed their own, or some counter to them – constitute a valid second-level deterence enhancing improvement in the quality of NATO conventional forces. But the fact is that the Soviets do not ap-pear to regard battlefield nuclear weapons as honorary conventional weapons. This may be due to their large investment in real conventional forces, or to difficulties encountered in manufacturing modern TNW. Whatever the reason, the contribu-tion TNW make to second-level deterrence in Europe will be uncertain for as long as the Soviet Union behaves as if she might well choose to see no difference between the use of nuclear weapons on the battle-field and their limited use against any other Soviet target; military or civilian, within or outside its frontiers.

Third-level deterrence in Europe, or rather the lack of it, illustrates this diver-

*Equipped for nuclear war: personnel on a British 'Rapier' SAM site,
dressed in anti-contamination gear*

gence between the military philosophies of the East and West. NATO reacts to increases (or rather what are believed to be increases) in Soviet conventional forces by increasing its TNW capacity, to which the Soviets appear to counter-react by improving their limited range strategic nuclear forces, closely resembling their intercontinental strategic nuclear forces but with a range restricted to 3,000 miles or so. There is nothing surprising about such a diverg-

ence. A similar and arguably more serious dialogue of the deaf occurred in the 1960s over anti-missile defences, with the United States not developing them partly because she believed them to be harmful to first-level deterrence, and the Soviets pressing on with development because they saw anti-missile defences as having nothing to do with deterrence. Eventually the American view was (tacitly) accepted by the Soviets and third-level deterrence at the

THE 'NEUTRON' WEAPON

The peoples of the Free World, and of NATO countries in particular, have a right to be outraged at the stupid and inaccurate way in which their journalists announced the so-called 'neutron bomb' in early 1978. For a start it is not a bomb, any more than a shell bursting in the air can be called a bomb. It is best described as an 'enhanced radiation, reduced blast' (EHRD) warhead for artillery and for short-range missile systems. Designed as a tactical battlefield aid to compensate for the West's suicidal run-down in conventional forces, it is grossly unsuited for wiping out civilian populations in strategic nuclear warfare.

All nuclear weapons are 'neutron bombs' in that their detonation releases neutrons. The EHRB is a tactical weapon exploiting the relatively short range of the neutrons and their great power of penetration to attack tank formations and other armoured troops. Its localized effect eases the problem of ensuring the safety of friendly troops and greatly reduces 'collateral damage' – the killing or injuring of thousands of civilians remote from the battle area, and the ruin of their homes.

The development of the EHRB was the result of gloomy but realistic studies concluding that a Soviet armoured attack could well breach the NATO front line and overrun rear areas, together with NATO tactical nuclear missile sites. The problem was the time taken to obtain top-level authority for nuclear release, and the inaccuracy and excess destructive power of orthodox nuclear warheads. Escape from this twin dilemma was arst indicated by two lines of non-nuclear development. One was improved methods of target designation and of command, control and communication; the other was the improvement of weapons delivery, reaching zero or very low error in accuracy. But a third development, that of a radically different warhead, offered a real breakthrough.

The process of fusion of hydrogen atoms, as used in the 'hydrogen bomb', produces a powerful flux of neutrons, and the yield of the explosion is not affected by the base limit of a critical mass. If the extremely high temperature to initiate fusion can be provided, even a small amount can be induced to fuse and release its energy. The giant megaton bombs are triggered by actual fission bombs. The 'neutron' warhead seems to be a miniature fission warhead united with 'hydrogen', in the form of lithium deuteride, yielding a neutron flux comparable to, say, a 1-megaton warhead but without the heat and blast.

What is claimed, and seems fairly certain, is that the EHRB reduces blast and heat to a minimum; and that the neutron flux is intense enough to kill or rapidly disable men behind thick armour over a tactically significant area (say a tank battalion deployed at the usual close Soviet intervals, or an armoured self-propelled battery). Outside this radius, perhaps 2–3 miles from the burst, there would be negligible effects.

Such a weapon, if combined with suitable weapon systems (guided missiles or guided artillery shells) and brought into service in sufficient numbers, could seriously depreciate the vast Soviet capital investment in tank armies. It may be another step in the grim dialectics of weapon and counter-weapon. But it also holds out the prospect of defending the present frontiers of NATO without demanding a suicidal self-sacrifice from the people of West Germany, whose country is the predestined battlefield of World War 3.

It was only to be expected that a storm of protest would come from Moscow over the announcement of the 'neutron' weapon, as over the B1 bomber and the cruise missile. But now NATO has renounced two out of the three – all in the doubtful interests of 'detente'.

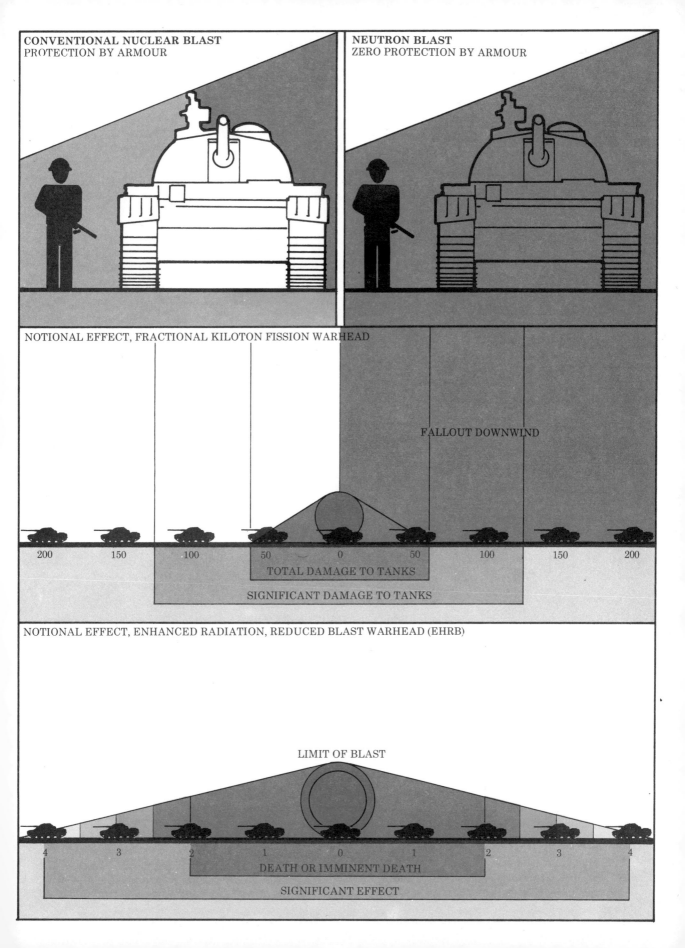

CONVENTIONAL NUCLEAR BLAST
PROTECTION BY ARMOUR

NEUTRON BLAST
ZERO PROTECTION BY ARMOUR

NOTIONAL EFFECT, FRACTIONAL KILOTON FISSION WARHEAD

FALLOUT DOWNWIND

| 200 | 150 | 100 | 50 | 0 | 50 | 100 | 150 | 200 |

TOTAL DAMAGE TO TANKS

SIGNIFICANT DAMAGE TO TANKS

NOTIONAL EFFECT, ENHANCED RADIATION, REDUCED BLAST WARHEAD (EHRB)

LIMIT OF BLAST

| 4 | 3 | 2 | 1 | 0 | 1 | 2 | 3 | 4 |

DEATH OR IMMINENT DEATH

SIGNIFICANT EFFECT

strategic nuclear level was put on a sounder footing.

THIRD-LEVEL DETERRENCE

Third-level deterrence at the strategic nuclear level is again a pursuit strictly for first-class nuclear powers. Only they possess the scientific, engineering and industrial resources necessary to permit reaction to innovations of weaponry or tactics by any other country, and by reacting to nullify. As the superpowers have become aware that each possessed this facility, each has been deterred from attempting dashes to numerical or technological superiority over the other. The latest striking example of the operation of third-level deterrence is the American decision (1977) not to build the new strategic bomber, provisionally (and optimistically) designated the B-1.

Of course third-level deterrence is not entirely leakproof. The United States has not added to its land-based missile launchers (ICBMs) or submarine missile launchers (SLBMs) since 1967, and its strategic nuclear bomber fleet has been almost halved in size since that time. But considerable improvements in quality have taken place over the same period. Multiple warheads of smaller yield but of greater accuracy have replaced single warheads on all SLBMs and on 50% of ICBMs; and the latest improvement to bomber payloads is the air-launched cruise missile (ALCM). This restores to the bomber some capacity to penetrate anti-aircraft defences, both by virtue of greater subdivision of its payload into some tens of ALCMs and through the property of the ALCM of flying with great accuracy under medium-range warning and anti-aircraft radar systems.

The Soviet ICBM and strategic bomber forces have also stabilized in size with their SLBM forces growing slowly towards the ceiling agreed with the United States, with

The undersea menace of MIRV: a 'Poseidon' is launched

similar improvements being made to ICBM and SLBM warheads to those made in the United States, though at a slower pace.

Some leakage is entirely to be expected. There are improvements to be made to first-level and second-level deterrence which cannot, by their nature, be cancelled by any practicable countermove by the other side, and such improvements are therefore, likely to be made.

The American submarine-based missile force has been fully equipped with multiple warheads and construction is well advanced on new submarines capable of carrying 24 launchers to their predecessor's 16, each launcher of nearly twice the range of its predecessor and carrying eight multiple warheads (two fewer than before, but each one of 50% greater yield than their predecessors). Since submarine missile forces are, by virtue of concealment, pretty well immune from countermeasures, any reasonable investment in them to improve deterrence at either level can be expected.

THE ROLE OF
MULTIPLE WARHEADS

Multiple warheads improve first-level deterrence by multiplying the destructive potential of those missiles likely to survive a surprise attack, thereby making such an attack less probable. This comes about because a number of small warheads of reasonable accuracy can more effectively destroy a large city or other extended target than one large warhead of the same weight. The technical reason for this is somewhat complicated and there are circumstances when the greater radioactivity associated with a large warhead gives it certain advantages; but generally a large warhead will damage the area close to its impact point considerably more than is necessary, and the districts more remote from impact point less than adequately, whereas a number of accurately spaced smaller warheads, even when of substantially smaller total megatonnage, will produce adequate levels of damage over the entire region. (The same consideration applies, on a much reduced scale, to the use of tactical nuclear weapons.) In addition, when each of these small warheads is capable of being guided to widely separate targets, as they are in most modern designs, this puts the potentially valuable capacity to destroy several small targets within the reach of each surviving launcher of the retaliatory force.

Improvements in accuracy are equally uncontained by third-level deterrence. Greater accuracy combined with multiple warheads improves first-level deterrence by giving assurance that an extended target will be efficiently blanketed by an attack relying on several individually small yield warheads. There is an increased assurance that even if only a few launchers were to survive a surprise attack, their warheads will nonetheless strike home on their assigned targets. Improvements in accuracy as a means of improving second-level deterrence of limited strikes against non-military targets are of equally obvious value.

Improving accuracy so as to better second-level deterrence of limited strikes against the strategic nuclear retaliation force itself – if this were all it accomplished – cannot hitherto have made much sense in terms of third-level deterrence. In the early days of intercontinental missilry, expensively-won improvements in accuracy were comparatively easily nullified by placing the land based missiles of a retaliatory force in well separated concrete silos; also by dispersing bombers widely and putting them on a continuous state of near-alert. The part of the retaliatory force concealed in submarines, of course, needs no special modification to cope with a more accurate attack, except perhaps design changes to reduce further the small proportion of vessels that are at any one time in port for overhaul.

However, important changes are occurring to weaken third-level deterrence of the search for greater accuracy to improve the prospects of limited attack against ICBM emplacements. The cost of incorporating better accuracy into warheads of all kinds, including cruise missiles in bombers, has begun to decline rapidly (largely because of cheaper and better micro-electronics) in comparison to the cost and practicability of countering this improvement by building thicker, heavier, and deeper concrete silos. The ICBM in its concrete emplacement will soon be of very little value to the maintenance of first-level deterrence; and it is for this reason that the modernization of submarine forces, and to a lesser extent of bomber forces too, have already established a priority claim on resources, at least in the United States.

The diminishing contribution of the ICBM to first-level deterrence does not seriously weaken it – it is too robust for that – but it does draw attention to the importance of having technologically diversified strategic nuclear forces, simply in order to win time in which to decide how best to react to all kinds of unforeseen developments. Without this diversity an opponent might be encouraged to try and beat third-level deterrence by disclosing a secretly-developed technology or tactic, not so dramatic as to provoke the other side into an immediate attack before his position got any worse, but important enough to create a sense of inferiority. As it is, the near impossibility of making substantial secret advances on three technological fronts at once is one reason why third-level deterrence works.

Maintaining third-level deterrence is the strongest argument for replacing the silo-based ICBM with an attack-proof land-based launcher. A good design would combine mobility with concealment, with each characteristic based upon different principles from those behind the concealment of the submarine or the mobility of the bomber.

Third-level deterrence is not sufficient by itself to ensure that first-level and second-level deterrence are kept in good repair while maintaining a crisis-free atmosphere between the two superpowers. For even if technological diversity gives a breathing-space, each side must still be able to form a reliable picture of any new developments in the other side's technology or tactics in sufficient time to be able to make suitable countermoves. It is also essential that there exists at all times a reservoir of scientific, engineering and industrial resources, and of political will, ready to be put at the service of an effective countermove to any dash by the other side for a margin of superiority.

Neither condition can be entirely met without the sort of reinforcement third-level deterrence can get from arms control agreements. Arms control agreements, in the process of negotiation and in their provisions when negotiated, nearly always add to the flow of information each side has about the strategic activities of the other and consequently strengthen third-level deterrence against surprise. And formal arms control agreements not to do what third-level deterrence itself already makes fairly pointless, such as deploying anti-missile defences, are worthwhile not only because pointless things are sometimes done but also because the political will for reacting to a move that involved violation of a treaty can be more readily relied upon to materialize.

Formal treaties have the bonus of making a bridge between strategy and the totality of a state's foreign policy. If violations of arms control treaties were inhibited only by third-level deterrence together with whatever moral cost attached to violation (not, usually, very great in bilateral treaties, where a belated discovery of 'unfairness' is all too easy) they would be worth less than is in fact the case where treaty violations in practice would almost certainly have repercussions on bilateral trading relations – and on other aspects of external policy where the wronged party could harm the interests of the violator.

First generation arms control (of the SALT-1 variety) usefully shores up third-level deterrence, but does not go beyond it. In the long run the problem for bilateral arms control is the reproduction of the regulation provided by third-level deterrence without the costs and other difficulties of maintaining at permanent readiness a huge sector of industry devoted solely to the research, development and production of strategic nuclear weapons.
IAN BELLANY

PART TWO

INTO THE ABYSS

IN THE SECOND PART OF THIS BOOK
WE VENTURE TO PEER AHEAD AND IMAGINE HOW,
WITHIN SO SHORT A SPACE OF TIME AS THE NEXT FIVE YEARS,
CURRENT INTERNATIONAL TENSIONS AND DEVELOPING WEAPONRY
COULD ACTUALLY BRING ABOUT WORLD WAR 3.

THE IMAGINARY SCENARIO CHOSEN BY OUR AUTHORS IS,
OF COURSE, ONLY ONE OF THOUSANDS ON THE THEME,
AND SEEKS TO HIGHLIGHT IMPORTANT DETAIL
RATHER THAN ATTEMPT A COMPLETE,
SELF-CONTAINED NARRATIVE.

EVERYTHING YOU ARE ABOUT TO READ IS ONLY TOO POSSIBLE.
EVERY IMAGINARY EVENT DESCRIBED FROM NOW ON
IS FAITHFULLY DRAWN FROM THE REALITIES OF TODAY.

11. THE LAST MONTHS OF PEACE

The North Atlantic Treaty Organisation had always depended on an accommodation of differing viewpoints. West Germany, being in the front line, was therefore predictably 'hawkish'. The Danes and Norwegians remained pacific, refusing to accept foreign troops and above all nuclear weapons on their territory. The French were perverse, maintaining their troops in position but withdrawing from any military staffs or machinery for co-ordination. The British claimed to be determined but acted 'dovish'. And the Americans, deeply conscious of their responsibilities for both war and peace, continued to promote detente while at the same time maintaining their defences in good shape, although they made some important sacrifices in the hope of detente.

It was easy to point to NATO's weaknesses, but repeated prophecies that it was about to break up had been proved false. In fact it was an extremely elastic structure, and the mutual respect of its members for the views of each other constituted its real strength. But the first signs of serious decay in the alliance appeared in 1980, and there was an increasing lack of cohesion which got steadily worse throughout 1981.

A key ingredient of the Atlantic Alliance, indeed, the very cement of the structure – had always been the historic *rapprochement* between France and Germany. Unfortunately, however, a sharp downturn in the German economy had encouraged the growth of a neo-Nazi party. This body commanded no serious support on a national scale, but its increased activities caused alarm in western Europe. Although 36 years had passed, memories of Nazi occupation were still vivid. As a result, Franco-German relations had sadly deteriorated.

There was an even stronger reaction in the eastern European states and above all in Soviet Russia, which had suffered worse than any other country at the hands of Nazi Germany. To make matters worse the neo-Nazi party succeeded, in the Bavarian local elections, in returning a deputy to the *Landsrat*.

Both *Pravda* and the organs of the Western press united in condemning this development in the strongest terms, until it might have been thought from the newspapers that the entire Federal Republic of Germany was about to return to Nazi rule. This naturally distressed the German government, for after all the process of de-Nazification had been long and conscientiously pursued. It also began to feel isolated, and to think that the more the country could defend its own frontiers against aggression by its own efforts the safer West Germany would be.

West German anxiety was unfortunately increased by the equivocal attitude of Great Britain, once one of the major pillars of NATO, towards European defence. While paying it lip-service the British permitted a steady weakening of their armed forces, at the same time embarking on an expensive expansion of social services financed from the North Sea oil bonanza. True, Britain imposed no further military cuts, but her government made no effort to repair the damage done in the 1970s, thus steering a course which satisfied neither its pacifist wing nor those who were seriously alarmed at the inability of Britain to play her promised part in European defence. All the economies of the 1970s had bitten deeply into the morale of the Army as well as its equipment. Substantial improvements in both pay and equipment were needed, plus an increase in manpower. The same applied to the other two services, especially the Royal Air Force.

All this was clear to the West German government. For a long time British officers had occupied a high proportion of senior military posts in Supreme Headquarters Allied Powers in Europe (SHAPE), Allied Forces Central Europe (AFCENT) and Northern Army Group (NORTHAG), in tribute to the early British involvement and British military skill. The West Germans now felt that the *Bundeswehr* was in fact, if not in principle, taking on more and more of the British share of guarding western Europe, and that the British share of direction exceeded the real British military contribution. It was therefore requested that a due proportion of these glittering appointments should be relinquished in favour of German generals. This was ill-received in London, and a marked coolness set in between the two governments.

In the United States there was a new President whose temperament and policy differed markedly from those of his predecessors. He lacked the firmness of a Kennedy or the naïve if sincere evangelism of a Carter. He was not an isolationist in the traditional meaning of the term, but he had to take account of strong isolationist feelings that had always existed in the United States, and which had been strengthened by the disastrous outcome of the long and costly war in Vietnam. Long after this defeat the American people, usually so resilient, were still going through a period of doubt and were questioning their own institutions.

The opinion-forming classes in America were also loud in their denunciation of the reappearance of neo-Nazism in Germany, which had been much exaggerated by press and television. The new President viewed the problems of foreign policy as intractable, being especially discouraged by American failures to play any decisive part in restoring peace to the Middle East. Foreign affairs did not inter-

est him: the two great problems he felt he had been elected to solve were inflation and the energy crisis, and all his attention was concentrated on them.

US defence advisers had urged the President to reconsider the decisions of his predecessor which in their view seriously restricted the variety of options open to them: the final cancellation of the 'neutron bomb' after initial deferment, the cancellation of the XB-70 and B1 bombers and the mobile, land-based missile system. American military weakness, they argued, could only encourage Soviet aggression – but the President remained unconvinced. In his crusade for economic stability, vast expenditure on arms had no place.

The American President wisely remained inscrutable in his general attitude towards defence, but the general consensus of all political commentators, including those in the Kremlin, was that he saw the arms race as economically wasteful, that he was determined to prevent the involvement of the continental United States in war, and that he was unlikely to do anything rash or provocative. He would be the last man to precipitate a direct armed confrontation between the conventional forces of the superpowers, let alone risk the nuclear destruction of the cities of the United States in a reaction to some minor infringement of the peace not directly threatening the USA.

As a result, the West German government began to feel more and more isolated. Bonn had no doubt about the hatred still felt for Germany by most of the Warsaw Pact countries. The feeling quickly grew that once West Germany was not merely isolated, but was seen to be isolated, strong pressure on her from the Soviet bloc was a near certainty, with a considerable likelihood of military invasion if that pressure were to be resisted.

The West German government therefore concluded that it must have its own, independent nuclear weapons: a deterrent to counter the Soviet SS 20 system threatening all the NATO countries, in whose introduction the United States and Britain seemed tamely to have acquiesced. Then there was the question of battlefield weapons. German technology was fully capable of designing a 'neutron' warhead, essential for German defence, yet irrationally put in cold storage and indefinitely deferred by the Americans.

The West Germans felt that they had no other course but to create their own weapon, and to this end they set up an establishment to begin research. Since it was foreseen that the decision, if it became known, would create an international furore, the West German government decided to keep the whole thing top secret. But, inevitably, this proved impossible. Soviet espionage soon got wind of the development. In addition, a number of West German scientists assigned to the project strongly believed that the Federal Republic should *not* have nuclear weapons of its own, and leaked the news to the press. It was a bombshell of a story, in every sense of the term. 'Nuclear proliferation', in all its aspects – the provision of reactors to Third World countries, the processing of nuclear waste, and the nuclear threat to the environment – was one of the most sensitive subjects in the world. Combined with the spectre, or fantasy, of a Nazi revival in Germany, it created an international sensation.

At most the *Bundeswehr* units were permitted, like the other NATO forces, to possess short-range launching systems which might, in war, discharge nuclear warheads under American supervision. This the Russians understood, however bitterly they denounced it. But the prospect of West Germany having tactical nuclear weapons under their own control for unilateral use, let alone seeking to possess intermediate-range systems for deterrence, was unendurable to Moscow.

The Soviet government made its objections clear to all the members of the NATO alliance. In Bonn the Soviet ambassador delivered a note declaring flatly that his government was not prepared to accept German acquisition of nuclear weapons in any circumstances or by any means whatsoever. At the same time the entire Communist propaganda machine went into action, aiming its message at world public opinion. It sharpened memories of German militarism and trumpeted the message that a Germany armed with nuclear weapons was a menace to world peace.

The member states of NATO were almost as reluctant as the Russians to see Germany in possession of an independent deterrent, or even nuclear weapons of any kind. Amid the uproar in the media in their own countries, they began to put intense and concerted diplomatic pressure on the West Germans in an attempt to persuade them to abandon the whole mad project. The US government was especially severe, as it had long set its face against any further nuclear proliferation.

The German response was reasonable. West Germany would not only be in the front line of any future war with Soviet Russia: it would be the cockpit in which the war would be fought. The West Germans had willingly accepted this burden and were making a powerful contribution to the common defence effort. They had every reason to demand that this total effort should be strong enough, first to deter any military aggression or pressure against her frontiers, and also to fight the battle as far to the east as possible.

West Germany's terms for giving up what was, after all, an immensely costly project involving much financial self-sacrifice were bluntly put. Her allies, and her European allies in particular, must recognize the West German viewpoint in a practical way. They must increase their own defence expenditure, and above all they must improve the strength, equipment and readiness for war of their contingents in AFCENT.

The diplomatic crisis raged unabated for month after month into the late spring of 1983. The NATO governments pressed West Germany with double-barrelled arguments which claimed that their contributions were in fact sadly understimated, and offered trivial improvements. These West Germany scornfully rejected. She also indignantly refused to give way to more forceful demands from the United States to close down the nuclear research establishment, or at least give a guarantee that it was confined to research only and that no actual weapons would be made or tested.

Some did feel that there was more sound and fury than real danger in the whole affair. After all, even for the United States with its vast nuclear technology, the process of taking a single weapon already researched – like the 'neutron bomb' – from test stage to the fully engineered product, complete with an appropriate delivery system, might take two or three years. This crisis, like many others, might easily have been contained by the deft use of the 'crisis management' machinery already in existence and directly connecting the two superpowers. But two separate factors now began to operate jointly in accelerating the course of events to runaway speed.

First, a West German scientist allegedly disclosed to an East German agent *that an effective nuclear weapon already existed.* This was astonishing, but not entirely inconceivable. It was possible, though unlikely, for any country with advanced technology to produce a crude fission weapon, and such a prototype *could* be delivered by adapting the high-performance aircraft or the Honest John and Sergeant missiles West Germany already possessed. But West Germany was looking for *sophisticated* weapons, and her chance of independently arriving at a 'neutron' warhead was still far in the future.

Nevertheless, the news was leaked from Moscow and the fat was now really in the fire. The clamour in the West rose to a new pitch of intensity. There were even suggestions that the whole affair was a piece of duplicity on the part of the United States (or that favourite bogey, the CIA), that the German establishment was a blind, and that this was really a cunning underhand way of dodging the ban on the infamous 'neutron bomb' *and* giving it to the Germans.

Second, and just as important, the Russians began to pay serious attention to the hesitancy and irresolution on the part of the NATO powers.

Only the extreme, inbred caution of the elderly Soviet leaders restrained them from taking prompt advantage of the West's political disarray, but now a more valid argument was advanced by the militant wing in their counsels. The danger was very great, it was argued; why wait until it was greater? If the Soviet Union was going to take any action at all, why wait until her most implacable enemy had the weapon in his hand? Surely the time to strike was now, and nip the danger in the bud? Why not let it be known that the Russian action was limited, pre-emptive and specific, with no intention of occupying territory or of hostile acts against other members of NATO?

These arguments prevailed. The Soviet leaders decided that there was no time left for further warnings, and that immediate action was essential.

Russia's 'police action' was to take the form of an invasion of West Germany by conventional forces of the Warsaw Pact: an advance to the Rhine with the aim of cowing Bonn, and a parallel advance across the North German plain to seize and destroy the nuclear establishment at which the weapon was being developed. (This establishment was located a few miles southwest of Hamburg). The Kremlin decided that the entire personnel of the nuclear establishment should be seized and taken to Russia. In order to prevent them from leaving the establishment at the first hint of real trouble and scattering throughout western Europe, the initial seizure was to be made by dropping an entire airborne division.

It would take a full day to mount the operation, so 'H-Hour' was fixed for early in the morning of the second day after the decision was taken, with no preliminary troop movements until dusk on D-1.

At 11 pm on D-1 the Soviet ambassadors called on the governments to which they were accredited to explain the reasons for the action which their government was about to take – action which, their hearers were dismayed to learn, was scheduled for 1 am – less than two hours away. The ambassadors emphasized that the sole purpose of the operation was to prevent the German militarists from getting access to nuclear weapons; that as soon as the West German government had agreed to renounce them, and had broken up its nuclear research establishment, and as soon as effective measures had been taken to prevent a future West German government from making another attempt to secure such weapons, the Soviet forces would be withdrawn.

The ambassadors went on to stress that the USSR was not interested in acquiring any West German territory: its sole purpose was to prevent a German militarist finger on the nuclear trigger. It was hoped that the other NATO governments would agree that this was a most laudable purpose, and that the whole world had a vital interest in preventing the emergence of a nuclear Germany. The USSR therefore asked the NATO governments to order their forces not to oppose the Soviet advance across West German territory, and not to come to the help of the *Bundeswehr*, should the latter decide to fight.

If, added the ambassadors, non-German NATO governments reacted belligerently and allowed their troops to resist the Soviet army, Moscow could only take this as proof that the whole affair was an imperialist plot to equip West Germany with nuclear weapons as a first step towards starting a war with Russia. Therefore Moscow, if faced with such resistance, would regard it as the opening shots of World War 3 and would retaliate accordingly. The 'hot lines' from Moscow to Washington, Paris and London worked flat out at elaborating the above.

All now hinged on the President of the United States, who had an awful and solitary responsibility. He could instantly threaten the Russians with the strategic nuclear weapon, with all that it implied. He could acquiesce, and see what could be salvaged from a diplomatic and military disaster of the first magnitude and the virtual end of the Atlantic Alliance and NATO (an objective of prime importance to Moscow), and a collapse of American military credibility. Or he could temporize. There were now barely 35 minutes before the Russian forces were scheduled to move. The President chose to temporize, keeping in touch with the Kremlin, frantically calling up his advisers, in his capacity as Commander-in-Chief, and alerting the armed forces.

The messages now reaching every capital from the Kremlin continued meanwhile to hammer home three points:
● The operation was not intended to upset the existing military balance between NATO and the Warsaw Pact because there was no intention of destroying the *Bundeswehr*, merely of denying it nuclear weapons. Once the crisis was over and the Pact forces had been withdrawn, the *status quo* would be restored;
● Compliance by the non-German NATO governments with the Soviet request not to resist the Soviet forces would be greatly assisted by an order to their forces to stay in barracks until the end of the operation. This would only hasten the moment when all could return to normal. Resistance on their part, however, would start a

major war;

● Surely none of the Western governments *could* want a major war, when they must obviously dread the prospect of a nuclear West Germany as much as the USSR itself.

As it was vital to win strategic surprise the Soviet leaders, after much soul-searching, agreed to renounce a number of preparatory measures which would have appeared, at first sight, to have been most advantageous to them. In particular they agreed to take no steps whatever to deploy their navy, because they knew that Western Intelligence regarded the movements of Soviet warships as an important indication of Soviet military intentions. A deployment forward into the Atlantic, for instance, would certainly have been regarded in the West as a sign that war was imminent; and it was crucial for the success of the Soviet operation that this should not be so.

Consequently, although their decision not to deploy their warships would make it harder to defeat NATO if their plans misfired and the operation escalated into a general European war, the Soviet leaders decided to accept this liability. In the debate that preceded the taking of this decision a number of senior officers tried hard to prevent its adoption on the grounds that it was only prudent to allow for things going wrong. But this was countered by three effective arguments.

First, surprise was all-important. If surprise failed, things would certainly go wrong. The Soviet invasion of Czechoslovakia in 1968 was cited: a complete success generally accepted to have been largely due to the attainment of surprise. Second, and still in connection with Czechoslovakia, it remained a simple historical fact that one of the measures by which surprise had been so completely achieved in 1968 had been the order to the Soviet fleet to stick to its normal peacetime routine and refrain from any unusual ship movements.

The third argument was that, given that the nuclear submarines would be on station anyway, the rest of the navy's part in a general war would only be of importance if the war were prolonged. As the entire Warsaw Pact strategy was based on fighting a short war, there would be no role for the Soviet Navy, even if general war materialized, unless the entire strategy somehow or other went off the rails. But such a disaster could only come about by a double failure on the part of the Soviet Armed Forces; and most of the Russian generals agreed that a double failure was the sort of thing of which only the Rumanian, Bulgarian or Hungarian armies could reasonably be deemed to be capable.

The first decision came from France, and came quickly. France was not a member of NATO, but the French armed forces were an important factor in any military operation in Europe. The French had always affirmed that if a Soviet invasion of western Europe were ever to take place, the French armed forces would collaborate with NATO to resist it. At that moment, however, Franco-German relations were poor while relations between France and the Soviet Union were particularly good.

With all the awful consequences of a blunt refusal in mind, the French leaders felt able to accept the official explanation of Soviet intentions as sincere.

The French reply – short, because there was no time for any long and carefully-phrased note to be drawn up – was that the French forces would not oppose the advance of the Soviet forces through Germany. But if any hostile act was committed against the French troops stationed there (who would be confined to their cantonments), or if West Germany's western frontier was crossed at any point, then France would retaliate with all means at her disposal, including nuclear weapons.

The French President and Prime Minister were able to consult sufficient colleagues to get this accepted as official policy as early as 3 am; and the French decision was immediately communicated to the world.

While the President of the United States was agonizing over the problem, examining all the long-prepared procedures drawn up for every variety of such an emergency and carefully assessing the advice being poured in his ears (some of it contradictory) by his many advisers, the centre of the stage was now occupied by the British.

The British Labour government of the day – the usual uneasy alliance of powerful left-wingers and timid moderates – was bitterly divided, finding it extremely hard to reach a decision of any kind. On principle, the important left-wing element in the British Cabinet would have been most unwilling to fight the Soviet Union under any circumstances. It flatly refused to consider doing so in this case, where the object was, according to the Soviet communiqué, to prevent the spread of nuclear weapons (always a desirable goal, not only in left-wing opinion) and, in particular, to prevent the spread of them to a notoriously militarist state – one experiencing a revival of Nazism at that moment.

The moderates of the British Cabinet found themselves in a dilemma. They argued for British resistance, but only half-heartedly. Even the right-wing or NATO-orientated members of the British Cabinet shared the intellectual and emotional dislike of their left-wing colleagues for the idea of resurgent Nazism coupled with nuclear weapons, unreal though this picture was.

In Britain the issue was closely linked with the antics of the extreme right-wing group calling itself the National Front, which in its limited but repellent manner commanded a degree of support in parts of England by exploiting racial strife, unemployment, bad housing and unsatisfactory social conditions in immigrant areas. In the mind of the British public, such extremism was still unjustly regarded as typically *German*. Even in the 1980s, the fascination with World War 2 and the image of the Nazi enemy was a popular and recurring theme in fiction and television drama.

Fears of the National Front were shared by a significant number of voters of every political hue; and the right-wing members of the Cabinet did not press their case with the energy and conviction they might have done. But the British Cabinet, in its emergency session, had just about reached this point in their deliberations when news of the French decision was conveyed to them. It was not likely to encourage them to stand firm, and it did not.

The British Cabinet agreed that:
- The commander of BAOR must be ordered that British troops would only fire on Russian troops in self-defence (a phrase representing the last stand of the defeated right-wing members, put in to pacify them);
- In no circumstances whatever would Britain agree to the use of any nuclear weapon, strategic or tactical;
- If the Russians were to advance through areas held by British troops, they were to be allowed to pass;
- British troops were not to go to the assistance of the West Germans, if fighting broke out between the *Bundeswehr* and the Soviet forces;
- In order to minimize the chances of any incident, the British troops were to be confined to barracks from now until further orders.

By this time – shortly before 3.30 am – Soviet forces were well inside West Germany and were advancing on two axes, one aimed at Bonn, the other at the nuclear establishment south-west of Hamburg. And earlier, at 1 am – precisely at the moment when the first of the Soviet ground forces began to move – the Soviet airborne division had taken off in its fleet of transport aircraft to seize the nuclear establishment, prevent the escape of any of its staff, and hold it until the arrival of the ground forces.

12. THE LAND WAR

rom the very start, the advance of the Soviet ground forces was fiercely resisted by the West German frontier forces, the *Grenzschutz*. In turn, their resistance activated the process of the call-out of the reserves and the Territorial Army. These at once began to put into action their programme of disruption and destruction of the West German communications systems in the area near the border. In particular, the bridges across the Weser were successfully blown.

This was a considerable setback to the Russians' hopes. Although they carried with them sufficient bridging equipment to enable them to cross the river, it would naturally take up time if they had to use it. Admittedly, the success of their operation did not depend upon being able to use the existing bridges, but it would obviously make things very much easier if they could. To this end, they had, years before, successfully planted agents in the area, who had been 'sleeping' there until the day they were required. In one vital area south of Hameln, however, German counter-intelligence had discovered them only a few days before the start of the Soviet invasion. This meant that, in that area, the *Bundeswehr's* programme of disruption had not itself been disrupted. The bridges consequently were blown; and the Soviet advance westwards had been temporarily held up.

The northern axis of the Soviet advance progressed steadily on a line roughly parallel with, and not very far away from, the Baltic coast. It was a Soviet aim to capture both Bremen and Hamburg, so providing Moscow with as many 'bargaining chips' as possible when the time came to negotiate with Bonn. Strict orders had been given by the Kremlin to the Warsaw

Pact commander that no German cities were to be heavily bombarded, whether from ground or sea or air, in order not to arouse in the NATO peoples a feeling of revulsion against the Russians, and therefore a wish to resist.

The Kremlin, however, had sanctioned the use of seaborne landings in co-operation with the advance of the ground forces, and so the Soviet naval infantry of the Baltic and Northern Fleets prepared to assault Kiel, while the naval infantry of East Germany and Poland got ready to seize Lübeck, march across the neck of Schleswig-Holstein and attack Hamburg from the north-east, while the Soviet Army proper attacked it from the south. A secondary thrust on that axis was to aim at Bremen, linking up on its way with the airborne division at Verden.

On that northern axis, resistance to the Soviet advance had passed from the hands of the *Grenzschutz* to the *Bundeswehr* proper. Heavy fighting developed in the area round Lüneberg and also in the country to the north, between Lüneberg and Lübeck.

The *Bundeswehr* put in a number of counterattacks at brigade and divisional level, but though these slowed the Russian advance they did not succeed in halting it.

Meanwhile, in the British sector, the British I Corps was busily engaged in taking up its prearranged positions.

The crossing of the frontier by the Pact forces and the outbreak of fighting with the *Grenzschutz* had resulted in British troops being automatically called out to their secondary positions, the ones to which they would move when warning time was not long enough for them to get to their proper positions. They got into some sort of fighting order and began to prepare to resist the Russian advance.

Their efforts at resistance, however, though heroic, were not effectual. The oncoming Soviet formations swept round and past them, leaving them to be dealt with by their second echelon. As a result of this, the British, so to speak, were put into the 'pending' tray; and consequently fighting continued in the area of Wolfenbüttel for a considerable period. However, apart from its initial messages back to its parent formation, the British garrison at Wolfenbüttel was quite unable to communicate with the rest of British I Corps. Once the Soviet troops had got beyond Wolfenbüttel, their EW equipment deprived the British radio sets of their ability to maintain communications, while the telephone lines had naturally been cut by agents.

Meanwhile, back in Britain, the Cabinet had decided that it was not enough to signal BAOR the decisions that had been taken. In all the circumstances the signal, it was felt, might not be regarded as genuine, and British officers might well be reluctant to sit back and watch their West German comrades 'being clobbered by the Russians'. In order to enforce compliance with its orders, the Cabinet decided to send the Chief of the General Staff and the other military members of the Army Board out to BAOR. In all, five very senior British officers got ready to fly out to Germany. It was agreed with the Cabinet that the CGS was to go to HQ, British I Corps, while the other four were to go to the respective divisional headquarters.

Moscow was informed of this arrangement over the 'hot line'. The Russians were asked to slow down the speed of their advance in the British sector, and, if necessary, to halt it, in order to give time to these generals to reach their destinations and issue their orders. Moscow willingly agreed; and the routes, the types and identification numbers of the planes that would be used to take these officers to Germany were then transmitted to the Kremlin.

The fate of the garrison of Wolfenbüttel was not then known in London.

The CGS and his brother generals all reached their destinations safely by 7 am. Their most pressing problem was to get hold of the troops in the field, ensure that they thoroughly understood that they were not to resist the Russian advance, and order them back to barracks.

A bitter altercation then ensued at the headquarters of the forward division. Reports had come in of fighting between the Russians and the *Bundeswehr*; and the division in question had developed cordial relations with its neighbouring German units.

The officers at divisional headquarters were not inclined to sit back and let the feared and detested Russians knock hell out of their German counterparts without making at least some effort to come to the latter's rescue. Furthermore, they had at the back of their minds a picture of the fate that they believed would befall the civilian population in those areas of West Germany that were overrun by the Russians.

The Adjutant-General, however, had come from London for the express purpose of seeing to it that the Cabinet's orders were obeyed, and he was not to be deflected from that purpose. He therefore gave the Divisional Commander, his assembled staff, and as many of the field force and battalion commanders as could quickly be assembled a direct order that they were to return to barracks immediately. There was a tense moment when it seemed as though his hearers would disobey him; but military discipline held firm. Slowly and reluctantly, the troops pulled out of their positions and began to return to barracks.

Everyone was thoroughly irked by having first had to rush to reach their positions, and then, a few hours later, to be ordered to move back from them. If it had been a peacetime practice it would have been understandable; but everyone had heard on their transistor radios about the

Soviet invasion of West Germany, and the noise of battle was plainly audible coming from the north and the east. They were about halfway back to barracks when the head of the Soviet columns caught up with their tail.

The Soviet commander was under strict orders to push westwards as fast as possible. He had been told that the British government had agreed to collaborate with the Soviet government, and that the British Army had been ordered not to oppose the Russians' advance. He had been told to slow down, so as not to clash with the British; but at the same time he had been equally emphatically ordered to be on the east bank of the Rhine within five days. He knew what would happen if he failed to comply with that order; and since at the same time he also knew that the British Army ahead of him, by virtue of the order given it, was no longer an army but a civilian rabble, he decided to treat it in the way in which Soviet officers are wont to treat civilians who have become a nuisance. He raced up with his forward tanks to the vehicle containing the officer commanding the rear British detachment, and ordered him to get off the road. When the officer demurred, he shot him dead. An attempt by the officer's companions to seize the Russian resulted in them being shot dead too. The sound of the firing attracted the attention of the other British vehicles, which turned round and moved back to investigate. They were immediately surrounded by Russian tanks; and the two sides faced each other, their guns at the ready.

News reached divisional headquarters that Soviet troops had caught up with the rear of the British column; that there had been some sort of trouble with a Soviet officer; and that British vehicles were surrounded by Russian tanks. The divisional commander wanted to order his forces to go to their assistance but this was countermanded by the Adjutant-General, who said they must return to barracks. He agreed, however, that they could not resume their movement until the present situation was cleared up; and a brigadier was sent back to sort things out with the Russians. The brigadier reported by radio that the Soviet commander insisted that the British forces clear out of his way; and that, as hostage for the good behaviour of the British forces, he was going to keep a couple of battalions prisoner.

The Adjutant-General now felt it his duty, as senior officer present, to go and argue personally with the Russians. No sooner had his staff car disappeared from sight than the divisional commander, ordered his forces to deploy for battle and to resist any further Russian advance. The first clash between Soviet and British forces took place a few minutes later; and within a few minutes the whole front was ablaze.

True to the promise conveyed in its communiqué, the Soviet Command told the British government over the 'hot line' that it regarded the British resistance as an act of contumacy, and that unless the resistance immediately ceased, the British Isles would be bombarded with nuclear missiles. The British Cabinet had no means, however, of securing compliance with such an order. It had no communication with the Army Board in Germany; and it had no notion itself of what to do. The Prime Minister in despair in turn called up the President of the United States.

By this time the President had changed his attitude. For one thing, the crossing of the West German frontier by the Russians had automatically put the Americans on to 'Red Alert'. For another, the gallantry shown by the *Bundeswehr* and the subsequent embroilment of the British Army had sufficed to nullify Washington's grudging acceptance of the course of action propounded by the Soviet ambassadors on the evening of the day before. For yet another, American public opinion was clearly showing itself to be violently anti-Soviet, and

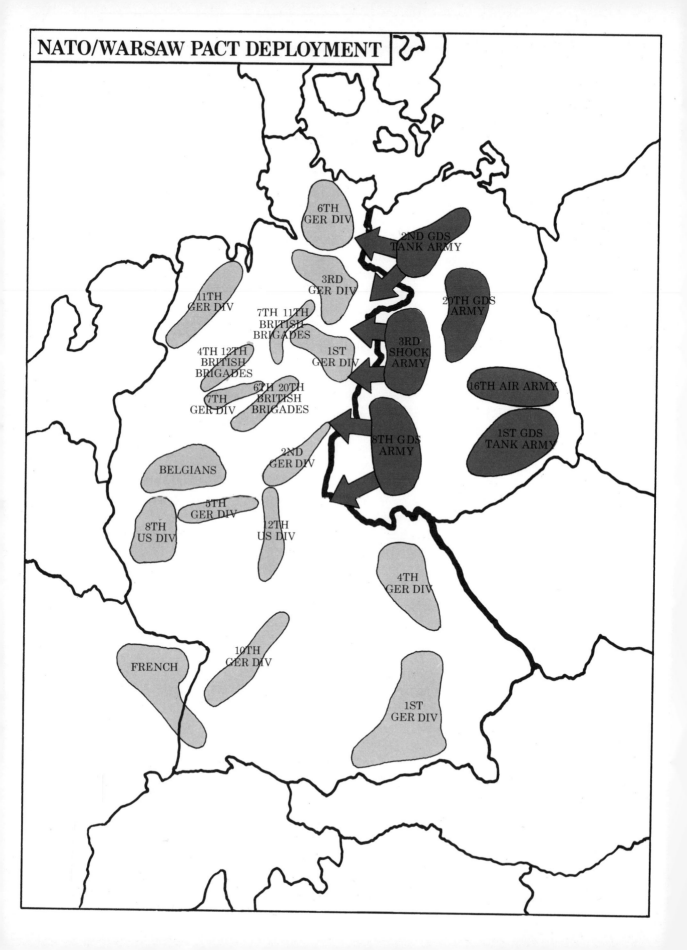

was demanding of the American President that he should get on and do something. In particular, it was demanded of him that he should stop the fighting in Germany.

At long last, the President acted decisively. Although he was convinced that there could be no question, and that furthermore that there was still no need, of embarking on a global war with the Soviet Union, he was not prepared to allow the Russians to create havoc in Western Europe. Over the 'hot line', he therefore requested the Soviet government to order all its forces, ground and air, to stand fast. He would take all steps to allay Russian fears (he said), but deplored their very dangerous action taken at notice so short that it precluded any peaceful or reasonable discussion. If Russian agreement was not immediately forthcoming he would throw the full weight of the United States into action to stabilize the situation. At the same time he unilaterally sent out orders to the high American officers who habitually occupied the posts of Supreme Allied Commander, Europe (SACEUR) and the Commander-in-Chief, Atlantic (SACLANT) as well as the commanding general of the United States Forces at Frankfurt in Germany. All American forces, ground and air, were to be used to bring the fighting to a halt, using force if necessary.

The American troops in Germany were located mainly in Bavaria. There was one brigade in the northern part of Germany, but this was soon embroiled in the general fighting and overrun. News of the destruction reached American headquarters in Frankfurt within less than a quarter of an hour and headquarters, in turn, passed the message on to its subordinate formations.

American officers are not, in general, noted for their pro-Soviet sympathies and the general commanding the 4th Division was particularly anti-Communist. Since his division happened to be nearest to the scene of the action, it was his division that was told by Frankfurt to get in and stop the fighting. The general's notion of stopping the fighting was to fall like a thunderbolt on the flank of the Soviet 55th Division, which, taken by surprise, was badly mauled. This victory greatly encouraged the Americans. A second American division, enheartened by it, marched towards the sound of gunfire with the greatest enthusiasm and the units of Soviet 3rd Guards Shock Army became suddenly gravely imperilled.

The situation was by then extraordinarily confused. Formations on both sides were intermingled, and the Americans were fighting in areas and in circumstances completely different from their planned operations. Headquarters on both sides were divorced from their units or destroyed by air action, and units obeyed such commanders as appeared, or fought such enemy as they encountered. Violent ECM jamming on both sides disrupted communications and the flow of information and orders. 'C³', in fact, broke down and no orders to halt could have reached the units in the field, even if they could have been obeyed in the excitement of close combat. While the Soviet commanders became alarmed at their losses, the Americans on their side, gallantly and successfully as their divisions were fighting, soon became conscious that (as they had always feared) in a conventional battle the successive echelons of Russian tanks arriving in waves would soon wear them down by sheer weight of numbers.

The view from the Kremlin was by now totally changed. Gone was the dream of a smooth deployment with a neutralized France and Britain and the prize of the German nuclear establishment in their hands, negligible casualties and little if any trouble from the *Bundeswehr*. All this had changed abruptly to something infinitely more alarming. What had been planned as a 'small victorious war' was suddenly appearing to be far from small and not necessarily victorious; and the fact that it had never been intended as a war, but merely as a punitive expedition, made little difference. Things were going wrong, and in the usual manner of Russians when thwarted or frightened, the men in the Kremlin instinctively reached for their sledgehammers. In other words, they gave to the Soviet commanders in the field the release for tactical nuclear weapons.

Their original intention for this dangerous step was that the missiles should fall upon the Germans and the British. The commander of the 3rd Guards Shock Army, however, expressly warned his superiors that the major threat to the safety of his force was now mounted by the Americans.

The original intention of the Soviet Defence Council had been to avoid any entanglement with the Americans at all costs. But now the strain began to tell, and their course of action ceased to be strictly logical. They agreed with the commander of the 3rd Guards Shock Army that the American forces must be a principal recipient of their nuclear strike. They renewed their threat to London that, unless fighting ceased immediately, they would attack the British Isles directly. As they did so they saw that they were caught between the devil and the deep blue sea – that an American riposte had now become as nearly inevitable as is possible in human affairs. That being the case, they began to consider abolishing London *and* pre-empting the American nuclears. In the meantime the entire mass of the Warsaw Pact land forces was unleashed upon West Germany and the Soviet navy was ordered to commence hostilities around the world.

World War 3 had begun.

D+2: THROUGH RUSSIAN EYES

It was not until the late afternoon of D+2, that is, some 64 hours after the first airborne troops had landed in the Hanover area, when the Soviet government decided to extend their punitive action to the purely British and United States sectors. All was ready. Every staff preparation had been made. All that was required was for the divisional and regimental commanders to issue the briefest verbal instructions and for the sealed packages of operational orders to be opened and issued to the units, who were to motor straight into action from their barracks and camps.

The major commanding the battle group formed on the Second Battalion, 180th Motor Rifle Regiment, 50th Motor Rifle Division, returned from the briefing to find his battle group, already paraded in orderly ranks ready to march off: the tank company, the three companies of motor infantry with their armoured carriers, the all important company of ZSU anti-aircraft guns, the battery of self-propelled guns. His column, like a dozen more across the army front, formed the vanguard, the trailblazers whose business it was to throw themselves on the enemy forward screen, drive it back, find the gaps and make way for the great steel-clad flood of battle tanks in the tank divisions to go racing through to smash the main enemy defences.

The major was a young man but he was one of the rare veterans in the Soviet Army. He had seen the real face of war in Sinai in 1973, and favourable as the situation might prove to be, as by all accounts the Americans were off-balance and unprepared, he knew he was in for a bitter combat resulting in heaven knows what in the way of destruction if things went awry and they started to fling nuclear weapons about.

These feelings he kept to himself. He was a good soldier and a practical leader and he saw his first task in this great test clearly. Accordingly he climbed without ceremony on to the engine hatch of a tank and called for the real key-men, the leaders of squads, the commanders of tanks, the non-coms to be gathered round him.

The soldiers knew it was more than the voice of authority: it was the voice of a leader. Their major, they knew, understood the ordeal they were about to face. Better, he knew how to fire a rifle, lay a tank gun, mend a track and knew their own work better than they did, and they were, as armoured soldiers, an elite.

'First, you infantrymen. I rely on you. When we go into the attack don't let me see you skulking inside your carriers. A carrier in the face of anti-tank fire is nothing but an armoured crematorium. Get out, and run like hell towards the enemy while we cover you. Get as close to them as you can. I want to know exactly where every enemy anti-tank gun is, and when you've passed the signal back, don't lie there on your over-fed bellies and go to sleep. Go for them.

'Tank-captains, don't go dashing about. This is not going to be an exercise and no-one is there in the spectators' stand waiting to be impressed. I've been over the ground as a tourist. It's not the steppe: there's plenty of cover – little ridges, trees,

hedges. Go from one good position to the next, showing just a rim of your turret, so the gunner can see the target: no more.

'Tank-gunners, some of you are new, or reservists. Take your time. One target, one shot: no more. Then you captains, move quickly and pop up again somewhere else.

'I expect that the enemy will jam all our command radios. Take no notice. You'll have a bearing of advance, just keep going along it: if you keep advancing you can't be wrong'.

He turned to the artillery officer, commander of a troop of ZSU self-propelled AAA guns, standing by. 'Comrade artillery-lieutenant. I can cope with the enemy tanks and infantry, but their aircraft are the very devil. I was in Syria 15 years ago, and I can tell you for sure a tank cannot fight an aeroplane. I'm relying on you to keep them off our backs. Remember what I've taught you during training.' The major continued:

'Don't let me see you skulking inside your carriers. Get out, and run like hell towards the enemy'

'You will ride right by me, and never mind waiting to ask me for orders. The moment we're held up even if by so much as a single squad, give them everything you've got, and everything you can call for from behind. Keep your own guns close behind, and your forward observers with the point, really forward. That's all I have to say. Go to your posts and good luck'.

The battalion commander had struck precisely the right note. On the order to dismiss they trooped off, chattering, to complete their last-minute jobs. He climbed down and watched his executive officer collect the officers and noncoms to issue them with the sheafs of documents needed to move a motor rifle battle group - armoured troop carriers, tanks, field and anti-aircraft artillery - into battle: maps, overlays, routes, orders, radio frequencies, recognition signals, positions of headquarters, medical aid posts and the mobile ammunition reserve. He supposed it was necessary: it gave the staff something to do, but privately he could never understand how you could stop and thumb through a wad of paper in the middle of a battle.

All he wanted was an objective and a route, not an order of 54 sub-paragraphs telling him what to do and how to do it. He knew what he was going to do. He was going to ride in a tank, as near the front as possible, with a red flag and a green flag, and if the battle group was stuck, he was going to get out and walk. He was going to take his troops not only up to the enemy but among them and as far inside their positions as possible; live or die, for that would be the safest place. But it was going to be a terrible affair. The battalion commander was an 'old sweat': he had jumped out of a burning tank in his time, and had lain paralysed by terror on the ground with cannon shells from Israeli aircraft bursting all round him. He was a fatalist, without fear, but without illusions.

His executive officer came up to him and saluted formally. 'It is 15 minutes before H-hour, we have just ten minutes to the initial point. Your permission to give orders to start engines and mount'.

There was no noise; no barked orders. The groups of men clambered into their vehicles, there was a chorus of coughs as the motors caught, a deep rumble of engines, an officer flashed a green torch and above the bass noise of the motors came the metallic chatter of the tracks on the metal of the road. They were off.

Across a hundred miles of front the road network was filled with similar columns of steel boxes carrying loads of men packed together in discomfort, in darkness except for the little red eye showing that the radio transceivers were switched on, ready to break silence when the enemy was finally met. Only the vehicle chiefs and the drivers, peering into image intensifiers, could see into the dark outside, and then no more than the back of the tank in front. For the rest, boredom was an anaesthetic for the thrill of going to war. It all seemed like an exercise and one by one they dozed off.

Their battle was to come. Up in the sky, one had already started, and in this they were as yet only the prey. Radar beams from above were scanning the roads below, the picture flashed back to the West and other aircraft taking off to attack, while yet others took off in the East to protect the advancing columns: they were being attacked in turn and volleys of SAM-6s arced up to drive them off. From a few hundred feet, where the American A-10As roared overhead, their sensors feeling the ground for moving targets, to the utterly remote battle for air control ten miles above the earth, the lethal technology of the war was hard at work.

The battalion commander, violating his own orders, had opened the hatch of his command carrier and was sitting on the roof. To the north and south he could see flashes, feel rather than hear the concussion of bombs above the clanking of tracks and roar of exhausts. Showers of tracer were floating lazily up into the night sky. Curious, he was thinking, how it looked so slow, and so pretty, when he was nearly blown off his seat, banging both his knees painfully on the edge of the turret hatch. Metal fragments whirred through the air, and ahead something went up in flames. It was a tank. The column stopped, shutting up like a telescope. Useless to shout. They've found us, he thought, well, damn radio silence. He seized a microphone and without a call sign, relying on his captains to recognise his voice, said 'Get off the road, right or left, it doesn't matter, but get off.' And to his driver: 'Left, quick left, through the hedge and halt by that burning tank'.

It was a rough night and it became worse. When dawn broke he had lost two more tanks and a squad of infantry had been roasted alive in their BRDM. They were left, screaming, to burn. The implacable voice on the radio simply repeated 'Get on! Get on!'

The battle when it started was bad enough, but at least then a man could see what was happening. The column reached the checkpoint a kilometre short of the border where they deployed into battle formation and spread out, the infantry thankful to be in the open, all three companies in lines of columns, the tanks behind them; the ZSUs spread out in a square, their radar saucers scanning the sky. There was no pause. As the vehicles filed past the check point the companies and platoons fanned out, every one to its planned position. Speed was safety. Along the whole frontier the same battle groups were deploying in the same way. Their mission, to meet the enemy, draw his fire, find his positions, smother them with tank and artillery fire, find the gaps, or make them, and press on. Behind, their comrades in the other regiments followed, then the tank divisions, echelon after echelon, queueing up to go through.

D + 3: NATO SUPREME HQ

The battle took an unexpected turn. SACEUR's staff could find out little of what was going on in the I British Corps sector, and what they heard was bad.

The fatal vacillations of the British had had three consequences. They were short of men. Tank squadrons could only man six or seven tanks, batteries of artillery only three or four guns out of six, for lack of the reservists who had never been called up or sent in time. Many units, forbidden to move to their action stations, or even the emergency harbours, were caught in their barracks or jammed among streams of refugees. Worst of all was the lack of ammunition. The troops were garrisoned in towns, but for reasons of safety the ammunition depots were in remote areas out in the country. It was a day's journey for many units to collect the first line war supply and this process, involving complicated road movements, should have been completed early in the mobilization plan, while other small forward depots were set up near the pre-planned defensive positions. Half the combat units were impotent. Some had been trapped in their barracks and had surrendered. Some moved out but were without ammunition. Only the 2nd Division was making a fight of it on an improvised position along the Weser near Verden and Nienburg.

The *Bundeswehr* was holding firm in its sector, but was hard pressed. It could not extend its front to cover the gap left by the British. The accident of history had placed the strongest foreign contingent, the Americans, well to the south of the most dangerous Soviet thrust line. SACEUR accordingly risked thinning the American front and sent three US armoured brigades to the north, to fill the gaps left by the British. Parts of the American sector were held only by the reconnaissance troops, who had only light armour

147

and armed helicopters backed with a few tanks. Had all gone according to peacetime planning their line of observation had the limited mission of providing warning of frontier crossings and identifying the main thrust lines, but the planned Main Line of Resistance was as yet unmanned. The new and sacrificial mission of the outposts was to fight for time, and the 7th United States Cavalry, the lineal descendent of the regiment which had fought at the Little Big Horn, gritted its teeth and prepared to match its mobility and firepower against armoured mass.

D+3: THE FRONTIER BATTLE

When the Russian motor infantry commander spoke to his soldiers he was doing no more than explaining in terms they understood the doctrine of a revised *blitzkrieg*, now the core of Soviet armoured tactics, well suited to and, indeed, devised by the new generation of well-educated junior officers and warrant officers which had grown up since 1973.

To put it bluntly, the NATO defensive plans and deployment had long been an open book to the Russians. Rigid and linear, it consisted in essence of islands of resistance like a string of beads across the map, backed by a formidable air force and forced to rely on nuclear counterattack at an early stage. The objectives of the Soviet offensive were to overrun the airfields and the nuclear weapon systems, beginning with the forward artillery, in an *attaque brusquée*. The task of the leading Soviet armoured units was to look for the gaps between the defended localities, then curl round them and neutralize their anti-tank fire while the tank divisions, moving in behind in serried echelons, poured on past them, with objectives 30 and 40 miles deep.

Like all the well-trained shock troops of the Soviet army, the 1/41 Tank Regiment was prepared for American land/air tactics and expected a stiff fight in the opening rounds of the combat, but they believed that with their own massive AAA defences and the support of the Soviet air force they must succeed. Their newest tanks with their composite armour were, if not proof against the heavier missiles, very tough and hard to stop. Success was all a matter of determination and pace.

What confounded them was not the strength of the outposts but the apparent lack of any resistance at all. Conditioned to expect a certain pattern, they were puzzled to know what to do next. Were they to press on ever more deeply until they found the defensive pattern it was their mission to detect? The division and army commanders listening to the first flow of signals before the radio jammers on both sides clamped down wondered, at first almost incredulously, whether deception had been complete and that the Americans had not had the time to deploy at all.

The battle on the morning of D+3 went no better, but no worse than the seasoned commander of 1/41 TR had expected. The surface-air battle had been a stiff one, appallingly noisy, but not traumatically so. The American A-10-As, the tank-busters, came tearing over the unit so low that men ducked in automatic reaction, as if to avoid being decapitated, to be met by the short burps of fire from the ZSUs and coveys of *Strellas*. Soon pillars of greasy black smoke marked the funeral pyres of the armoured infantry carriers, but from time to time a huge explosion and a sheet of flame also showed a hit on an aircraft, somersaulting into the ground and shedding wings and engines in all directions. The worst moments were when the companies closed in to pass the gaps in the frontier wire and minefields made by the engineers. The battalion commander climbed one of the watch-towers behind the frontier fence to observe his units crossing, disregarding the protests of the East German non-com in charge. (How like a policeman, he thought, to tell him that he

'The Bundeswehr's *heroic resistance' inflamed the British to resist as fiercely*

required a special pass before he could be allowed up – in the middle of a war!) and from there he watched the first phase of contact. There was no sign of his opponent, only a sprinkling of artillery shells; the bursts inaudible in the general din of aircraft and AAA fire, and therefore not alarming.

There was danger apparent enough to the discerning eye, however. Without any good reason a ZSU suddenly blew up. A distant aircraft wheeled in a vertical bank and disappeared, having left a radar-seeking missile to back-track the pulses down to the gun. Some of the artillery fire was equally and disconcertingly unerring. Single shells hit or near-missed tanks without even an adjusting round: somewhere in the edge of the woods in front was an observer with a laser indicator. In fact the quicker his infantry was into those woods the better. The battle group was almost through the gaps in the frontier wire. The battalion commander ran down the ladder

with as much haste as was decent in an officer, as a long shot from a distant enemy tank knocked splinters from the cabin he had just left.

It took some time to clear the woods, which were big enough to swallow all the infantry, who peered about in the trees to see where the odd burst of fire was coming from. The battalion commander called for artillery fire support but it only hit the air, or rather trees. By the time he had cleared that bound, all that anyone had seen was an enemy carrier or two racing off through the young corn in the fields beyond, to disappear behind one of the neatly barbered copses which decorated the orderly German landscape.

A signal from Regiment at HQ, penetrating the increasing mush of jamming told him to get a move on and, fatally, he ordered his riflemen back into their BRDM carriers. They cheerfully mounted, and encouraged by their battalion commander riding with them, sitting on top of his command vehicle and waving his green flag, the whole group set off fully deployed and at a fair pace. The air attacks had slackened (in fact, the forward units had passed the air interdiction line, and the American air force was concentrating on the echelons of following Soviet tanks.) War was not too bad, the soldiers felt, their confidence restored after firing their own weapons at the enemy, at last, and relieved to find themselves alive. It was then that they ran into trouble.

Or rather, trouble ran into them. The supporting artillery had been closed up behind the battle-group, when, one after another, four missiles came floating over from the right rear, black dots with ruby coloured flaming tails, and four 122mm SP guns were struck. The reserve tank platoon was ordered to switch round and drench the area with fire. 'With respect', said the lieutenant of the AAA, 'That will do no good. It was a chopper. I saw it. It just showed above the trees and let fly, it's away by now. Here's another'. This time the green metal dragonfly emerged skimming the ground at left front, flying fast and sideways, keeping its chin-shaped turret towards its target, gun twinkling. Sparks flew from the leading carriers as the shells struck and their crews came tumbling out. A ZSU fired a burst, but missed as its target disappeared. Then another came up right front, to fire and dodge again. Another carrier stopped; another ZSU fired and missed. AH-64-As, with 30mm gun, noted the anti-aircraft lieutenant. He began to worry about his ammunition supply.

He would have worried more had he known that his vehicle following with the reserve supply a kilometre behind was already burning and his reserves exploding in an unwelcome firework display. The helicopters, some with Gatling guns, some with 30mm, some with ATGW, attacked in depth from ambushes. Others, at a safe distance from the *Strellas* and ZSUs, looked for targets and signalled the Cobras sitting,

with rotors turning ready to take off, in forest clearings, in the courtyards of farms, behind ridges. They rose, hovered briefly, shot and disappeared westwards at 100 knots, hugging the contours of the rolling terrain.

As the day wore on the frustrating battle continued. There was an occasional check when the tank-gunners, almost thankfully, saw something solid and still to shoot at, and the air was torn by tungsten carbide bolts speeding in both directions and impacting in a white hot shower of metal as they struck armour. The field artillery observing officers called for fire to suppress the infantry who greeted the armoured spearheads from each successive crest line with volleys of ATGWs, but the enemy never stood and fought for long, while the toll he took mounted hour by hour.

Every thrust line was marked by a trail of damaged and burning tanks. Still the orders were to drive on: the regimental commanders came up in person to urge on the battalion commanders, conscious of the divisional commanders behind them and the army commander's relentless drive behind all of them.

'There's nothing stopping me getting on, comrade colonel', said the battalion commander. 'Every position I've attacked has proved empty by the time I've reached the objective: the bastards have slipped away. The only thing is, by nightfall I won't have anyone to advance with. I'm down to four tanks and I've formed one company out of what's left of three. And I must have a complete refill of AAA ammunition. We've shot away every round, with little enough to show for it.'

The accidents of war had thrown the rival forces together in what was a brutal trial of competing theories. For a decade the airmen had been waging a war of words with the tank-men; arguing the case of expensive, high-speed combat helicopters built as weapon systems and relying on missiles and mobility, while the tank-men defended the gun, armour, and hordes of cheap tanks. From neither side was the view encouraging. 'Sure', said the colonel of the 7th Cavalry to a newsman who had found his way to his command post. 'We're attritting them all right, and my own losses so far have been moderate. But they've got enough troops to start fresh, all over again; while my boys are getting awful tired. All I can do is to trade territory for time, and we haven't much left of either'.

Numbers gave the attacker an incontestable advantage against a defence rely-ing on darkness and a pause in the operations to assess the situation, to replenish ammunition, to reorganize and to position the reinforcement units as they arrived. No such reprieve was granted. The second echelon of 15 tank divisions allotted to complete the break-in on the American sector had started from a line of departure carefully calculated to bring them without a pause to the line of contact at about nightfall. They never ceased to move, and so never gave the air forces or the nuclear weapons systems a worthwhile, compact target. The dark was no longer an obstacle:

'We're attritting them all right, but they've got enough troops to start fresh, all over again'

rather it was an aid to tanks fitted with night-vision and night sights. When the early summer dawn broke there was no longer a front: only hundreds of square miles of dogfights deep in German territory.

It was fortunate that SACEUR was both a student of military history and a man of massive calm, for he needed both these qualities when he listened to his staff briefing on the morning of D+4. The chief difficulty was to piece together what was happening. Communications had been cut, radio had been jammed, satellites had mysteriously ceased to transmit, headquarters had simply disappeared. The news came in, somehow, from liaison officers who had set out in helicopters, from telephone calls on the post office lines, by microwave and secret circuits set up for just such an emergency (a whole jam-proof alternative system had been designed by the NATO planners, but was only part built, owing to lack of money and endless national delays.) It was bad, but no worse than he had expected.

In the far south the 1st German Mountain Division had not been under heavy attack and was holding its own comfortably. From east of Munich north to Nuremberg and round to Coburg the German 4th, 10th and 12th Divisions had had a day's desperate fighting. Their losses had been heavy, but they had slipped the Soviet night offensive, leaving the invading tank divisions to flounder in a maze of minefields. Their line was intact, though battered.

In the south-centre sector Fulda had gone after a night of confused fighting, with Americans firing on Americans, Russians on Russians, both stumbling into new minefields as they were laid by mechanical minelayers, engineers blowing up bridges before friendly forces had crossed them. Both sides were wincing under the desperate and random blows descending from the airforces of both sides. A reserve line had been established, and the Fulda gap was still safely blocked astride . . . 'but only one tank deep, and then, *phhhuttt*', as the corps commander said to himself.

Up in the north the 3rd and 6th German Divisions were holding, but from the north-centre the news was dire indeed.

There was a complete breakthrough along the natural line of invasion: Brunswick-Hanover-Minden. No front existed, but islands of resistance holding out behind the columns of Soviet tanks which, driving flocks of motor-borne refugees before them, or driving them off the roads with bursts of machine-gun fire, had reached Rheine, where the Dutch were fighting an encounter battle with their advance guards.

The brigades despatched from the German 11th Division and from the 3rd and 8th US Divisions were hanging on the flanks of the tank army pouring through – with what success was not yet clear. Fragmented British forces were joining them, but the only firm news of the British came from the 2nd Division, fighting in perimeter defence. The only crumb of consolation was that more Soviet airborne troops had been intercepted and where they had not been shot down had landed in small scattered groups. The French, who had at last decided to act, were usefully employed in rounding them up.

Had it been World War 2, now was the moment for the classic counterattack, for forming reserves for a counteroffensive, accompanied by orders of the day demanding sacrifices and heroism: 'with our backs to the wall'. But there was no wall behind the NATO back. There were no mighty reserve armies: there was not even a reserve stock of munitions. It would not be long before the last missiles were shot away. There was nothing left to stabilize a line. The air forces reported the almost endless columns of enemy armour stretching back for a hundred miles and more, broken by their attacks from time to time like a procession of ants when a foot is scuffed across them, but ever reforming and coming on. As SACEUR was briefed fresh items came in.

The Soviet ambassador at the United

Nations had formally stated that it had never been the intention of his government to clash with the NATO forces. The present disaster had been precipitated by reckless provocation and aggression but his government would agree to a cease fire and a stand fast in the present positions, provided that it was implemented immediately and that the NATO military leaders who had acted so wantonly against Soviet troops merely carrying out a necessary police task were punished. Otherwise the Soviet field commanders would be ordered to destroy all NATO units east of the Rhine.

The President of the United States wanted the latest situation. That was easily given, and it was dire. In words of the command of 4th Allied Tactical Air Force: 'If the ground forces can stabilize the line and my reinforcements of aircraft pilots and missiles can be flown in, I can go for two days at this rate of attrition, maybe three, and take the pressure off the ground. But we can't stabilize. By tonight it will all be over and I'll have lost my forward airfields. It's that, or nuclear release, and I mean now: not after a day spent in talking.'

A staff officer flung the door open.

'Sir', he said, 'I have important information: a 2 ATAF pilot has seen four nuclear bursts in the British sector'.

'By God, they've used them first! But why now, when they've almost won the war?'

'Sir, they're not Soviet weapons. We have part of an intercept from the British 2nd Division command net on the warning frequency. They're ours. Three of one kiloton and one of ten.'

The Soviet leaders received the news that the nuclear weapon had been unleashed in the Nienburg sector unilaterally by the British with calm, even with satisfaction. The demand by the army and the air force, already terribly mauled in the fighting, to retaliate in kind, preferably on the sectors being defended with such fanaticism by the German divisions, was dismissed without argument. Things were going their way. The physical battle was three parts won, and if they denied themselves the general use of nuclear weapons they would win the moral battle as well. After all, the military had always expressed that they could break the NATO defences if both sides held back from the use of nuclear weapons, even if the NATO units were given time to mobilize and occupy their chosen positions in an orderly manner; so why did they want to use them now? In any case they wanted Germany intact, inside the Socialist camp, not as a radioactive desert.

This sensible decision was reversed only too soon. The President of the United States, forced to choose between what he read as a total surrender and a defeat for American arms, authorized the use of nuclear weapons strictly according to the preplanned programme: on military targets in the combat zone and extending only as far back as the tactical airfields in East Germany and Poland.

It had at least the effect of bringing operations briefly to a staggering halt. The Soviet response was one of mistaken subtlety. They decided to take out as precisely as possible and without collateral damage the United States Air Force bases in East Anglia in England. This had a triple aim. It would force the British Cabinet to throw its whole weight on the side of capitulation, it removed the only American air bases inaccessible (for the moment) to the Soviet ground troops, and it was a demonstration to the President of Soviet resolution. The Soviet leaders would refrain from a strategic exchange however severely they were provoked, but they would not hesitate to punish those guilty of aggression. Were the NATO commanders in the field the servants of their governments, or not? It was too late. The President, forced to choose between the complete destruction of the NATO defences and nuclear war, gave the fatal order.

SHELFORD BIDWELL

13. THE AIR WAR

In the early months of 1983 the usual reluctance to discuss anything that might be construed as 'shop' was forgotten in the messes of the 2nd and 4th Allied Tactical Air Forces, and the frighteningly select group of skilled and professionally dedicated officers and airmen found themselves talking of nothing else. The main questions around which the arguments revolved were variously: 'What ought NATO to do?' and 'What will NATO do?' - and the answers were not the same. Unlike the feeling everyone had expected in a future war - a united bond of courage and determination to see it through - nobody knew either what was to be done or what should be done. Determination had evaporated and had been replaced by a chill feeling of fear that Western Europe just might fall without a shot.

By first light on D-Day that fact that Warsaw Pact forces had crossed into West Germany was the only certain information anyone possessed, apart from confusion and a general belief that fighting was bound to break out. It was obvious that there was plenty of ground fighting, though air activity was virtually nil; and the air bases were a scene of silent engines and noisy voices.

A thousand things were wrong, but could not be put right. Virtually every aircraft was at a known base. Even the Harriers were neatly arrayed at the sites of 3 and 4 Sqns at Gütersloh, when they - of all aircraft - could have been safely hidden in a million hectares of forest. At least half the other aircraft, inevitably vulnerable, were not even in shelters.

Then came the stunning order from London that the British forces in Germany were to be confined to barracks. This was interpreted at 2ATAF HQ as meaning that aircraft, especially combat aircraft, should be kept on the ground. Several requests from operational squadrons for permission to maintain an aerial presence, and in particular to update the reconnaissance cover and 'Elint' operations along the border, were met by a flat negative.

AT LAST: A POSITIVE ORDER

By 7.30 a.m., when most of the arguers had breakfasted, a large group of Jaguar pilots at Brüggen knocked on the door of the station commander and formally requested that surely all aircrew should be at cockpit readiness, fully tanked-up and armed for whatever kind of sortie might appear best. After brief telephone calls, one of which confirmed that the Americans of 4ATAF were already fuelled and armed for action and would man their aircraft as soon as last-minute briefings had been completed, the HQ of RAF Germany did manage to issue a positive order. The day's flying programme was cancelled, but all serviceable aircraft should be ready for immediate takeoff of a combat mission, details to be left to squadron commanders. This single order did much to restore morale and inject a sense of purpose into a force whose previously unsurpassed skill and *esprit de corps* had been all but demolished by the prevailing mood of ambivalence and uncertainty.

Still nothing stirred near the RAF bases, but it was obvious that heavy fighting was going on in the distance. In fact the *Luftwaffe* had been heavily engaged since first light, and from soon after 4 am had not only been trying to get every available com-

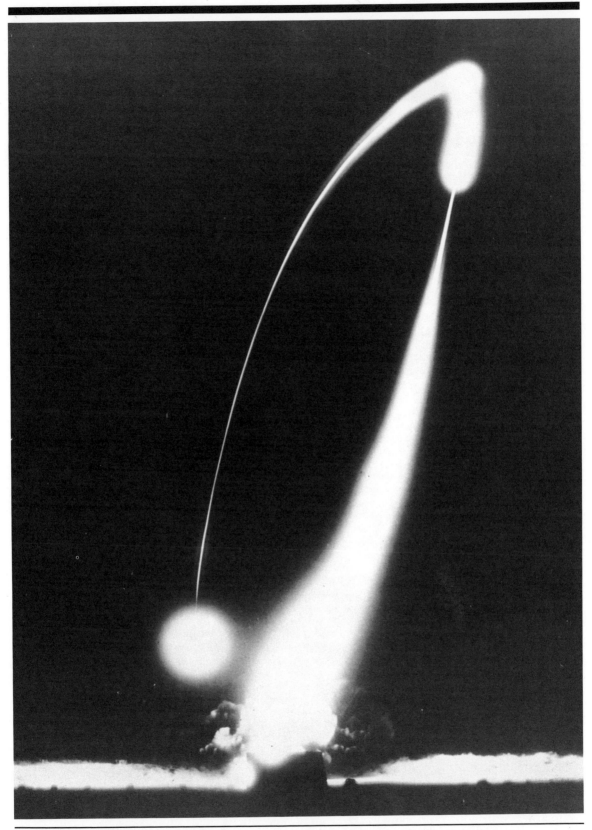

West Germany's SAMs hit back – 'the shattering noise of a Hawk departing'

bat aircraft airborne but had suffered several damaging attacks on its bases by Warsaw Pact fighter-bombers.

More than 200 aircraft, believed to be mainly Russian but including swing-wing Su-20s of the Polish PWL, had been plotted at 6.10 am crossing north-west in a loose gaggle, heading for Schleswig-Holstein at treetop height. By this time few serviceable aircraft were left at the northern complex of bases – such as Husum and Leck for the *Luftwaffe* and Eggbek and Schleswig for the *Marineflieger* – and the last uncommitted machines quickly took off to fly over the approach route from the south-east. Within minutes the radars of these scattered aircraft, a mix of old F-104Gs and F-4 Phantoms, had locked-on to the approaching low-level force. It was at about this time that the first traces became visible on NADGE displays, but there was no helpful AWACS in north Germany at the time – only a single USAF E-3A far to the south over Bavaria.

Several attacking aircraft had been brought down by fire from the ground in the small hours, but this major raid was the first full-scale air confrontation. It was obvious that the attacking force was using strong ECM, and observers west of Lübeck had actually seen lead aircraft strewing chaff, which remained as a glinting band when lit by searchlights, for all the world like the Milky Way. There had been no time for proper consultation between *Luftwaffe* SAM and fighter units, but each knew what the other might best do. Hawk batteries south-west of Kiel were locked-on and ready, and their interception process worked without a hitch. Whether or not any missiles had made mistakes and locked-on to the stationary chaff was conjectural, but all should have 'looked' at the oncoming aircraft. Frequently changes and inter-unit locks automatically assigned each missile to different targets, and at ranges of around 15 miles one FCO (Fire Control Operator) after another heard the shattering noise of a Hawk departing.

This particular attack appeared to have been over-confident: it would have been better to have gone round via the Baltic. The 28 Hawks fired all seemed to find their targets. Minutes later the surviving attackers ran into a succession of AIM-9L Advanced Sidewinder AAMs fired head-on with encouraging results, and as they neared their objectives were attacked from the flanks and rear by gunfire and more Sidewinders. By this time the attacking force had split up into five or six sections, but some appeared to comprize single aircraft uncertain of their position.

All the lead aircraft were Su-19s, with self-contained inertial navigation and a singlemindedness that made them deadly. Still in pre-dawn darkness, they reached their targets and put down heavy loads of GP and cluster-bombs, but the results were far from devastating. Hardest hit was Schleswig, where one clutch of 'iron' bombs went right into the station buildings, causing over 100 casualties and temporarily severing external communications. Even here the field remained usable, while at other bases damage was surprisingly light. Several further aircraft were shot down close to their targets by Twin-Gun 20 mm flak, which despite being optically sighted managed to fire remarkably accurately on attackers illuminated by the occasional searchlight and their own bomb-flashes.

Further heavy raids were mounted at about the same time, mainly on army targets in the areas of Celle and Soltau, while the whole front increasingly flashed with the heavy explosions of what were obviously tactical rockets. Telephone lines were very active between *Luftwaffe* and *Marineflieger* units and Bonn, and with the HQ of NATO and Allied air forces. *Luftwaffe* units further west and south quickly scrambled to fly attack missions against Warsaw Pact bases, and some 20 RF-4E reconnaissance Phantoms took off from Bremgarten in the 4ATAF area to the south to provide detailed coverage of the ground situation.

There was clearly a massive armoured thrust both north and south of Hamburg, but no report yet of activity further to the south. The objective was obvious, and the possibility of an airborne landing had occurred to the German staff even before the Antonov transports had taken off from their East German runways. Preparations to counter it included scrambling the vital Tornadoes of *JaboG* 31 at Noervenich, the only wing fully equipped with this extremely valuable multi-role aircraft, and embarking more than 600 airborne troops of the *Heeresflieger* in CH-53 and UH-1D helicopters for immediate despatch to likely landing-zones. It so happened that the commander of TR 25 (Transport Regiment), equipped with CH-53Ds, had thought aloud a few days earlier and decided that a Warsaw Pact airborne assault on the nuclear establishment was highly likely. A quick conference had pinpointed probable para-dropping and air-landing areas, and a plan had been drawn up to counter it. Telephoned orders, using scramblers, had informed all units of 'Plan Kontra-Air', and ensured that nobody would mistake it for a Pact invasion force.

The helicopters took off in small groups from six *Heeresflieger* bases. They carried special ECM and IFF to make for a safe passage, and avoided any base occupied by RAF or other non-German anti-aircraft forces. For some it was a long flight, and it was 1.30 am before most had reached their destinations, which were selected stretches of open country in the immediate neighbourhood of the isolated establishment. One of the first helicopters had put down on the lawn in front of the establishment's main offices, furiously shouting its identity in German through a loud-hailer. No shots had been fired, and with the situation explained the establishment and its newly-arrived guards waited. They did not have long to sit and think: at 1.36 am word came by field telephone that a large force of AN-12 ('Cub') transports was flying in across the Heligoland Bight. NADGE radars had been watching for some time, and had notified the substantial forces of *Luftwaffe* and *Marineflieger* aircraft already airborne.

First to pounce were F-4s of *JG* 71 at Wittmundhafen, right in the path of the great formation. Surprisingly there did not seem to be any fighter escort, and within seconds all hell had broken loose as Sidewinders by the score exploded among the big transports. About half the AAM bursts took off a wing, resulting in a crash within seconds from a height of barely 150 feet. With their missiles gone, the Phantoms raked the transports with fire from their M61 guns, trying to aim accurately at the flight decks but finding it far from simple. Almost at once it was clear that the inboard wing was the best target, and before the DZ came up more than half the force had ceased to exist. Of the 20-odd transports still flying, fully half flew over the target fields without anyone getting out. Fresh fighters kept arriving and picking off stragglers, and the few hundred paratroops who did reach the ground were mopped up almost to a man by the *Heeresflieger* helicopters, which had just enough fuel left to reposition the defenders alongside each stick of the enemy.

The Soviet airborne assault had been a key feature of the Soviet plan, and it was a complete disaster. This was due largely to the countermove having been judged correctly in advance by the West German air forces.

JaboG 31's Tornadoes had not had any work to do, and rather than land with bombs on the entire force was assigned to hit the lead elements of the oncoming ground forces. Accurate information was coming in from the reconnaissance centres, which were processing the digital signals from the RF-4Es in real time. A continuous stream of optical, infra-red and SLAR pictures was spewing forth from the automatic, computer-controlled machines, which not only produced pin-sharp pictures but drew attention to everything that had changed in each scene since it had been last flown over, usually a matter of days earlier.

JaboG 31's Tornadoes were naturally tied into the system, and the signals processed by the reconnaissance centres were within a few hundredths of a second creating clear pictures on the middle screens of the British-built displays in the rear cockpits. Within minutes the squadron commander of *II/JaboG* 31 had assigned targets to each of the 11 aircraft flying with him, and the whole system went into action 'for real' for the first time.

Inertial navigation systems were given the digital coordinates of each target and tied-in with the multi-mode radar in the terrain-following mode. Defensive electronics, already operative, were tuned to that morning's hostile emissions and programmed for maximum cover in the planned attack. Chaff, flare and jammer payloads were quickly checked in their dispensers, and as the target area was reached the ECM pods were turned on and the tail warning linked with the main defensive system to eject payloads automatically.

Most of this group of 11 aircraft had external ordnance loads of around 10 tonnes, far more than the limit with any other tactical aircraft and much too much for snappy manoeuvrability. They knew they had to be right on their first run in, and as the last kilometres ticked away on the HUD (head-up display) sights all eyes were strained to see good targets. The weakness of the attack was that a good target might be spotted by two aircraft at once, who could duplicate and dilute effort and get in each other's way. Thinking they would have to deal with air-landed forces, most crews had about half their load in the form of *Streuwaffen* (scatter weapons), and these would be useful even against an armoured

spearhead. Nobody had 'smart' (precision-guided) weapons, but there were plenty of retarded GP bombs, air-to-ground rockets (most with heads able to pierce airborne armour, such as the ASU-85) and twin 27 mm Mauser cannon.

Flak came at them as they approached, and it was unpleasantly accurate. Several aircraft were shot down on the final run-in, and many wished for the missiles that homed on the source of gunfire, extensively tested but still in the laboratory. Mauser cannon were going full blast as the Tornadoes swept in with wings at maximum sweep in two ragged line-abreast groups at a height not greater than 100 feet.

There was no opportunity to aim anything, though radar-homing missiles would have been useful. Certainly the textbook mission in which an attacker calmly gets a target in his electro-optical display, or whatever else is used, and then fires a homing 'fire and forget' missile, did not apply in attacking a Warsaw Pact field army. There were too many SAMs and ZSU-23-4 vehicles, all seemingly very much on the ball. At least it could be said that eight aircraft let go their whole load pretty much on top of enemy troops, and as the attack direction had been directly along a main road just east of Hildesheim it had certainly been effective. The Pact vehicles were following the road and also the fields on each side, so that there could not be any particular holdup or bottleneck.

As the Tornadoes thundered ahead of the invading force they were warned of SAMs coming from the rear. The formation opened out laterally, went even lower and, throttling back, ejected flares and jammers tuned in the last split-second to enemy radars. Crossing Hildesheim, one aircraft simply disappeared in a great explosion. The rest were luckier: their decoys and jammers had put the SAMs, assumed to be SA-6 ('Gainful'), off the scent.

But the survivors were under no illusions. They had lost four out of 11, and it could easily have been 11, for only a modest return. They had probably not held up anyone, except possibly a handful of vehicles of no consequence to hard-minded Russian generals. It was extraordinary that the attackers had not seen or detected enemy fighters, and next time – if there was one – they would have to plan properly and precede the main attack with aircraft carrying missiles homing on the deadly SAMs and flak. Better still, leave forward troops to tactical missiles, and make air strikes against the enemy rear.

Two West German Tornadoes, damaged and short of fuel, put down at RAF Gütersloh. They were made welcome, and given what help could be provided – an entirely on-the-spot decision by the station commander, who did not even bother to seek advice – but both the *JaboG* 31 crews expressed sarcastic regret that the British government had been unable to make up its mind whose side it was on. Several RAF hosts expressed themselves, defensively, as disgusted with the situation; but Harrier pilots who had watched the arrival of the battle-scarred Germans began to ask over their telebrief wires for permission to reposition in hidden locations, partly as an act of prudent self-preservation and partly to give an impression that the British were at least doing something. At this moment, 2ATAF was told via the local British army commander of the outbreak of fighting between British and Soviet troops. Within one minute 2ATAF had authorized combat units to go into action against the Russians, and as a start the two Tornado crews, still shaking with reaction and stained with sweat, gave the nearest Air Operations Centre a clear idea of where the nearest enemy forces were and how their own attack had gone.

The CO of No 3 Sqn immediately ordered his Harriers to disperse into prearranged positions in surrounding woods. He himself went over to Army Corps at Detmold and found frantic activity there. After hours of frustration, every available Lynx and Gazelle, and even a few old Scouts, were being readied for missions against Soviet armour, mostly with the American-designed but part-British-made TOW missile. A previous exercise had shown that Harriers and anti-tank helicopters could in some cases work together. Air defence of the most forward elements of the invading armies appeared to be left entirely to intense Triple-A flak and SAMs, the Russian fighters being strongly in evidence ahead of the FEBA along with tactical Frontal Aviation attack aircraft, and possibly in the rear areas too. Harriers had often been proved the most elusive of all battlefield serial targets, except for small RPVs. Their small size, smokeless engines and odd shape made it hard to see them, or decide which way they were going.

The CO of 3 Sqn got on the telephone to his units, and asked them to be airborne within one minute and listen out on the R/T. While the helicopters throbbed away to the east, the first Harrier started its engine, lifted off and within seconds was tearing across country at low level.

In a little more than four minutes the nimble Harrier was a few miles south of Hildesheim, hugging the ground and flashing down wooded slopes towards the *autobahn*. This area was clearly not in dispute, but battle was joined further east. A few quick turns and the Harrier was speeding north over Bockenem and through a gap in the hills. The whole area beyond was covered by an army on the march, and as he flew over the scene the Harrier pilot reported in detail exactly where the Russians were. For good measure he let them have his six BL 755 cluster bombs, each of which spread four tailfins, unscrewed a nose fan and then opened to reveal 147 deadly bomblets, which were scattered by the sudden inflation of central gasbags by a cartridge. Each bomblet burst on impact, scattering its square-section, notched-wire binding into about 2,000 shrapnel-like frag-

'Harriers had often been proved the most elusive of all battlefield aerial targets'

ments. A total of 1,764,000 potential killers from one Harrier seemed at least to go some way to redressing the prevailing balance of power.

The Harrier went straight back to Gütersloh, only to find the field a shambles. MiG-27s ('Flogger' D) had simply ignored casualties in doing so much damage as possible. At least 18 had been shot down out of about 50, almost all by the Rapier missiles of the RAF Regiment; but now the field was defenceless because no reload missiles were immediately available. The squadron leader had radioed ahead for fuel and laser-guided bombs so that he could join in the action with the rest of his men, and with No 4 Sqn also.

No fewer than 30 Harriers, all but two of the serviceable aircraft in RAF Germany, were at that moment engaged in the most effective attack yet on the oncoming armies. Lynxes and Gazelles were trying to hide in the wooded slopes to get in pot-shots with their batteries of TOW missiles.

The Lynxes had also been able to offload small combat teams who not only went into business on their own account with TOW and Vigilant missiles, backed up by a handful of Milans, but also sighted on choice enemy targets and marked them with Ferranti lasers. This was vital. Every few seconds Harriers would scream over the ridge in pairs, never in quite the same place, and within seconds release 'smart' bombs which plummeted unerringly on to the marked targets. As soon as one group had been dealt with, fresh targets were waiting. In five minutes the ground markers and Harriers took out 14 battle tanks, ten other armoured vehicles and – of great significance – every visible ZSU or SA anti-aircraft missile, a total of almost 40. Three Harriers had been hit and the hills had been plastered in return with enemy artillery and rocket fire, though mostly in the wrong places.

Before the last Harriers had attacked, the sky had become full of Soviet fighters of all types, a probable change of plan and an admission that the army's own defences could not cope. One Mig-23 lined up on a Lynx hovering just above the ground, only to run straight into one of the extremely effective Super Blowpipe missiles launched by one of the Lynx team waiting for just such an attack. (Smaller helicopters were more limited, and with six TOWs could not carry a laser designation team, a SAM operator and plenty of missiles). This one operator alone destroyed nine Russian aircraft in about five minutes with his nine rounds, though in the same space of time several of the British Army helicopters were destroyed and casualties suffered from the fighter gunfire and air-to-ground rockets.

Super Blowpipe had long ago been recognized as a vital weapon, able to engage aircraft approaching head-on (unlike the US Army Redeye, which did not even have an IFF facility). But the scale of issue was pathetic, and the nine rounds fired by the member of the Lynx team were not to be replaced. The Americans, Germans and their other NATO allies had thousands of Redeyes but only a handful of Stingers, the replacement that had been awaited for a full ten years and which even now was rated inferior to the Super Blowpipe.

This was the pattern of the air war on D-Day, and it had long been foreseen by those in the know. NATO's excellent aircraft were indeed able to inflict damage out of all proportion to their numbers – but the odds against them in a deliberate battle of attrition were impossible. Unlike the RAF in the Battle of Britain 43 years before, the West was not enjoying a constant stream of replacement aircraft – there were none, let alone reserves of thoroughly trained aircrew with which to replace the human losses. Above all there were not enough replenishment missiles ready to hand, and this was a missile war. NATO's missile consumption on the first day – as excessive as it was essential – threatened total disaster in the first 48 hours.

NATO's air forces were only kept in being as combat units by a frantically-improvised airlift of every available missile from the UK. As the transports shuttled their vital loads into Germany at zero feet they were forced to put down at airfields far in the rear, whence *ad hoc* lorry convoys rushed the missiles forward.

Thanks to repeated defence cuts over the last 15 years aimed at 'trimming the tail without blunting the teeth' the British rear areas inevitably saw the worst snarl-ups and delays in traffic and supply. It was a miracle that deliveries of the wrong missiles for the wrong aircraft were kept as low as they were. But by the morning of the second day just enough replacements had got through to enable the hard-pressed NATO air forces to renew the one-sided struggle over the land battlefield.

SECOND DAY

By 9 am the high-flying E-3A AWACS was already flying a new orbit on a line roughly between the Ruhr and Bremen. Gradually it took stock of the whole air situation, its wonderful secure, clear data-links bringing order and lifting morale – which in any case had recovered wonderfully with the beginning of action. The big Boeing platform had requested cover by two American F-14A Tomcats from the carrier *John F. Kennedy* in the Mediterranean, and very soon two fine contrails announced their presence. The stratosphere was a remote and special area where attack aircraft never went; but the E-3A was doing a vital job, and the Russians surely knew it. Too clever to be confused or jammed, the E-3A could nevertheless be shot down – with a bit of luck.

In the first 30 minutes after taking up its new station the AWACS was subjected to at least ten engagements by SAM batteries, using the big ramjet-propelled SA-4 ('Ganef') and SA-6 ('Gainful'). The latter were all at extreme range and were quite ineffective, but the big 'Ganefs', of the long-range type specifically designed to kill the AWACS, were well within effective limits. With each shot the AWACS had to divert its attention slightly and save its own skin by confusing the missile.

At first the SAM's own 'Pat Hand' radar steered the missile accurately, but the nearer the missile got to the E-3A the more completely it responded to the latter's own guidance commands. It eventually completed a wide-ranged 180° turn and headed back to earth. Unfortunately, the USAF crew had no means of detonating the warhead before impact with the ground. The Frontal Aviation MiG-23S interceptors never even succeeded in getting past the two Tomcats, which picked them off at extreme range with AIM-54B Phoenix missiles. The job of defending the AWACS was taken over by a Belgian F-16A squadron from Florennes which managed perfectly well with the recently-adopted British

Skyflash, a medium-range missile much cheaper than Phoenix and compatible with the F-16, turning it into a valuable interceptor able to kill from a distance. No aircraft with short-range Sidewinders could do the job.

This left the two Tomcats still on station with four of their original 12 Phoenix missiles still unfired. While a replacement pair was called up from the Mediterranean, the Tomcats were advised of 'customers at flight level 610' – 61,000 feet. This was the visiting card of the MiG-25 ('Foxbat'), which indeed could fly many kilometres higher still. The Foxbats were reported as 250 miles distant and rising, closing speed 1,500 mph.

Working together, the Tomcat pilots were told there were only two targets. Boldly, they decided to use only two Phoenix: there might be more Foxbats before their relief aircraft took over. For six minutes both Tomcats obediently wheeled round and headed east, their radar intercept

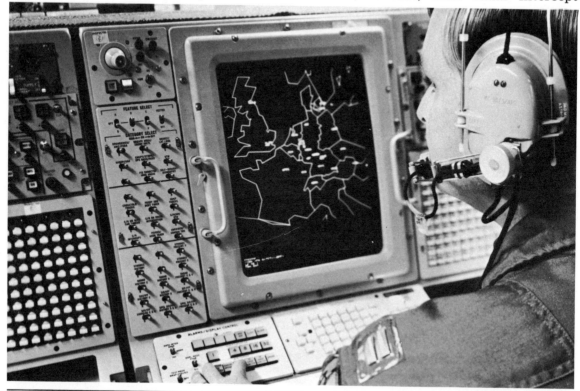

AWACS – 'its wonderful secure, clear data-links bringing order and lifting morale'

officers searching at extreme range on their AWG-9 radar displays – still the best in the business, they thought. At the same moment the two targets slid in from the side of both displays, far enough apart for each to be visible. Each might, of course, prove to be more than one aircraft, but the fine-discrimination IR seeker suggested that this was not the case. Automatically one Phoenix on each fighter was prepared for launch, locked-on at 135 miles and fired at a little over 100 miles.

A passing speed of over 4,000 mph was quite a challenge for the Phoenix, which even in 1983 had never been tested against so fast a target. Soon one trace disappeared from the radars, but the other kept coming. One F-14, ready for this, was about to launch its last missile when the Foxbat arched slowly forward into a dive. Nobody saw it, but either through pilot incapacitation or battle damage from the AAM warhead it went steeply 'downhill' and suddenly broke up in the air. Everything was clearly visible on the displays in the Tomcats and in the AWACS.

Lower down every Allied aircraft had joined battle by about 9 am, including the air forces of Belgium, Holland and Denmark. Long-range attacks were launched from RAF Upper Heyford, England, by the USAF 20th Tac Fighter Wing with F111E swing-wing bombers, and by the more powerful F111Fs of the 48th Wing at RAF Lakenheath.

Committing these valuable aircraft in daylight was the subject of some argument. Their great asset was that, unlike every other Allied aircraft except the Tornado, the F-111 could hit any target at night or in the worst weather, making its attack from treetop height in the terrain-following mode. In daylight, provided the location of a target was known, almost anything could have a go. The RAF's excellent Jaguars could do almost as good a job as the much larger F-111, and even the simple Belgian Mirage 5BA could put down a useful bomb-load. There were many who argued that the 'One-Elevens' should be hoarded, doing nothing until either a storm blew up or night fell; but they lost the vote. Most of the 20th Tac Fighter Wing went out to hit naval units bombarding German air bases with missiles from the Baltic, while the 48th was assigned four major strategic targets near Magdeburg and Salzwedel.

It was a long way, and 40 years earlier would have taken a Lancaster or a B-17 about five hours on the outward trip alone. The swing-wingers had no help from the terrain but flew the whole trip at treetop height, cruising fairly effortlessly at the start but going to afterburner 100 miles from their targets and accelerating to a speed close to Mach 0.9 – less for the E, more for the powerful F. The F-111s were held back by their draggy triplets of bombs, 24 per aircraft. They knew just where they were going, and passed under most of the Soviet Frontal Aviation without even being seen. Some had panel lights warning of hostile radars illuminating from astern; but carefully-judged chaff and, in one case, a jammer payload, caused the radar – obviously fighter-borne, possibly by one of the new MiG-29s – to break-lock and become uncertain.

To the amazement of most people other than the 'One-Eleven' crews, every aircraft that started out reached its target, in a little under 90 minutes' flight time. Every bomb released cleanly and was thought to have been right on target. Somewhere on the return leg four aircraft were hit and not seen again, believed to have been caught by MiG-29s or Su-15s ('Flagon' D) despite the ability of the unloaded F-111 to run at Mach 1.2. It was well-known that, since the mid-1970s, the Russian AAMs had become depressingly sophisticated and hard to put off the scent. It was also appreciated, too late, that the widely-believed NATO estimates of Russian AAM effective range had been pure wishful thinking.

From dawn there had been increasingly widespread air combat over the northern part of the front just west of Hamburg, and by 9 am this had extended all the way south to the southern edge of the thrust in the Hildesheim area. Everyone in the Allied air forces now had a healthy respect for the SAM and Triple-A defences that rolled ahead with a Pact army, and were especially shy of the ZSU-23-4. Time and again the ZSU had been proved lethal over just the ranges that mattered, and its streams of shells were not to be turned away by clever countermeasures.

To some degree, tangling with Russian or East German fighters was the lesser of two evils because, where they were, there was no fire from the ground (though sometimes even this rule did not hold good). In general the USAF F-15 Eagle was regarded as king of the sky, because in most situations it could destroy its opponent in seconds and stay whole itself.

But the Allied air force also knew that trading one-for-one was fatal. The Warsaw Pact forces could replace each lost aircraft ten times over, but an Allied aircraft could not be replaced at all.

As in so many vicious *mêlées* in World War 2, the fighting over the battle area was hectic and followed no predictable pattern. There was no doubt that the Allied aircraft had the edge, but it was doing them no good at all. Probably most encounters were ending in a 2–1 ratio of kills, in the Allies' favour – but it was obvious that on this basis there would be nothing left at all on the Allied side after a week. Each of the Eagles of the 36th and 49th Tac Fighter Wings was likely to take with it as many as four or five of the enemy, maybe more, but there were only 72 Eagles against thousands of enemy aircraft. To make matters much worse, every Allied pilot knew that the imbalance in the air was as nothing compared with the imbalance in bombardment missiles. Once nuclear warfare began – and everyone took it for granted that it was not 'if', but 'when' – their airfields would no longer be usable. Nuclear bombardment would be the quickest way to knock out the entire NATO air power – except for the unique RAF Harriers which, now that battle was joined, suddenly seemed doubly desirable.

One of the worst shocks on the morning of the first day had been a Russian AAM that seemed particularly eager to meet Allied fighters. In one heavy air battle involving Dutch F-16s and RAF Phantoms, Jaguars and Harriers, all engaged by various MiG and Sukhoi interceptors, ten or a dozen NATO aircraft blew up within the first few seconds. The Jaguars and Harriers, returning from a bombing mission, were concerned mainly to get away alive, and were surprised that they all did. Indeed, some of them did good work with Aden cannon and advanced-model Sidewinders. It was not until the debrief record and combat films had been studied that it was suddenly realized that the Russian missile might be designed to home on the Allied fighter radar. The Jaguar and the Harrier both had Westinghouse radars, but of totally dissimilar type. Could the enemy AAM be tuned to the known Allied radar in the course of a dogfight?

As the day wore on, this became increasingly likely. More than once an AAM zipped fairly close to an Allied fighter without homing on it; the inference was that the Soviet pilot had mistaken the Allied type and tuned his missile's wavelength incorrectly. This was a matter for urgent investigation, and within two hours 'Elint' missions were being flown by special RPVs which, acting as decoys for the Russian fighters, drew their fire and sent back complete data on the results. As soon as the RPVs began to simulate an Allied fighter radar, they went up in a ball of fire.

Had there been time to debate the matter, this would have been extremely interesting. As it was, the news was bitterly ironic. A few years earlier the Americans had cancelled their own very promising 'Brazo/Pave Arm' programme. This was to have led to an ERASE (Electro-magnetic Radiation Source Elimination) weapon which, back in 1974, had scored three out of three in its very first series of tests at Holloman Special Weapons Center. Though the original idea had been to build a sure-fire Foxbat-killer, it had soon become evident that with adequate 'Elint' information it would be possible to have a missile programme to home on any radar-using aircraft, with standard interlocks triggered by the IFF to protect friendlies. This had been one of many valuable items axed from the budget by the Carter administration.

THIRD DAY

As the grim morning wore on, faces became more sombre and determined. Still there was no nuclear holocaust, but the entire front was in flames and it was clear that the tip of the Warsaw Pact advance had come virtually to a halt. Behind the Soviet front were thousands of vehicles of all kinds, which despite severe losses from the few surviving SAMs and ZSUs were being pounded to pieces by small groups of Allied aircraft. But total losses by many NATO units since the small hours exceeded 50%, and one or two units – especially *Luftwaffe* and *Marineflieger* in the north – had virtually ceased to exist. The enemy had got a bloody nose; for the time he was stopped in his tracks; but what of the morrow? Basic commodities such as missiles and cannon ammunition were fast running out, and the impoverished British had once again used up nearly all their tac-air weapons.

By 11 am air strikes of varying weight and effectiveness had been flown by Warsaw Pact aircraft, nearly all of them Russian, against every chief NATO air base in the 2ATAF area. Several *Luftwaffe* aircraft, mostly F-104Gs and Alpha Jets, had been lost when they ran out of fuel looking for alternative runways. Messages, some of them in plain voice, filled the ether as air defence stations in the NADGE chain tried to vector aircraft to usable airstrips. The lone E-3A AWACS worked overtime in identifying people in trouble and getting them back on the ground.

Many tactical aircraft overcame frightful problems and intense danger to reach friendly bases, steered their way past craters on the runway and then parked – out of the battle for lack of either the right fuel or compatible ordnance. Lack of NATO uniformity reared its ugly head as never before. A Dutch F-16 put down at RAF Brüggen, only a stone's throw from its own base, and then had to wait while maintenance tools were brought by car because its own base had been hit and no helicopter was readily available. Likewise, four RAF Jaguars from 14 Sqn, which should have returned to Brüggen, were forced by lack of fuel to put down at the *Luftwaffe* base at Rheine-Hopsten, where the ground staff racked their brains to solve compatibility problems.

One base which had not been attacked by 11 am was Bitburg, home of complete wings of USAF F-15 Eagle fighters and A-10A attack aircraft. Both were among the latest American combat types, though both designs dated from the 1960s and both were present in Europe only to the extent of two wings totalling 72 aircraft.

The F-15, with perhaps the best radar computer/display/sight system in the air-combat business, went out from Bitburg with AIM-7 Sparrow medium-range AAMs, Sidewinder close-range AAMs and a gun, plus a flight performance almost the equal of the smaller MiG-29. The Eagle was probably the aircraft most NATO aircrew would have voted 'the plane I'd most like to go to war in', but it was hard hit by the Russian radar-homing AAM which was very evidently tunable to the Eagle's APG-63 radar. There was no point trying to out-fly this AAM and devising a counter-measure would take time. After the loss of

12 Eagles, the drastic decision was taken to switch off the APG-63 and intercept visually as long as daylight lasted, using the remaining elements in the cockpit display; sight and computer. This was a feasible procedure, but had the drawback of not having figured in F-15 training.

The other Bitburg resident was the large and ungainly A-10A, which had the great advantage of no radar. At first this had been considered a grave drawback, as it had with the Harrier and Jaguar; but now the A-10A jocks were beginning to appreciate that their tank-killer – officially described as 'having an austere avionics fit' – might just save their lives. Moreover, the idea that in a modern land battle any aircraft can be made 'survivable' had become somewhat discredited. The A-10A had been designed to fly home after being plastered with ZSU-23-4 fire, with a fair sprinkling of 57 mm or SA-7 infantry SAM warheads. The pilot sat in a great titanium bathtub the best part of an inch thick, and every vital part of the aircraft was protected or duplicated. (One of the *JaboG* 31 Tornadoes had flown home with one engine blown completely out of the aircraft; this impressed the A-10 merchants because they thought their own ability to do this impressive, and their TF34 turbofans were hung outside the aircraft, not inside.)

Despite their nominal 'survivability', the A-10A crews knew they might last only a few seconds in the European environment. In most wars they could do a fantastic job. They could kill any known tank and destroy any battlefield target, using their monster GAU/8A gun and Maverick missiles steered to the ground by various radar, command, EO (electro-optical) or IIR (imaging infra-red) guidance systems – but they had not been designed for operations in which command of the air over their targets seemed pretty much to belong to the enemy.

The advantages of the A-10A were long endurance, deadly accuracy, a formidable weapon load (such as 28 bombs in the 500 lb class) and amazing power to evade trouble and trade punch for punch; but no aircraft had yet been invented that could shrug off a hit by a SAM-6, or even the majority of Russian AAMs. Its one saving grace seemed to be the 'Pave Penny' laser tracker, which with the AGM-65C version of Maverick offered a near-certainty of hitting the target. The 'Long Knife' designator was also flying in some A-10s, doing the entire guidance task unaided.

But the biggest problem remained that of staying alive. Maximum distance from the target helped; so did minimum altitude. Yet on least one occasion an A-10 was almost knocked out of the sky by a massive explosion that, it was afterwards judged, must have been caused by a Soviet artillery rocket aimed to impact at a point immediately in front of the slowly-moving A-10 crawling along right on the deck. The A-10 was also all too easily spotted by Russian fighters, but in one amazing combat one A-10 out-turned its opponent and blasted it to pieces with its mighty gun. One such lucky victory could not be counted upon as a regular technique, calling as it did for unique judgement and guts.

In the afternoon they preparationed to pull out every kind of sensor and guidance system for use as dusk fell. The most important single device was unquestionably 'Pave Tack', with its stabilized sighting head combining FLIR, laser and EO, all fed to a single brilliantly-clear cockpit display on which also appeared all the radar information. This promised to ensure pinpoint weapon delivery in bad weather or at night. It was widely hoped that results after nightfall would be better than by day, though there was healthy respect for Soviet night sensors and missile guidance.

The AVQ-25 Pave Tack pod was available to most USAF F-4E and F-111 squadrons, and was in the process of being fitted in the late afternoon when a nuclear warhead exploded on RAF Lakenheath in

The A-10 'long endurance, deadly accuracy, a formidable weapon load and amazing power'

England. It missed by maybe half a mile and by no means killed everyone on the base immediately, but it stopped all operations at once. Nobody was in any condition to get on the telephone and warn Upper Heyford, and that airfield also received an identical Russian missile a few moments later. These were the first of many nuclear attacks against the key NATO air bases, and they marked the end of the conventional air war.

BILL GUNSTON

14. THE SEA WAR

When the announcement of the forthcoming Soviet 'police action' against West Germany was relayed to the naval chiefs of NATO, their immediate reaction was one of disbelief quickly followed by a momentary elation. It hardly seemed possible, but Moscow had dealt NATO an ace in the very first hand.

This was the situation, as it appeared to the Western naval chiefs. After years of crises and false alarms, the Russians were actually going to invade West Germany. They were playing on the time-honoured spinelessness of the Western politicians and hoping to get away with a major coup on land without armed opposition. Only time would reveal the Warsaw Pact's real objectives, but for the moment these did not matter so far as sea power was concerned. To start with, at least, the stakes were going to rest on land operations in North Germany. Hastily-checked surveillance reports all confirmed the same story: the formidable Russian submarine and surface fleets were being deliberately held back – and that gave NATO time to take out maximum insurance by sea.

Against all expectations, golden opportunities lay waiting to be seized by the sailors of the Western Alliance. The Baltic exits and the Dardanelles must be blocked. Surveillance of the Greenland-Iceland-UK (GIUK) gap must be stepped up, and patrols pushed forward as far as receding ice conditions would permit. Soon the Commander of the Baltic Approaches would be clamouring, perhaps in diplomatically muffled terms, for the release of forces to his control for minelaying, and for the blend of air, surface and subsurface craft by which the sea could be denied to the Soviet Baltic Fleet. It had long been a reasonably-held view that Warsaw Pact naval units which did not deploy before D-Day were likely to be trapped as far as the wide oceans were concerned. But they still had plenty of scope for mischief, particularly the amphibious forces within the Baltic.

In the south, the same applied – at least in theory – to the Soviet Black Sea Fleet and its reinforcement tasks in the Mediterranean and the Indian Ocean. The latter task had assumed a new significance in the late 1970s, when the Soviet fleet had increased its regular deployments to the Indian Ocean from 25 ships in 1976-7 to 50 in 1980. There were obvious measures which the Soviet Command could have taken to improve their state of readiness, by passing more ships through the Dardanelles and the Suez Canal on the pretext of 'exercises'. But there was no sign that this had been done – indeed, the Soviet Indian Ocean deployment on D-1 was, if anything, below its normal level.

As the minutes ticked away towards the deadline for the Soviet 'police action' to begin in West Germany, the NATO High Command at least knew that it faced no immediate menace from last-minute deployments of the Soviet navy. But this relief was no more than transitory. If the Soviet gamble in Germany came off, the entire credibility of NATO would lie in ruins; Moscow would be able to pose as the triumphant defender of world peace; a host of Third World governments, now knowing for certain which horse to back, would open their ports to Soviet mercantile and naval shipping; and the Soviet navy, given the security and shelter of new bases around the world, would be left poised for a decisive offensive against the vital sea lanes of the West whenever Moscow should choose to give the word.

None of this was the product of unwarranted pessimism or fevered imagination: it was a picture whose outline had been drawn by the events of the past 20 years, ever since the Soviet High Command had sat down to assess the reasons for the failure of Krushchev's Cuban adventure. And the apparent inactivity of the Soviet navy in this latest crisis was the exception that proved the rule.

As repeated talks on naval limitation in the Indian Ocean had been fruitless, the potential for trouble in that theatre had remained high. However, Australian initiatives had led to a Commonwealth agreement on joint action against piracy, unlawful detention of shipping and acts of terrorism at sea. One result of this agreement was the establishment of a Commonwealth Ready Force (CRF), to which the United Kingdom contributed one, and sometimes two, destroyers or frigates and the almost permanent allocation of a patrol submarine. As a multi-national force, the CRF was an invaluable symbol of Free World naval solidarity. It was modelled on the successful Standing Naval Force Atlantic (STANAVFORLANT) of five or six frigates and destroyers, flying the flags of their respective countries but directly responsive to the orders of their commodore. The latter appointment was held in rotation by officers of the navies represented in the force; and the commodore, in turn, came under the orders of an Allied Supreme Commander.

Ever since the Suez Crisis of 1956 the Canal, and progressively the whole of the Red Sea, had become a disputed passage; but since 1981 in particular the CRF had proved invaluable in making it clear that it was unwise to interfere with the free passage of ships under Commonwealth flags in the Red Sea and off the Horn of Africa. Aden, once just a source of fuel, was now just a source of trouble. A very firm line by the United States, Commonwealth countries and a group of Arab states

led by Saudi Arabia had been needed to convince the Russians that they would be stirring up a hornets' nest if they encouraged their local clients to terrorize the area.

The situation could have been far less dangerous if only resolute action had been taken in 1978, when Soviet fortunes had hung in the balance in Eritrea, Somalia and Ethiopia. Since then, however, action against vessels bound for West Germany had been an early sign of Soviet anti-German pressures outside the European zone; and during the recent war of words over West German neo-Nazism and nuclear aspirations, the Soviet Union had put considerable pressure on suppliers and shippers of oil for West Germany.

The 300,000-ton Liberian tanker *Monarch of the Glen*, bound for Hamburg from the Gulf, had blown up in the Mozambique Channel, ostensibly through an accumulation of explosive gases. The Malagasy Republic had led the howls of protest aroused by the ensuing (and hideously extensive) oil pollution. Another supertanker was seized by Mozambique coastal forces – including a missile-equipped fast patrol boat – and held hostage against payment of compensation for the environmental damage. It was no coincidence that the second tanker's cargo was also destined for West Germany. As tanker owners took the hint and re-routed ships to the eastward of Madagascar, the Soviet Union promptly declared an exercise area to the north and east of the island as 'dangerous to navigation'.

The dubious legality of this declaration was dressed up, with bare-faced hypocrisy, as compliance with the Helsinki Accord's provision for notification of major exercises. None of this helped an outsize container ship which very soon afterwards suffered a heavy explosion. This appeared to have been caused by a missile rather than any internal accidental cause. The ship (German-owned in this case) was beached, after a great struggle, just north

Russians in the Mediterranean: 'Kashin' class destroyers refuelling from a tanker

of Tamatave on Madagascar's east coast. German protests went unheeded, but a task group was detached from the US Seventh Fleet and moved to the general area of Diego Garcia in the Chagos Archipelago. A Royal Navy Task Group consisting of the elderly support carrier *Hermes* with Sea Harrier aircraft embarked, two 'Type 42' class destroyers, four frigates and several auxiliaries, was ordered to cancel a world cruise which had begun in September 1982 and to remain in the western Indian Ocean. When it was clear that this show of Western naval strength was exerting a cooling effect upon Soviet and Soviet-inspired malpractices, the British group had sailed to spend Christmas in Cockburn Sound, Western Australia.

For the West, the most dangerous situation had been created by Soviet pressure in the Persian Gulf itself. In late August 1982 the Soviet government had demanded a restriction on oil supplies for West Germany and threatened to seal off the Straits of Hormuz. But the Shah of Iran ordered anti-submarine patrols in the area of the Straits and moved mine-countermeasure vessels to sweep channels wide enough for the normal heavy traffic in and out of the Gulf. For this purpose, modified hovercraft adapted to the mine-countermeasure role proved invaluable.

This, then, was the general naval situation east of Suez at the moment when the first Russian spearheads thrust into West Germany:

● The Russian force operating in its self-proclaimed exercise area off Madagascar included the 'Kiev' class aircraft-carrier *Minsk* with her Yak-36 V/STOL aircraft, two 'Kresta II' cruisers and two 'Krivak' class destroyers, and two of the 'Modified Kashin' class destroyers. Several Soviet destroyers and frigates were at Aden or in the vicinity, two were at Beira in Mozambique, and yet another group was on passage to the Java Sea through the Sunda Strait, presumably heading for home in Vladivostok. It was this Soviet Pacific Fleet base which had normally maintained routine deployments in the Indian Ocean, with little reliance being placed on the Black Sea Fleet and the Suez Canal route.

● Ships of the US Navy's Task Group 77 were patrolling in the general area of their forward base at Diego Garcia. The Task Group Commander was flying his flag in the nuclear-powered aircraft-carrier *Dwight D. Eisenhower*; his force included another nuclear-powered ship (the cruiser *California*) and a mixed escort of guided-missile destroyers and conventional destroyers, with an underway replenishment group in support.

● The Royal Australian Navy's aircraft-carrier HMAS *Melbourne*, with the missile destroyers *Perth* and *Brisbane* and the newly-modernized frigates *Yarra*, *Stuart* and *Derwent*, was steaming west to rendezvous with the Royal Navy's Task Group off Mauritius for a prearranged exercise period. They were to be joined by:

● An Indian group led by the aircraft-carrier *Vikrant* (built in Britain as the 'Majestic' class *Hercules*) and three Indian-built 'Leander' class frigates, *Dunagiri*, *Vdaygiri* and *Vindhyagiri*.

● Strong elements of the Imperial Iranian Navy were patrolling the Straits of Hormuz and regularly check-sweeping channels.

● Pakistan's navy was not involved, although the Pakistani government had expressed its support for the stand taken by the Shah over the maintenance of free passage through the Straits.

● The Commonwealth Ready Force was off the coast of Oman, ready to move back towards the Horn of Africa if need be.

Apart from the US Sixth Fleet and its watching brief on the Soviet naval forces in the Mediterranean (of which more later), these were the only Allied naval forces actually in contact with the Soviet navy on the first day of World War 3. And elsewhere, contrary to all NATO forecasts and reason-

ing – nothing at all out of the ordinary. The Barents Sea, the North Atlantic, the North Sea, the Channel and the Western Approaches – all remained innocent of any suspicious Soviet moves at sea. Agreeably surprised but determined to waste not a moment of what could only be a respite, the NATO commanders prepared to take the initiative in containing the immediate crisis unfolding in North Germany.

When the British Cabinet made its decision to order the Army and RAF units in West Germany not to resist the Soviet advance, the politicians had the comfort of knowing that at least the British would be seen to be doing something at sea. NATO's naval structure involved the Royal Navy intimately; the Soviet diplomats had seen fit to make no stipulations immobilizing NATO's fleet movements; and so the British admirals had far more muscle to exert on the Cabinet than their Army and RAF colleagues.

NATO's three top military commands were ACE (Allied Command Europe), ACLANT (Allied Command Atlantic) and ACCHAN (Allied Command Channel). The Supreme Allied Commanders of the former two SACEUR and SACLANT) were American officers but the Channel commander (CINCCHAN) and Deputy SACLANT were British. Moreover, the most important subcommand of ACLANT – Eastern Atlantic Command, responsible for the Western Approaches to the UK and European mainland – shared its HQ with that of ACCHAN and the Royal Navy's own Fleet Command HQ at Northwood, Middlesex. The British were intimately bound up with NATO's naval reaction to the Soviet 'police action', whether they liked it or not.

SACLANT and CINCCHAN were in total agreement on what should be done at sea, and urged the American President and the British Prime Minister, as well as NATO Headquarters in Brussels, to release forces to their commands, so that the following measures could be implemented at once:

● ACLANT's Western Area Command, WESTLANT, would plan for the collection and sailing of the biggest possible fast convoy to ship fuel, tank engines, ammunition and above all replacement missiles across the Atlantic to Europe. If a conventional war did break out these replenishments would be desperately needed as soon as possible, and not nearly enough of them could be brought in by air. If nothing happened and NATO was left to pick up the pieces from a bloodless humiliation, they would still be needed to create the vestiges of military credibility. As every surface warship in SACLANT would be needed to escort the convoy if it sailed as a whole (at the same time presenting the biggest and juiciest target ever known in naval history), the convoy would be sailed in escorted sections, keeping in touch with the latest European situation, and holding the choice of eventual destination open as long as possible.

● ACCHAN was to begin mine-countermeasures at once – precautionary check-sweeping to keep open the Channel, and above all the approaches to Antwerp and Rotterdam, the two most important supply ports on the North Sea coast. ACCHAN's secondary priority was to send all help that could be spared from the Narrows to assist the West Germans, Norwegian and Danish blockade of the Soviet Baltic Fleet.

● North of the Atlantic convoy route, STANAVFORLANT's priority was to form a temporary surveillance picket-line across the Greenland-Iceland-UK gap. This would be reinforced by US and Canadian units from Western Atlantic Command, with carrier support and strike capacity from task groups centred on USS *Kitty Hawk* and the nuclear-powered giant carrier, USS *Enterprise*.

The English Channel was not only crucial for the passage of essential raw materials: it also had to be kept open for the major reinforcements of reservist troops, vehicles and equipment without which the forces deployed in Germany would not be at war strength. In two world wars it had been the proud boast that the British Expeditionary Force had been conveyed to France without loss. In 1983, despite the confident reassurances which Parliament had been given in past years, the threat was greater but the resources considerably less than in 1914 or 1939.

By 1978 the number of Royal Naval mine-countermeasures vessels (MCMVs) available was little over half the force available in the early 1960s. Splendid new British designs in glass-reinforced plastic had evolved into the new 'Hunt' class; but as these ships combined the roles of mine-hunters and minesweepers, they were not provided as replacements on a one-for-one basis. It is all very well to have versatile warships at one's disposal, but there must be enough of them. Versatility in the wrong place is not an undue advantage, and this was the cause of some anxiety at ACCHAN and RN Fleet HQ. But there was one considerable relief, and this had been achieved by a change of heart in 1979.

The British services had been amazingly slow in adapting the hovercraft to military use. The Royal Navy had bought a Wellington (BH7) Type for evaluation in 1970, after considerable experience with various types of early hovercraft. The hovercraft's very high speed, minimal pressure, acoustic and magnetic effects, and its relative invulnerability to underwater shock, made it a great potential asset to mine-countermeasure operations. Moreover, the big SRN4 cross-Channel ferries could carry 450 passengers and over 60 vehicles – ideal for military movements in an emergency – and their ability to shuttle half a battalion across the Channel in 35 minutes made them highly attractive. At last, in 1979, it was decided that four BH7s would be purchased for the Royal Navy's minesweeping force, and sets of equipment were purchased for the conversion of the

British Rail and HoverLloyd ferries to minesweeping; but the conversion of the SRN4s must wait until the cross-Channel reinforcement had been completed.

Even with the help of hovercraft the cross-Channel movement would be hard to protect; the waters of the Channel's eastern approaches were not the easiest for anti-submarine operations. But this was a fact which cut both ways. Modern submarines were not going to find these waters ideal for their purpose, either; and no Soviet submarines had been sailed in advance to patrol these busy routes.

In the early hours of D-Day, however, the Prime Minister and the Cabinet insisted that there must be no troop movements across the Channel: this might provoke the Russians. The restriction was lifted as soon as the news of the first clashes between Soviet and British forces in Germany filtered in around 9 am. Order and counter-order might well have produced chaos in the time-honoured style, but in fact it gave ACCHAN an eight-hour start with the minesweeping programme.

Wearing both of his hats as CINCCH-AN and Fleet Commander, Royal Navy, the Commander-in-Chief, Channel brought all his MCM forces to maximum readiness for precautionary sweeping at 1.30 am. It was a national responsibility for each member of NATO to see to the defence of its own coastal area, and in his national capacity the C-in-C called out all his Royal Naval Reserve MCM vessels. Two years earlier this would have been impossible; but in October 1981 UK legislation had been passed to enable reserves to be called out selectively without the ponderous procedures of the past. Without these powers the MCM preparations might have been delayed until all reservists had been called out and the reinforcement of the Continent begun. The six extra minesweepers thus made quickly available were more than welcome, for it soon became clear that the mining threat was a grim reality.

Many warnings had been given about the Warsaw Pact's resources for mine warfare, and some of these had already been brought into play. In the late afternoon of D−1 two Russian factory ships, the *Gherman Titov* and the *Zaporozhye*, had been returning independently from a thoroughly successful spell of ruining Britain's western Channel mackerel fishery, when they received a cleverly disguised executive order. All Soviet merchant and fishing vessels formed part of the Soviet naval defence apparatus, and their big trawlers and factory ships were capable of carrying a good deal more than fishing gear and electronic intelligence equipment. They proved it now. As the two factory ships passed through the Dover Straits (*Titov* at 10.15 pm and *Zaporozhye* at 10.55) ports opened silently below their waterlines to release random mines across the approaches to Dover, Harwich, Ostend and Antwerp.

For a minimum of effort, just as the mine warfare textbooks said, the maximum discomfiture was soon caused. Mysterious explosions in main channels, the sinking of one vessel and serious damage to three others brought traffic in the Narrows to a halt, just as the NATO governments were agonizing over how not to offend the Russians by making any precipitate moves. STANAVFORCHAN was quickly on the scene and as early as 3.30 am on D-Day British and Belgian forces were clearing a swept channel into Antwerp.

When confirmation came through five hours later that British forces were in action in Germany, and the reinforcement programme began, vital preparations had therefore been made. Resourcefulness was not lacking but resources were, and in spite of all the efforts made ships were still blown up and men and vehicles lost. The reinforcement programme was only kept going by narrowing the frontage to Ostend and Antwerp and stretching the timetable. The commercial hovercraft were invaluable, the only vessels able to maintain a full rate of operation; they could, of course, ignore the water depth and skirt round danger points where subsurface objects awaited the attentions of a minehunter. By dusk on D-Day one-fifth of the top-priority reinforcements in the programme had been landed on the Continent and intelligence confirmed that no fresh Soviet minelaying moves seemed likely. For this the blockade of the Baltic exits could justly claim credit.

But this definite success was also won at heavy cost. A group of Dutch, German and British frigates was detached to supplement the blockade; they had to take their chance with mines and HMS *Argonaut* was blown in half. The culprit was a presumed delayed-action acoustic mine over which all of *Argonaut*'s consorts had passed safely. Twenty minutes later the Dutch frigate *Banckert* lost her bows in an explosion and sank shortly after being taken in tow. *Banckert*'s loss was all the more keenly felt because she was about to finish her first commission. This is the kind of war sailors hate: no enemy to fight, but all the risks of sudden death and drowning almost within sight of home.

It was some comfort for the Allied sailors to know that their comrades had not been idle in providing Soviet vessels with a taste of their own medicine. The development of the Captor mine, which can home onto its target, and its distribution in considerable quantities, was a story not only of clever technology but also of its wise application. The factory ship *Zaporozhye*, making for the Baltic, was sunk by a Danish-laid Captor as she negotiated the Belt. *Gherman Titov* escaped the mines of the Belt – she was routed for Murmansk via the Norwegian coast and the North Cape – but ever since she had slowed to drop her mines off the Belgian coast the night before, the *Titov* had been shadowed by the Dutch submarine *Potvis*. The Dutch submarine commander was patched into STANAVFORCHAN's communications net and was incensed to hear of the loss of the *Banckert*; he was also fully capable of putting two and two together from a quick check of *Titov*'s course, speed, and time lapse. Without hesitation he attacked, putting two torpedoes into the *Titov* at a range at which it was impossible to miss. *Titov* took just under an hour to sink: the first Soviet naval casualty of the war.

FIRST BLOOD TO THE FEDERAL NAVY

Neither the Danes nor the Dutch, however, could claim the honour of having drawn first blood in the war at sea. That distinction had already gone to the West Germans, and their victims had been the massed air transports flying-in the Soviet airborne division for its drop on the nuclear research station.

After taking off from Neustrelitz at 1 am the transport fleet dropped to under 100 feet and headed north-west for the coast. They hugged the sea as they traversed the Bay of Mecklenburg, still in East German air space, before turning west for the second leg of the approach: a daring flight across Schleswig-Holstein at top speed and zero feet. It was a still night and the massed roar of their engines was clearly heard in Kiel as they passed to the north. Although the transports presented little or no radar target at that low altitude, the West German warships on station in the Heligoland Bight alerted by Kiel, had their missiles ready and fully depressed by the time the transports began their final approach run from the sea.

Immensely cheered by the sight, sound and radar contacts of *Luftwaffe* fighters tearing in to attack, the sailors of the destroyer *Hamburg* and the new frigates *Heimdall* and *Fafnir* managed to get in one full salvo as the harried transports shot past at extreme range. One of *Hamburg*'s four 'Exocet' missiles and no less than five of the 16 'Sea Sparrows' fired in flights

The US Sixth Fleet's primary task – supporting the Greeks and Turks – is fulfilled

'Good information was available on Kiev's movements and a strike was launched against her'

of eight by the frigates scored hits, vivid flashes mirrored by the waiting sea, before the range opened impossibly and the fighters were left to tear at the shredded formation.

The first round of the sea war – securing the Channel and blockading the Baltic – had been won by NATO. But naval supremacy in home waters depended absolutely on control of the air. Heartening though it was, this first naval success could be regarded as no more than temporary, given the Warsaw Pact's terrifying preponderence in resources for the air war.

Seven hours after receiving confirmation that the first Soviet units had crossed the West German frontier, the Allied and Soviet admirals out in the Indian Ocean found themselves in a uniquely difficult situation.

Were they in fact already at war? As fighting was undoubtedly going on between NATO and Warsaw Pact forces on the other side of the world, and seemed to be getting worse from minute to minute, a state of war could be said to exist in all but name. Yet Moscow and the governments of the West were still in close telephone contact, apparently striving desperately to localize hostilities to northern Germany. As long as that state of affairs lasted, any precipitate move at sea, anywhere in the world, could easily convert what might yet turn out to have been a gross misunderstanding into a war of global destruction.

Forced as they were to shoulder this tremendous responsibility, the Russian and Allied admirals faced an agonizing dilemma as they waited on station. How long could they remain there, staving off World War 3 by ostensibly doing nothing to each other? And above all, would the other side make the first move, and gain the vital prize of the initiative?

On D-1 the naval situation in the Indian Ocean, as mentioned above, had looked good from the Allied point of view. The American admiral in *Dwight D. Eisen-*

hower knew that he would soon be able to call on no less than three other carriers – the British *Hermes*, Australian *Melbourne* and Indian *Vikrant* – with which to counter the biggest Soviet menace in those waters, the carrier *Minsk* and her task group off Madagascar. Every other Allied grouping was placed where it would be able to do the most good, should there be any resurgence of Soviet naval interference in the Gulf traffic. But it was too good to last; and the first Allied piece was quietly but firmly removed from the board within hours of the Soviet announcement of the forthcoming 'police action'. In retrospect it is hard to blame the Indian government for its reaction to the Soviet announcement of the imminent 'police action' in Germany. Relations between Delhi and Moscow were particularly good at the time. In fact, after years of abortive negotiations with the British for the purchase of Sea Harriers for the Indian Navy, the Russians had virtually made a present of a batch of Yak-36 V/STOL aircraft six months before. The fighters were in *Vikrant* already, and the scheduled Commonwealth exercise off Mauritius was to have been their first sea trial. Observers had been looking forward keenly to seeing how the Yaks' performance measured up to that of the Sea Harriers of *Hermes*. But the Soviet ambassador had known his business, stressing the excellence of Indian-Soviet relations and dropping thinly-veiled warnings about Pakistan's ambivalent attitude to Iran's 'high-handed' behaviour in the mouth of the Persian Gulf.

Delhi therefore issued a firm order. *Vikrant* and her escorting frigates were to return at once to Indian home waters; and the Russian admiral had one less Allied carrier to worry about.

He also had the advantage of a considerable lead in news received of the unfolding drama in Germany. As soon as the news came in of the disastrous fate of the airborne drop, on which so much had turned, the naval chiefs in the Soviet High

Command had bitterly upbraided their army and air force colleagues. Thanks to their over-confidence the Soviet Navy had been persuaded to yield the benefit of initial deployment to the other side. That deployment must be ordered now, and orders passed to the remoter units of the fleet releasing them to take what action might prove necessary. Although the West Germans were still fighting there had still been no clashes between Soviet and British or American forces, and until such a clash took place the American and Common- wealth naval units in the outer oceans were almost certain to act with caution.

As it happened, the Soviet High Com- mand slightly underestimated the excel- lence of the NATO data links with *Dwight D. Eisenhower*, and the Soviet admiral's advantage was not as great as it might well have been. His opening moves were:

● Order every available warship in the southern Red Sea to make feint sorties from the Gulf of Aden – this to tie down the Commonwealth Ready Force off the Saudi Arabian coast;

● Take his own task force west round Madagascar's northern tip and lay every mine the ships carried in the Mozambique Channel (hopefully blocking one of the key routes for Western Europe's tanker fleets);

● With this task completed, steam due north towards the Horn of Africa in order to make it as hard as possible for the Americans, British and Australians to combine against him.

HUNTING DOWN THE MINSK

The American admiral may have been only ten years old when the last great carrier engagement of World War 2 – the Battle of Leyte Gulf in October 1944 – had been fought, but he knew very well what his first priority must be: seek and destroy the enemy carrier. His knowledge of naval history reminded him that the Russian

admiral was in much the same position as Admiral Graf von Spee in 1914 – as Winston Churchill had put it, 'a cut flower in a vase; fair to see, yet bound to die' – yet, as long as his ships remained in being, a paralyzing threat to Allied sea power. The American admiral placed himself in his opponent's shoes with little difficulty because the Russians had so few choices open to them. If they cut and ran for the South Atlantic they would be abandoning the whole reason for their strategic presence in the Indian Ocean, leaving the Allies with a free hand to secure the Gulf shipping routes and mop up the few Soviet warships left off the Horn of Africa and in the Red Sea. As they re- treated the Russians would moreover be exposed to attack from the missile craft, submarines and formidable air force of South Africa for over 2,000 miles. If the Russian admiral headed east he would run right into the British and Australians. He must go north.

The American admiral therefore re- quested the British and Australians to head for a rendezvous 600 miles due east of Dar- es-Salaam. His own Seventh Fleet task group had the shortest distance to cover in order to reach his rendezvous, and set off from the Chagos Archipelago at full speed with a permanent air patrol of two Tomcat fighters to guard against surprise air attack. As they headed west, the Americans mulled over their plans for attacking and sinking the *Minsk* when the time came.

The task seemed straightforward when the positions of the ships were plotted on a chart, but it was not. The Russian task force was known to bristle with SAMs and although *Minsk* would be unable to replace lost aircraft the same applied to the Allies. One carelessly executed air attack would be quite enough to push the odds back on to an even keel. The American admiral knew that he must cherish each and every one of his strike aircraft, and a series of conferences with the *Eisenhower*'s air operations officer persuaded him to try a plan so novel that it could well succeed.

Modern defensive AA weapons were, the Americans agreed, seriously type-cast. They homed on engine emissions, electronic emissions, or both, and they were geared to the speeds of extremely fast and sophisticated jet aircraft. But the admiral recalled an intriguing case-study used as a salutary object-lesson during his time at Annapolis. When the crack German battle-cruisers *Scharnhorst* and *Gneisenau* had raced through the English Channel in February 1942, their fire-power and swarming, land-based fighter cover had proved more than a match for all modern aircraft sent against them. But the British had given the Germans a severe shock by using antique Swordfish biplanes with a speed so low that the warships' fire-control systems could not adjust to it, and the fighters of the air cover had been forced to fly with wheels and flaps down in order to fly slow enough to attack the Swordfish. That particular lecture had been accompanied by film shot aboard the German ships, showing how close the old British museum-pieces had got (comfortably inside dropping-range) before the fighters and the flak clawed them down.

There were no old biplanes aboard the *Eisenhower* but there were two Grumman S2-E trackers: twin piston engines, 230 mph at sea level, cast in the anti-submarine role. The S2-E was therefore designed to carry those twin concomitants of modern AS warfare, sonobuoys and depth-charges; it could carry rockets – and it could also carry torpedoes. Talking it over with the Tracker pilots, the admiral and his staff sketched out plans for an extremely unorthodox attack on the *Minsk*: a torpedo attack from two sides, using both Trackers guided to the target by radar, but making a slow and erratic approach right down at sea level. With any luck this would give the Russian fire-control system a wretched headache and catch the carrier in a converging web of torpedoes.

'The two oddly-behaving blips on the Russian radar screens baffled the fire-control computers'

INTERCEPTION
AND ATTACK

The American admiral's guesswork had been sound. At 1.25 am on D + 1 (local time) the first ships of the Russian task force began to show on *Eisenhower*'s radar. *Minsk* was steaming barely west of north at 20 knots, flanked by the two 'Kresta II' cruisers, the three ships sailing in a lozenge-shaped screen formed by the two 'Modified Kashins' ahead and to starboard with the 'Krivaks' astern and to port. Three Kamov Ka-25 'Hormone' helicopters preceded the fleet, carrying out a standard 'dunking' sonar sweep and listening-out for possible submarines.

The two Grummans took off from the *Eisenhower* an hour before dawn. They had a long way to go on the approach flight and the plan was to get the Soviet air defences thoroughly mystified during the run-in before attacking at first light. Both carried a brace of torpedoes and an ASM rocket pod. The Grumman with the task of attacking *Minsk* from the starboard approached on a long, lazy zig-zag, now seeming likely to pass ahead of the Soviet task force, now astern; the other one flew off on a near-semicircular course to pass astern of the task force and come up on *Minsk* from the west.

Five miles out from the target the starboard-side Grumman was welcomed by a salvo of SAMs from the 'Kresta II' and 'Modified Kashin' on that side of the screen – eight missiles in all, none of which seemed properly 'locked-on' and which proved surprisingly easy to avoid by executing flat, skidding turns – automatic gunfire would have been more dangerous. But all the pilot's skill was needed as he edged his heavily-laden Grumman closer and closer in a flattening zig-zag, flying at wavetop height with his engines throttled back as far as he dared. The other Grumman pilot was meanwhile coming in on the far side nearly 100 mph faster; and the two oddly-behaving blips on the Russian radar screens baffled the fire-control computers. There was, however, no mistaking what was coming, and *Minsk* ordered her escorts to open out in order to give the threatened carrier maximum room for evasive action.

The escorts were still carrying out this order when the two Grummans simultaneously cracked open their throttles, went into straight-and-level flight and dropped all four torpedoes simultaneously. Their timing was perfect and a narrowing chevron of torpedo tracks streaked across the sea, aimed to intersect right under *Minsk*'s clipper bow. *Minsk*'s captain went into the classic anti-torpedo parry, turning towards the torpedoes (in this case, selecting the ones coming in from the starboard) in order to 'comb their tracks'; but the carrier had only just begun its turn when the starboard-side torpedoes hit, one fair and square in the engine-room and the other under her square stern. Only three of the Yak-36 V/STOLs managed to get airborne before the doomed carrier's increasing list made further operations from the flight-deck impossible.

The triumphant Grumman pilots had meanwhile followed their drop with an inward turn that took them away down *Minsk*'s wake. Unfortunately, this escape manoeuvre also carried them within range of the rearmost escorting 'Krivak' destroyer, which put up a withering barrage of AA gunfire from its four 3-inch guns and blasted one of the Grummans out of the sky. The other was furiously set upon by the Yak-36s from *Minsk*, none of whose pilots had had any training experience in attacking such a slow and agile opponent. Constantly out-turning his enemies, the Grumman pilot held on just long enough for a quartet of F-8H Crusader fighters, catapulted from the *Eisenhower*, to arrive on the scene and make short work of the Yaks.

There was a grim postscript to the

action. In the missile age there was little future for a warship stopped dead in the water to pick up survivors, and in the Soviet Navy standing orders on the subject were draconian. Rescue work over *Minsk*'s grave was therefore left to the three 'Hormone' helicopters in the air at the time of the attack, and only about 40 survivors from *Minsk*'s complement of 2,000 were saved. The surviving warships sped north towards the Horn of Africa with the triumphant American task group in pursuit.

Three days later they were wiped out in the Gulf of Oman after a battle fought, on both sides, 'without fear and without hope'. Human ingenuity coupled with high-order technology had swept the Indian Ocean of Soviet warships. With the South African Navy already at work clearing the Russian mines from the Mozambique Channel, the tanker sealane from the Gulf to Western Europe was once more free. But with the coming of strategic nuclear warfare to the Northern Hemisphere, Europe's tanker fleets would never see home again.

The grim engagement off Oman was only the first of a series of sea battles in which 'victory' and 'defeat' had lost their traditional meaning.

Much of the peacetime navies' *raison d'être* had been deterrence, but could their undoubted combat efficiency do much to change the course of Norld War 3, once that conflict flared out into its brief and terrible life? Nowhere was this question posed more urgently than in the Mediterranean, as the rival fleets fought their first and last battle.

'To deter, but if deterrence fails, to fight' had always been a fundamental motto of NATO's military existence. For more than a generation the US Sixth Fleet had patrolled the Mediterranean at the southern extremity of the NATO line. And in its deterrent role the Sixth Fleet had always been seen to have a full range of capabilities appropriate to the area, from small US Marine Corps boat units to the ability to fly nuclear air strikes.

One obvious strategic task of the Fleet was to help the Greek and Turkish armies repel any Warsaw Pact attempt to thrust to the Mediterranean coast, and, more particularly, to the Dardanelles. At one time the Sixth Fleet could only have been opposed by submarines and shore-based aircraft, but over the years the Soviet Navy had built up a formidable Mediterranean fleet of its own. Now the fight was on.

NATO'S CONFLICTING PRIORITIES

The Sixth Fleet Commander, flying his flag in the aircraft-carrier USS *John F. Kennedy,* took his orders from the C-in-C of NATO's Southern Region, the latter also acting as the Fleet Commander's national superior in the chain of command for nuclear release extending from the office of the American President. This saddled the American admiral with the following sequence of priorities:

● Land the leading elements of a Marine Amphibious Brigade in conjunction with Italian and Spanish troops as reinforcements for Allied Forces South-East Europe and as evidence of Allied solidarity (a well-practised NATO manoeuvre);
● Give air support to the Turkish Army;
● Give specialized air support, as requested, to the NATO forces in Germany;
● *Lastly*, to deal with the Soviet warships in the Mediterranean.

Naturally the American admiral would have preferred to tackle the last task first; but in his final deployments he resolved these conflicting priorities as best he could.

● The Amphibious Group, led by the command ship USS *Mount Whitney* and including the Amphibious Assault Ships USS *Nassau* and *Inchon*, was deployed to the selected landing area in Turkish Thrace. Both the latter ships had AV-8 Harrier aircraft embarked and these would have to suffice for immediate needs. (Air defence was not likely to be crucial. Warsaw Pact aircraft would have to pass through the NATO Air Defence Region to reach the ships, and no bases on the North African coast were available to Soviet aircraft.) Italian and Spanish warships were directed to reinforce the escort provided for ASW and other tasks needed for the protection of the Amphibious Group;

● To support the Turkish Army, two squadrons of medium-attack A-6 Intruders should be flown off to make an initial show of force in the eastern frontier area, one squadron from *John F. Kennedy* and the other from her elderly partner USS *Independence*. This would leave one medium squadron and two A-7 Corsair light-attack squadrons in each ship to tackle the Soviet surface fleet;

● Pairs of Tomcat fighters from the *Kennedy* were to be flown north to Germany as requested, and rotated so that one pair could always remain on station.

The biggest worry was the variety and range of the anti-ship missiles in the Soviet fleet. The first objective was therefore to reduce the number of aircraft of all types which might provide these missiles with in-flight guidance or other information.

The main sources of these aircraft were the V/STOL carrier *Kiev* and the helicopter-carrier *Moskva*. Good information was available on *Kiev*'s movements and a strike was launched against her, using the four squadrons of Corsairs in a co-ordinated attack. This seemed to have paid off, although the attacking aircraft suffered heavily in achieving their objective; the Soviet Navy's first aircraft-carrier was sunk in her first engagement, and severe damage was caused to a 'Kynda' class guided-missile cruiser and two 'Kanin' class destroyers in the same group.

But these early successes did not give rise to much euphoria in the Sixth Fleet. Even without the potential of their surface consorts, everyone knew what a tough proposition the Soviet submarines in the area were likely to prove.

The Soviet reply began when one of the destroyers on the Fleet ASW screen, USS *Moosbrugger*, was hit by a missile and sank within minutes. As a matter of standard procedure selected ships in the force immediately fired chaff projectiles, which ejected foil strips to confuse any other missiles launched. At least two more missiles were believed to have been frustrated by the chaff, and an hour later two more were shot down by two ships on the screen fitted with the ASMD close-range anti-missile system based on Sea Sparrow. More satisfactory still was the report from a Sea King helicopter that she was in contact with a submarine.

The Fleet altered course to the southward to clear the scene and two frigates, USS *Capodanno* and *Donald B. Beery*, were detached to join in the hunt, the latter flying off her own helicopter to assist the Sea King.

This was only the beginning of a drawn-out mortal combat: a battle in which the great Sixth Fleet faced certain decimation and probable destruction for the technical 'achievement of the objective': holding the Turkish Straits. Some might call it a futile struggle, but after all there was a precedent, and a precedent established in these same waters 40 years before. As his fleet was progressively shredded to near-extinction during the Battle of Crete in 1941, the British Admiral Cunningham had signalled to his ships: 'The Army is just holding its own against constant reinforcement . . . we *must* not let them down. At whatever cost to ourselves, we must land reinforcements and keep the enemy from using the sea.' Cunningham had also reminded the battered and exhausted British fleet that 'It takes three years to build a ship. It takes three hundred to build a tradition'. And another, earlier voice could be heard, urging on the present custodians of the tradition built upon his words: 'We have not begun to fight'.

The first message needed by all NATO warships, surface and sub-surface, was the national order to 'chop' to NATO commands. The word 'chop' in this naval context signified the formal assignment of forces from one Allied commander to another, with logistic support for the units involved remaining a national responsibility. As soon as it could be spared from the GIUK Gap, STANAVFORLANT was 'chopped' to the operational control of SACEUR so that its ships could fit into the pattern of coastal operations off north Norway. Two Royal Marine Commandos, 45 and 42, were already deployed in the Norwegian frontier zone in readiness for the time-honoured ritual of the 'Northern Lights' annual summer exercises.

Tremendous advantages had accrued to the Royal Marine Commandos in the very recent past. The first were the very handsome allocations of anti-tank and AA weapons which had transformed the Commandos' order of battle. The second was the ready availability of air power in the shape of Sea Harriers V/STOLs flown from the support carrier HMS *Bulwark* and the aged cruiser HMS *Tiger*. The combined resources of the two ships were not impressive numerically, but both friend and foe took note of these reinforcements for the Allied air support group now at Bardufoss and Bodö, long in advance of any kind of heavy carrier support.

Like the Far North, the Baltic area no longer attracted the might of the Strike Fleet Atlantic with its huge carriers, but there were other cards for SACLANT to play in support of his land colleague SACEUR. As the Russian land forces rolled forward, well-practised NATO reinforcement options were put in hand. Under the operational command of CINCEASTLANT at Northwood, a brigade of US Marines was landed in southern Denmark and a British air portable brigade was put into Schleswig-Holstein. A mixed airborne drop from the old US 82nd Airborne Division and the resurrected British 16th Parachute Brigade spearheaded both these flank attacks and gave them both brief security in the landing areas. The prompt arrival of such well-equipped mobile anti-tank forces was greatly appreciated by the hard-pressed *Bundeswehr* and again helped restore inter-allied confidence so grievously sapped over the past months.

The safe delivery and support of seaborne elements, and the air cover furnished from the sea, were perhaps the most important contribution of the modern navies to conventional war. Specialized ships carried men and vehicles, or V/STOLs and helicopters, or both, and they were the result of a minor revolution. This revolution had enabled more ships to be produced within limited budgets, by improvising from commercial hulls and accepting small units in each package, replacing the old commando ships and assault ships of the Royal Navy with smaller hulls. The more generous resources of the USA had produced the *Tarawa* and *Iwo Jima* classes of assault ships their Sea Stallion helicopters and Harrier V/STOLs, and such ships were both designed and available for just the sort of quick-response operations called for by the present situation.

Casualties were soon suffered, and USS *Da Nang* did not survive her first full commission. She sank in the North Sea after being hit by two missiles, apparently from a Soviet submarine from the Soviet Northern Fleet.

The origin of that submarine – sent to the bottom by a German submarine soon after the sinking of *Da Nang* – lay in the absence of 'reinforcements' from the Soviet Baltic Fleet. Part of the significance of the land battle in north-western Germany lay in the defence of NATO's blockade of the Baltic exits. Minefields and obstacles on land or at sea should always be covered by fire for as long as possible, as the Royal

Navy had found to its cost at the Dardanelles nearly 70 years before. At the same time, however, Soviet commanders were being urged to clear the land flank and prize open the exits, all of which drew off resources from the main forward thrust.

Thus the Allied navies, for all their slender lines of communication, had played a vital part in denying the Warsaw Pact a bloodless victory with its 'police action'. The most successful demonstration of Allied solidarity, the European naval force had more than fulfilled its promise. But in so doing it had helped bring forward the moment when World War 3 moved forward from conventional to nuclear war.

By D+2 the impressive NATO Strike Force Atlantic had taken over from the light units of STANAVFORLANT along the GIUK Gap, ready to meet the expected mass challenge of the 200-odd Soviet submarines expected to break into the North Atlantic.

Gone were the days when NATO had been forced to rely on air patrols and sonobuoys to watch for Russian submarines. There was now a complex web of electronic surveillance posts – airborne, shipborne, and underwater – which furnished SACLANT with ample data. The problem, however, remained the numbers available to the enemy, which might well swamp the Allied systems. On one occasion in the 1970s the Soviet Navy had put a mere 60 submarines into the North Atlantic during a NATO exercise, and only the most strenuous efforts managed to keep them all covered.

By D+3 the entire GIUK line was a frantic scene of AS activity with practically every NATO helicopter in the air, at the end of 'dunking' sonars and hunting down submarine contacts. The Russians had begun with a 'first wave' of 80 submarines, all of their older and noisier (to sonar) classes, which predictably stretched NATO resources to their limits. Once the submarine countermeasures were under way a 'second wave' of 30 came streaking through the Atlantic entrances, faster and quieter than the first. Nearly all of these broke through to the open Atlantic and prepared for offensive operations, granted an interminable endurance by virtue of their nuclear reactors.

The first of the emergency RESCUE ('Reinforcement Emergency Services Convoy Unto Europe') had sailed from the St Lawrence amazingly early, on the evening of D+5: 18 15-knot freighters crammed with replacement missiles and aircraft spares being virtually press-ganged by the US Coast Guards from the Chesapeake to the St Lawrence, the latter only just freed from the winter ice. The American carrier *Midway* and six A/S frigates formed the escort for this stage of the convoy, which had been designated RES-1.

The story of RES-1 forms what is probably the most heartbreaking naval story of World War 3. Long before it was even halfway across the Atlantic – D+10 – the circumstances prevailing when the convoy was formed and loaded no longer existed. The NATO front had been buckling when RES-1 sailed; by D+10 it lay seared and shrivelled after the exchange of over 50 tactical nuclear weapons. Land fighting continued, though with little or no cohesion, and France was now the last NATO bastion in Western Europe. Units of the French Navy sailed to meet RES-1 and bring the convoy into St Nazaire, the designated reception port; but only eight of the merchantmen ever saw the French coast. The others had fallen victim to Soviet 'Charlie' class submarines, recklessly expended in a war that was now fighting itself. The war at sea had come down to the massive hulls of the strategic missile submarines, hidden in the Arctic pack or beneath the open oceans, hurling their ICBMs into the fiery ruin of the Northern Hemisphere.

E F GUERITZ
RICHARD HUMBLE

15. DOOMSDAY

Between the long focus generalizations of destruction per megaton, and the close-up observation of the fate of individuals based on the experience of Hiroshima and Nagasaki and nuclear test programmes, there lie vast uncharted regions in our understanding of nuclear war. What a nuclear attack of even moderate heaviness would mean for *society* is anyone's guess and as much the domain of science fiction as of science, with the one proviso that what is postulated for society should be consistent with what is known for a fact. Whatever the literary merits of *On The Beach*, Nevil Shute's celebrated novel of nuclear war, his particular guess about postwar society is in the end uninteresting as prediction because he wrongly believed radioactive fallout from a nuclear war in the Northern Hemisphere would spread quickly and substantially to the Southern Hemisphere. In fact there is very little mixing between the two halves of the atmosphere, and it was a surprising mistake for someone with Shute's scientific background to make.

This chapter's context is little more than a restatement of what can be said for a fact about nuclear war. The only justification for going over this narrow ground again is that popular ignorance of what these facts are shows that previous attempts to educate have been ineffective. The reason for this may possibly be indifference, but it is more likely to have been due to the over-technical language of the few accurate accounts that have been attempted. It matters that these facts become better understood if only because no more than a minority of any population will be killed in the first hours of even the heaviest plausible nuclear attack, and the rest will depend in part on their already having some understanding of the peculiar risks to life presented by the highly radioactive dust that will settle like windblown sand hundreds of miles downwind from the centre of gravity of a strategic nuclear attack.

One of the unknowns about nuclear war is whether, once begun, it can be managed and confined in some way through bargaining between the belligerents. If it cannot, we need concern ourselves only about one kind of nuclear war, one where the participants exhaust their nuclear stockpiles in massive attacks against all targets previously identified as worthy of attack. This all-out kind of war will produce about the same degree of devastation whatever the pace at which it is conducted, within reasonable limits. Compressed into a few hours, there will be comparatively little opportunity for putting together any kind of measure to protect populations, but at the same time there will be some squandering of stockpiles on targets already hit or no longer worth hitting, such as empty silos from which ICBMs have already been fired. Spread over days or even weeks the attack will be more efficient, but some protective and adaptive measures are likely to have been instituted in the meantime (always assuming the minimum of public order required to implement these measures can be maintained).

If nuclear war can be confined, there is naturally an infinity of possible stopping places short of the extremities of devastation, but of these, two are of special interest for they correspond to stopping places for which the United States, at least, has already made plans. One is a nuclear war limited to attacks made on military installations (airfields, missile silos, submarine bases) actually within the territory of the superpowers themselves. The other is a nuclear war limited to the battlefield use of nuclear weapons, in particular a war in Europe where conventional and nuclear weapons are yoked together in order to achieve some kind of decision in a contest between armies.

Both types of limited nuclear war are interesting, partly because wars are sometimes fought to plan and partly because each type does possess natural features favouring limitation. Limitation is favoured when there is a shared incentive not to exceed the limits; and limitation is practicable when the exercise of restraint (or not) is clearly discernable to the parties involved. An incentive not to exceed the limits is just another way of speaking about deterrence. A limited strategic nuclear war may stay limited because each side is aware that redirecting its attack from military installations to cities will meet with retaliation in kind: a battlefield nuclear war may remain at battlefield level because each superpower is deterred from striking directly at the territory of the other. In neither instance will the distinction between what is being done and what is consciously being avoided be perfectly clear. As we shall see, radioactive fallout from limited nuclear attacks is likely to reach cities many miles downwind in potentially lethal amounts, and a tactical nuclear war in Europe will be fought on the fields and in and around the cities of the European allies of the superpowers.

Yet the lines American planners see as dividing a contained war from an uncontained one can reasonably be described as thresholds, stopping places of universal significance as readily appreciated, in principle at any rate, by a Russian as by an American; imperfect, certainly, but much more likely to be converged upon and far less arbitrary than alternatives based upon the accumulation of a particular amount of destruction, without regard to where or of what kind.

One possibility is an accident, either due to mechanical failure or the unauthorized action of an individual. A missile once launched cannot be recalled, and unless a remotely controllable self-destruction device has been implanted there is nothing to prevent it proceeding to its targets and destroying them (a high proportion of modern US ICBMs and SLBMs carry multiple warheads which in some instances at least are pre-programmed to land on widely separate targets; the Soviet Union is beginning to adopt the same technique).

Even if the victim of the accident were convinced that it *was* an accident, there would be a natural anxiety to obtain some compensation or redress. A loss of a million or so dead (and, if the accidental attack had focused on New York or Moscow, the destruction of an important centre of governmental, commercial and cultural activity) might be great enough to weaken the authority with which the injured party could demand redress, and embolden the party 'responsible' for the accident to resist any demand.

There would be no obviously evenhanded way of arranging compensation, even if the unharmed party were prepared to concede a generous settlement. A fine, amounting to a transfer of resources to the cost of rebuilding the destroyed property, would be sensible if properly disinterested and sufficiently authoritative arbiters could be found to pass judgement on the amount. A settlement of account by a retaliatory strike of equivalent destructiveness might be less sensible but could be the choice of a shocked government in the first minutes or hours after the accident. That could not seem a wholly reasonable act to the government responsible for the accident, however, and it would be unlikely to agree with the aggrieved party's definition of what constituted an equivalent target. Delay and due consideration by the aggrieved party would improve the chances of a 'sensible' settlement but would put the government responsible for the accident in a quandary about what precautionary moves to take in the meantime. It would seem obvious to evacuate the largest cities, if only to keep panic under control; but behaviour of this kind could persuade the aggrieved party that an attempt was under weigh to deny it justice, even that further nuclear strikes were being planned.

Enough has probably been said to show that a nuclear accident is something to be taken seriously. The public acts of government to contain the consequences of any accidentally launched nuclear attack include, most notably, the 1971 Soviet-American agreement to get in touch when an accidental launch has, or appears to have, been made. The United States has instituted admirable precautions against human error in the command and control of its bomber and ICBM forces, though what has been done with respect to its submarine forces is more of a mystery. The Soviet Union has taken the opportunity presented by the terms of the 1972 treaty with the United States on the deployment of anti-missile defences to build a ring of anti-missile defences around Moscow, which could probably cope with a light accidental ballistic missile attack on that city. It may be that more has been done. Remotely controllable self-destruction devices may have been implanted in missile warheads, but secretly so as to discourage the other side from looking for ways to trigger them deliberately, although they too would be capable of failure.

A more familiar and far more extensively explored route to the outbreak of nuclear war is through the failure of deterrence or, more accurately, the failure of some part of the supporting framework upon which deterrence is believed to rest.

The intervening stage between the failure of deterrence and the outbreak of nuclear war is an interlude, which may be very brief, of substantial advantage accruing to the side that strikes the first blow of the war. This might arise through a previous failure of third-level deterrence: a growth in the ability of one side to strike at the retaliatory forces of the other to which the disadvantaged side had failed to react. Both sides would then have an incentive to go to war quickly. The advantaged side would secure a winning position if it struck first; and the disadvantaged side would be *relatively* better off if it struck first, not to obtain victory but to avoid defeat.

The present condition of third-level deterrence makes a central nuclear war between the Soviet Union and the United States, as a direct result of its failure, seem rather improbable.

In Europe the story is different. The interlude of substantial advantage to the side striking the first nuclear blow might arise in peacetime; but once a conventionally fought war had already broken out it would be almost inescapable.

The side that was the most hard pressed would presumably be presented with two tempting classes of target for its tactical nuclear weapons: the airfields, missile launchers (and for a Warsaw Pact strike on NATO, aircraft-carriers) from which a retaliatory tactical nuclear strike could be launched, and, equally important, the concentrations of conventional force that were precisely what was making conventional resistance difficult.

The side that was coming out of the purely conventional war best, on the other hand, would be anxious to deny its opponent this rewarding recourse to TNW and would aim to forestall it by attacking the other side's airfields and missile launchers before they could be used in a TNW attack. The conventionally superior side might contemplate using conventional weapons for this pre-emptive attack, but since anything less than complete success would trigger a TNW response, there would be little reason for such restraint.

If the conventionally inferior side got

his TNW blows in first something approaching a stalemate might ensue. Additional TNW will no doubt be brought into play from reserve forces at sea, in the case of NATO, or from bases inside the Soviet Union, though some husbanding of stocks will become evident. Conventional reinforcements will be organized and their assembly points at Channel ports and other ports on both sides of the Atlantic, and within the Soviet Union, will be touchstones for the future of the war. If they are not attacked, the limitation of the war to the region from the Soviet Western border to somewhere not very far west of the Rhine will be virtually assured. If they are attacked the risk of an all-out nuclear exchange, involving the superpowers together with Britain and France, will be substantially heightened.

THE FALLOUT FACTOR

By this time the war zone will have become heavily contaminated with radioactive fallout emitting hazardous gamma rays (a particularly penetrating form of X-ray). Infantry operations in the open will be impossible for several days at a time, except in narrow corridors of country where local weather and geography will have reduced contamination to safe levels. The dimensions of these corridors will obviously fluctuate for as long as nuclear bursts continue to be made, but aerial mappings of the extent of safe terrain can be quickly and accurately carried out. Whether these corridors will have any strategic value will depend very much on their width and how far they penetrate beyond the prewar boundaries of the belligerents.

The traditional dugout or slit trench will, even in highly contaminated areas, provide infantry with adequate protection against fallout gamma rays, which are effectively stopped by 3 or 4 feet of earth or sandbags. In theory, there would be no great difficulty in keeping a network of trenches supplied from the air. And even artillery operations could be maintained if the pieces were placed in sunken areas cleared of the radioactive topsoil. In practice, any return to static or quasi-static war would be made unlikely by the free rein still available to tanks and aircraft, neither of which will be restricted to low contamination corridors. For the most part, tank armour will be thick enough and aircraft will fly high and fast enough to stop gamma radiation from reaching their crews.

Operations at sea will be much less hampered by radioactivity. Vessels that remain afloat will be free to sail in any direction provided they are hosed down periodically to wash away the radioactive dust that will settle on the superstructure and upper decks from land and sea nuclear bursts upwind. Ships in coastal waters in the eastern Mediterranean are likely to find repeated hose downs necessary in the first (and presumably most intense) days of a European nuclear war, given the direction of the prevailing winds. Any reversal in wind direction will reverse the process; nuclear bursts as part of the war at sea will produce radioactive fallout of their own, in land, in the form of contaminated (and salty) rain.

If the conventionally weaker side did get its nuclear blow in first – and it is likely, though not certain, that it will be the NATO forces that will find holding their own in a purely conventional war difficult – to a first approximation the result will be to equalize the contest and at the same time change its rules, temporarily redefining mobile warfare for both sides within the narrower limits set by the extent of radioactive contamination. Provided the war had in the meanwhile not extended to the territory of any of the nuclear powers involved (radioactive fallout will almost certainly have drifted over the western part of the Soviet Union, but it may not be too intense to be lived with), both sides might feel that further hostilities had little to offer and a ceasefire might at this point be negotiated. This seems to be about the best outcome NATO planners could reasonably hope for.

If, however, the European nuclear war has begun by the conventionally superior side getting its nuclear blow in first, the regional military imbalance will have been accentuated. Defeat for the weaker side will now be just around the corner; although some delay might be imposed on the superior side by radioactive contamination of the territory whose occupation would be the usual consequence of victory. In all probability, we are talking here of a Warsaw Pact victory, and another turning-point in the nature of the war. The British and the French strategic nuclear forces would be of no significance at this point (except in so far as they are always of significance in denying the Soviet Union a cheap surrender-or-else option); they could not credibly be used to deter a march by Warsaw Pact forces to the Channel or beyond by threatening attacks on Soviet cities, since the Soviet response would be devastating. Only the United States could act to prevent the Warsaw Pact gathering in the fruits of victory, by threatening strategic nuclear strikes against Soviet targets if the Pact armies advanced beyond some designated line on the map.

This threat, if successful, could not operate indefinitely. If it could, there would have been little point in NATO maintaining conventional forces in being at any time since 1949. For the line to hold the Americans would have to organize a rapid reinforcement of NATO conventional forces from whatever reserves remained on either side of the Atlantic. This would be NATO's second best hope.

If the threat was ignored, containment of the nuclear war to Europe would be at an end and a strategic nuclear war will have begun, unless the American threat turned out to be bluff. If the threat had been ignored because it had been assumed the Americans were bluffing, and this assumption proved false, the Pact forces might still be prevented from invading by a small scale American strategic nuclear attack on Soviet targets, launched probably by ICBMs, the intended effect of which would largely be psychological, communicating to the Soviet government that the Americans were fairly desperate and ready to run risks to achieve their objective.

But a small strike would indeed be risky. If the threat had been ignored simply because the Soviets believed they could absorb the largest blow the Americans would dare to strike, mindful that the heavier they struck, the heavier the Soviets would strike back, Warsaw Pact forces will presumably press on into Western Europe and a measured Soviet retaliatory strike will be launched against American targets. The size of the Soviet retaliation will be governed not only by the weight of the American first strike, but also by its effectiveness.

If the American strike had demonstrated that, for instance, 30 warheads launched by ten Minuteman III ICBMs were capable of putting out of action 15 or 20 Soviet ICBMs, the Soviets will not be inclined to leave many of their remaining ICBMs in their silos as sitting targets for the second wave of American attack that would probably follow their measured response. And for a war in the near future, fought by forces resembling those in service in 1978, ICBMs will be precious to the Soviets, since they account for 64% of the destructive capacity of the entire Soviet intercontinental nuclear force (American ICBMs carry 22%). If a discriminating, small-scale, American strike has its dangers an undiscriminating strike could be as bad. If Soviet cities were hit directly, or affected by radioactive fallout from strikes on military targets, the Soviets would be less strongly motivated to avoid American cities in their counter to the American strike.

If the above paragraph is broadly correct, it follows that the United States will not be able to afford the luxury of a shot across Soviet bows that a small, precisely executed, attack on Soviet ICBM silos or bomber airfields would correspond to; its own remaining ICBM force would be too much at risk from Soviet retaliation. Less would be left to chance, it would be more prudent, if the American will to resist a Soviet victory in Europe were communicated by a comprehensive attack on as many Soviet ICBM silos and airfields as possible.

Whether this would mean harming civilian targets is, as we see below, partly a technical matter depending on the yield, accuracy, and burst height of the American attack, and partly a political matter for the Soviet government to decide how blind an eye it could turn. The ingredients of a settlement would now be available. The strategic nuclear advantage would be with the United States, since it would have ICBMs in reserve while the Soviets had lost most of theirs; the advantage in conventional forces would be with the Soviets, with stretches of Western Europe under occupation. This would be NATO's third best hope.

Of course, it is right to ask why the Soviets should allow themselves to be manoeuvred into having to negotiate and surrender part or all of their gains. It would be more consistent with Soviet doctrine on nuclear war for them to fight a nuclear war as an indivisable entity incapable of compartmentalization into tactical or strategic kinds. This would suggest (allowing for some dilution of doctrine by common sense) that their initiation of tactical nuclear war in Europe will be timed to coincide with an ICBM attack on American ICBM silos and bomber airfields (but, again, carefully avoiding population centres).

Four things suggest that however doctrinally sound this may seem, it is not part of Soviet thinking, or at least, not yet:

● Soviet hostility to American feelers that a capacity to fight a limited strategic nuclear war is worth having;

● The large megatonnage and indifferent accuracy of Soviet ICBM warheads which would produce intense radioactive fallout over thousands of square miles downwind of American ICBM silos, resulting in heavy casualties in urban areas;

● The small proportion of the American retaliatory force based on ICBMs;

● The large proportion of available Soviet megatonnage that a reasonably successful attack on American ICBMs would consume.

The precariousness of limited nuclear war is evident and is a common theme in any forecast of how it might come about; at every stage there will be arguments for going to greater extremes. Once the submarine nuclear forces of either side come into play, for instance, there are technical reasons for thinking that restraint will become almost impossible. If a single missile launch from a submarine is enough to give away its position, as seems to be the case, prudence will require that submarines fire in broadsides, 16 (or in the new American Triton class, 24) launchers at a go, carrying 160 warheads. Their targets will be cities; by the time submarine forces enter the war, airfields and ICBM silos will already have been hit or not be worth hitting, since we can expect the most vulnerable nuclear weapons to be used first.

This account of a European war and its extra-European implications is semifactual, and conventional where it cannot be factual. It is possible that the Warsaw Pact armies are a paper tiger; their equipment always seems to be at least half a generation behind the best Western kind, and the fighting qualities of their conscript armies and inexperienced navies are largely untested. It is possible that Soviet nuclear forces are strong on paper only. The reliability of their ICBMs and bombers may be low, as low as the reliability of their com-

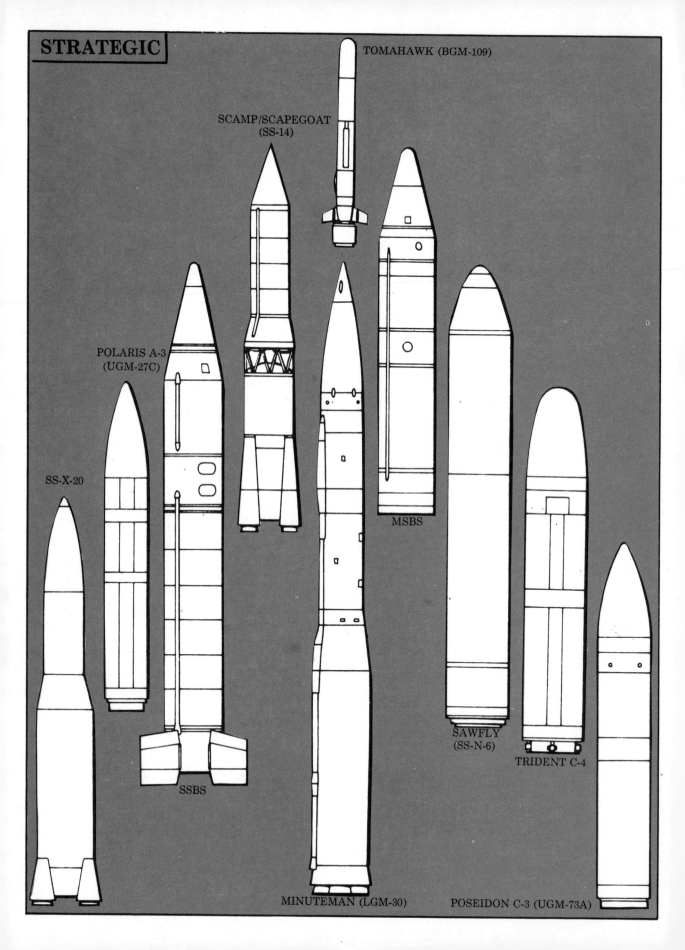

STRATEGIC

TOMAHAWK (BGM-109)

SCAMP/SCAPEGOAT
(SS-14)

POLARIS A-3
(UGM-27C)

SS-X-20

MSBS

SAWFLY
(SS-N-6)

TRIDENT C-4

SSBS

MINUTEMAN (LGM-30)   POSEIDON C-3 (UGM-73A)

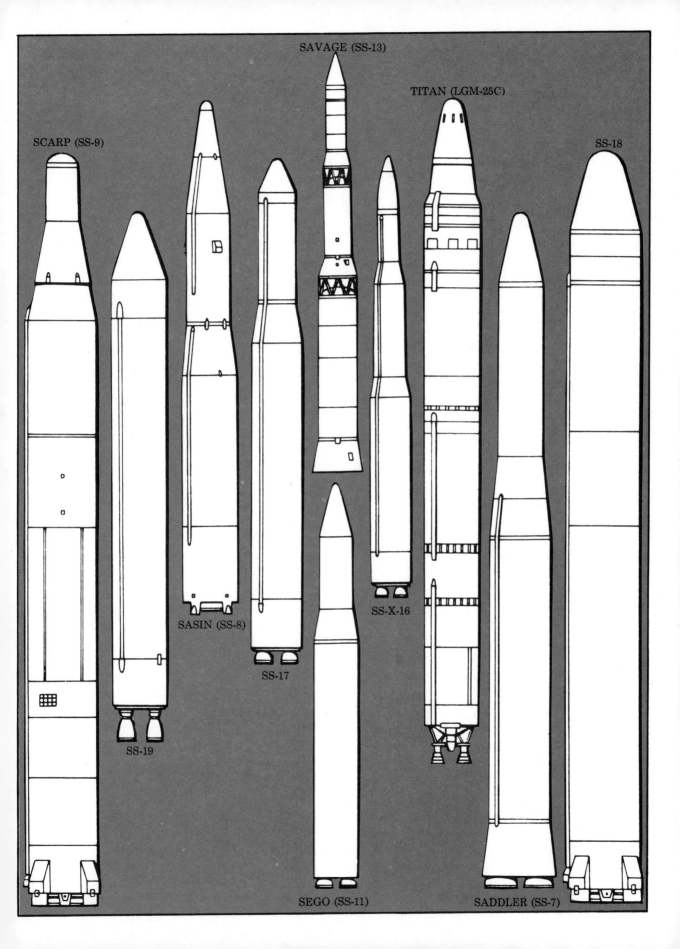

mercial airliners is known to be. The backwardness of Soviet micro-electronics may mean their command and control of ICBM and SLBM launchings is full of holes, and vulnerable to disruptive attack. The motors of their missile-carrying submarines may be as noisy as they were at the time of the Cuban missile crisis, which means Soviet submarines can be easily tracked by the listening apparatus of the other side and sunk at will. The Soviet military communications network may have been penetrated by Western intelligence and codes broken, something likely to have as influential an effect on the next European war as Allied interception of German communications had on the last. These are the kinds of 'surprises' whose omission makes a conventional account of how a European war will be fought unreliable, and whose incorporation any unconventional account capricious.

It has already been mentioned that a factual description of the effects a nuclear attack would have on society is impossible. The reason for this is that there is nothing we know of that nuclear war would sufficiently resemble. Allied bombing of Germany in World War 2 was spread over six years and amounted in total to less than one and a half megatons (of conventional bombs). A Soviet attack on American cities (or vice versa) could be over in six hours and use five or six hundred megatons. The simple comparison of megatonnage understates the relative damage done to Germany, but not by very much.

It is relatively easy, on the other hand, to be precise about the physically destructive effects of a single nuclear detonation, and it is equally possible to make a tally of the deaths and destruction caused by the burst of several hundred nuclear weapons, spaced across the length of a country.

The effects of a single nuclear burst depend upon three factors: its megatonnage or yield; the proportion of its yield derived from the fission process; and, least obvi-ously, on the height above the surface of the earth at which it is exploded.

The yield of the explosion is the principal indicator of the strength of the immediate effects of the explosion, those occurring within a minute or so from the time of the burst. The fission contribution to the yield, and the height of the explosion together determine the strength of its delayed effect, the radioactive fallout.

The immediate destructive effects of a nuclear burst increase with yield but not in direct proportion. For yields up to about ten megatons each eightfold increase in yield increases the area subject to destruction by four times (125 kilotons: 1 megaton: 8 megatons – 1:4:16). Beyond ten megatons even greater increases in yield are required to produce fourfold increases in area destroyed. The strength of the delayed effects, however, for a given design of weapon, rises pretty well in direct proportion to the yield.

The immediate effects are of three kinds; the blast wave, the pulse of heat from the fireball, and the initial nuclear radiation.

The blast wave and the heat pulse carry away most of the energy of the burst. The initial nuclear radiation, made up of neutrons and gamma rays (basically similar to those emitted by radioactive fallout), is given off directly by the nuclear processes responsible for the explosion. Radioactive fallout, appearing several hours later, if at all, is from the debris left over at the end of the nuclear processes that produced the explosion and is dangerous as a temporary emitter of gamma rays. Initial nuclear radiation has a shorter range than the blast and heat effects, except for very low yield bursts. At Hiroshima and Nagasaki, after 20-kiloton bursts, blast and heat accounted for many more casualties than neutrons and gamma rays. There were survivors with symptoms of radiation illness but they recovered for the most part. Any shelter that gives its occupants protection from the blast and heat effects of bursts of 20 kilotons and above will automatically shield them also from initial nuclear radiation. The inapplicability of this statement to smaller bursts is the basis of the so-called neutron bomb: nor does it apply to shielding from radioactive fallout, which can carry hundreds of miles and be a threat to life at points so far distant from the explosion for people to be unaware that an explosion had occurred.

The destruction caused by blast and heat on an inhabited area is normally a compound, greater than the sum of its parts, of the destructive effects of each singly. There are exceptions. In open areas on clear days the heat flash can be biologically harmful out to distances far beyond the point where blast had become insignificant: persons actually looking at the point of the burst can have their retinas permanently damaged, although the impairment of sight that would result would not be severe. It is also possible, in similarly clear conditions, for the heat flash to start fires in areas too far out for blast to matter, but this would depend upon their being somewhat artificial concentrations of highly combustible material lying out in the open. Closer to the point of burst, largely within the area exposed to blast induced pressure (overpressure) of five pounds per square inch (5 psi) or greater, blast and heat work together.

The heat flash comes first and starts fires by setting alight curtain materials, upholstery, clothing – anything inflammable not shaded from the flash. The blast wave follows, demolishing most buildings of normal construction within the 5 psi zone. It is accompanied by winds which even out at the 5 psi point (ten miles from a ten megaton burst) will be travelling at 160 miles per hour: at the 15 psi point, five miles closer in, winds will reach 350 miles per hour. Fragments of buildings – bricks and glass – will be picked up in the wind and thrown against whatever is in their path. Many casualties will be caused by this urban shrapnel alone. Buildings that are damaged by the blast but still standing will form the nuclei of fires; gas mains will be burst open, oil tanks will be split and wooden beams will be exposed. Fires will be most intense in areas of densest habitation and least serious in the more spacious suburbs, partly because of the firebreak effect of space between buildings and partly because a neatly-tended, freshly-painted neighbourhood is less vulnerable to fires begun by the heat flash, or so Nevada test site experiments seem to show. The so-called 'firestorm' seen in World War 2 is not expected to be a typical result of nuclear attack on a modern city, whose building materials are less combustible and whose building regulations are more strict than those of the mediaeval towns that saw the worst fire-storms of World War 2.

Curiously, under certain circumstances, evasive action can be taken by alert individuals even after the nuclear burst has occurred. For very large bursts (10 megatons), the heat flash is spread over a few seconds, and people in the open will have time to shield themselves from burns by looking away. The blast wave (at 5 psi) will take half a minute or more to reach buildings ten miles away. Individuals inside might possibly have time to go down into a basement in the time between the flash of the burst and the blast wave striking. Smaller bursts (20 kilotons) produce briefer head flashes of a tenth of a second or so during which time no evasive action will be possible, but for a city-dweller in the open, the two or three seconds between the flash and 5 psi blast wave (a mile from a 20 kiloton burst) will be long enough for him to fall to the ground (facing towards or away from the point of the explosion) which will give him some protection from the urban shrapnel.

Destruction within the '5 psi zone' will be massive. Falling masonry will block streets, and fire-fighting services, even if they survive, will be unable to get to burning buildings. Here and there buildings of particularly robust construction will be left standing, protected from fire by the firebreak created around them by the demolition of flimsier structures. A proportion of the population within the 5 psi zone will survive even a surprise attack. In round figures a third to a half of the population within the 5 psi zone will be killed: the proportion will be smaller for a city built on uneven terrain – where hilly areas shelter the folds from blast and heat flash. If the population of inner London was evenly distributed in concentric circles around St Paul's, a 1 megaton explosion above St Paul's, producing a 5 psi zone ranging over 80 square miles, would kill some 3-400,000 in a surprise attack. In an actual attack, deaths will be fewer because of the low population of the city centre and the irregular distribution of population with distance from the centre.

So far we have assumed that the nuclear burst takes place at or near the height that produces the maximum amount of blast damage on the ground. Very high bursts produce no blast damage at all; bursts very near ground level (surface bursts) do produce considerable blast damage but because the blast wave is not reflected from the surface, blast damage at some distance from the point of the explosion is less than if the burst had been higher, when a wide region is exposed, not only to the direct blast wave but to the lethal echo of the reflected wave as well. Extensive targets, like cities, are then most efficiently struck by bursts at a height that maximizes the area underneath subject to destructive blast. Small targets, such as missile silos, are most efficiently struck by bursts nearer the ground, when the maximum overpressure at a particular point – on the ground – is what is wanted, and the nearer the point the better.

When a burst takes place at the optimum height for the destruction of an ex-

tended target, the fireball of the explosion does not touch the ground. This has the extremely important consequence that all the radioactive debris of the nuclear explosion is carried into the upper atmosphere where it stays for weeks rather than days, and returns to earth, not only very much less radioactive than before because of radioactive decay, but also spread extremely thinly over several continents. (As a useful rule of thumb, strongly radioactive isotopes in the debris decay quickly, and present no danger to health in a few weeks; weakly radioactive elements take much longer to decay, hundreds or thousands of years, but are never a serious health hazard).

The danger to life from this long-term fallout (to be distinguished from the short-term fallout associated with surface bursts) is exclusively from two radioactive isotopes (strontium 90 and caesium 137), whose decay is both moderately slow and moderately harmful. Neither is much of a threat outside the body but they can become a danger when eaten. Strontium mimicks calcium, potassium, and both are taken up by the roots of plants and find their way into the human food chain. Caesium is a gamma ray emitter and attacks internal organs and fairly indiscriminately; strontium concentrates in the bones. The moderate radioactivity of both at such close range to living tissue can cause damage, notably genetic in the case of caesium and bone cancer in the case of strontium, the latter probably the more serious because of the tendency of the body to retain strontium for very long periods. It should be noted, however, that thousands of megatons of fission explosions would be needed before people would inevitably carry concentrations of strontium 90 in their bodies greater than that reckoned currently to be safe for workers in industries exposed to this kind of hazard – which is not to say it would be perfectly safe.

Bursts at optimum height for the destruction of cities then, have the oddly conventional property of causing deaths and destruction almost exclusively as a result of blast and fire. The radioactive debris is carried more or less safely into the upper atmosphere and the pulse of initial nuclear radiation of neutrons and gamma rays is of such short range (for 20 kiloton bursts and greater) as to add very little to the deaths already caused by the physical effects of the burst. The secondary radioactivity in the soil and debris of collapsed and burning buildings close to the point directly underneath the burst, induced by the pulse of neutrons and gamma rays, decays to harmless levels in a few hours. The bombs at Hiroshima and Nagasaki were exploded at or near optimum height, and as we have seen, survivors of the physical effects of these bombs also survived for the most part the biological effects (radiation deaths were about 10% of the total, which is to say that if the nuclear burst had emitted no nuclear radiation at all, the death total would have been 10% lower). In the longer term, the after effects of radiation push up the death rates among survivors noticeably, but not dramatically.

Still-births increased among mothers who were pregnant at the time of the explosion and who themselves had been exposed to radiation at the 500 REM level and survived. (500 REM is about the radiation dose which, when received in a brief space of time, gives the victim a 50% chance of survival. Slightly greater exposures can be tolerated if spread out over longer periods). Among persons surviving doses in the region of 500 REM an increased incidence of cancer – especially leukemia – was later noted at perhaps twice or three times the normal rate, with radiation induced leukemia reaching a peak six or seven years after exposure. Among children of survivors, conceived after the attacks, abnormalities through the inheritance of genetic defects did not show a sharp rise, although information as to what radiation

dose their parents had received, on average, does not seem available.

The proportion of the 5 psi zone overlapped by the zone of 500 REMs for a 1 megaton burst is considerably smaller than that for a 20 kiloton burst, and in our fictitious example of a 1 megaton burst at optimum height above Central London, we can expect radiation of all kinds to be responsible for only 5% or so of the deaths.

It cannot be assumed that nuclear attacks on cities in a future war will be based on optimum height bursts. More likely some mixture of surface and optimum height bursts will be employed. A second-class nuclear power, with relatively few weapons at its disposal, forced to retaliate against a superpower, might target entirely for surface bursts, exchanging physical destruction (a surface burst will demolish only about 30% of the area demolished by an optimum height burst of the same yield) for the extended biological hazard presented by the heavy short term radioactive fallout that accompanies the surface bursts of any nuclear weapon that derives a substantial portion of its yield from fission. This includes the most common and cheapest form of thermonuclear bomb that has its thermonuclear (fusion), and therefore fallout free yield doubled by a blanket of fissionable uranium.

The mechanism of short-term fallout production depends on the fireball of the explosion touching the surface and gathering up vaporized earth and masonry (or water in a sea burst). The radioactive debris of the fission part of the explosion distributes itself within the fireball, which as it cools, starts rising into the atmosphere at several hundred miles an hour. On further cooling the vaporized materials sucked up from the surface begin to condense in solid form as sand-like and sometimes larger particles, encapsulating within a high proportion, 50% or so, of the radioactive debris. Fairly quickly, after about 30 minutes, these radioactive particles start to fall back to the ground, the heaviest and largest fall first, the lightest more slowly, taking 20 hours or more. Much the same effect occurs with water droplets. If a 15 mph wind is blowing at the time, lighter particles may reach the ground 300 miles (20 × 15) downwind of the explosion. Because there are always some crosswinds, especially at altitude, the pattern traced out by an imaginary line joining points on the ground of the same intensity of radiation from fallout, at any time after the explosion, will be cigar-shaped, with the point of the explosion itself near one end.

The hazard to life from short-term fallout is largely from long-range gamma radiation emitted by fallout settling on the ground and other flat surfaces such as roofs. Fallout actually settling on the skin and not washed off is additionally harmful to the skin, through the very weakly penetrating phenomenon of beta radiation, but this is generally a trifling matter in comparison to gamma radiation. Neither breathing fallout dust into the lungs nor swallowing it through eating contaminated food is especially hazardous compared to external gamma radiation: fallout particles are generally too large to be inhaled, and the body expels ingested radioactive matter rather quickly (strontium 90 and caesium 137 being important exceptions). Stocks of food washed clean of fallout dust and subsequently stored in shelters are perfectly safe to eat.

Gamma radiation is dangerous in exactly the same way the gamma rays of the initial nuclear radiation are dangerous. Because it is so penetrating, radiation damage affects the whole body. Death is unlikely to be immediate, even for people exposed to 1000 REMS (double the dose for which the long-term survival probability is 50%). Those exposed to 500 REMs show signs of illness within the first day, chiefly nausea, vomiting, diarrhoea and loss of appetite. After the first day or so these symptoms disappear, only to return with renewed force after a week or two. They are then likely to be accompanied by internal bleeding, including spontaneous bleeding from the mouth and the intestinal lining, and the loss of hair from the head. The body's defences against bacterial invasion will, at this point, be extremely low and the chances of fatal infection fairly high, with rising body temperature producing fever and delirium. At some point in this period or in the following two months, 50% of those receiving a 500 REMs dose will die; the rest will recover.

Shielding from gamma radiation is difficult. Brick walls cut down radiation only by a factor of 2 or 3; the basements of large public buildings cut it by around 100; and underground shelters (under three feet of earth or more) by 1,000. A trench similar to those dug on the Western front during World War 1, with a 3–4 ft wide area to the front and back cleared of fallout, will cut down radiation for the occupants by a factor of 100. Three thousand feet of air shields by a factor of 1,000, something that makes flying fairly safe even in the most heavily contaminated zones and something which makes a mooring in offshore waters a reasonably safe haven. But to be effective, a shelter of any kind will have to be occupied more or less continuously for two weeks or longer.

The actual extent of hazardous contamination is governed by three very simple principles. The danger to life from radioactivity does not begin until the fallout particles reach the ground, which may be several hours after the burst has occurred. Second, the fission content of the explosion governs the intensity of the radiation from the fallout when it arrives. Megaton range explosions are usually assumed to derive half their yield from fission, and fallout calculations speak of so many 'megatons of fission'; in an especially clean device the fission blanket may be left off and the fission contribution could be down to, say, a tenth of normal with a corresponding decrease in fallout radioactivity. But some fission contribution is believed to be present even in the 'cleanest' bomb. Thermonuclear (fusion) explosions without a fission trigger of some kind are theoretically possible, but no one has ever claimed to have produced one of military useful size. Third, fallout radioactivity becomes less hazardous with distance downwind from the explosion, for two reasons: the dust settles more thinly the further out it travels; and by the time the dust falls to ground at remote locations, the process of radioactive decay will already have been in operation for the several hours the dust was suspended in the atmosphere.

These principles, together with the empirical discovery that the average pattern of radioactive decay of fallout is of a tenfold decrease in gamma ray dose rate for every sevenfold increase in time after the explosion, can be used to predict the extent of potentially dangerous fallout, given a knowledge of the fission yield of the explosion and weather conditions in the region of the burst.

A representative danger zone calculation is carried out as follows. Assuming a total radiation dose of 600 REMs to be fatal in 50% of cases when this dose is spread over several months; assuming the inhabitants of the zone make no special effort to restrict their exposure to fallout, but spend two-thirds of their time in buildings with a shielding factor of 2; and assuming no effort is made to leave the contaminated zone, a dose lethal to at least half the inhabitants will be received in a cigar-shaped zone up to 75 miles long downwind of a 1 megaton fission (2 megaton explosion) surface burst (assuming a steady 15 mph wind) and about 12 miles across at its widest point. Nearer to the centre of the explosion, there will be a cigar-shaped zone about 25 miles long and 5 or 6 miles wide of such intense radioactivity that it

will be unsafe to re-enter for permanent occupation for at least a month after the explosion. For a 1 megaton surface burst (500 kilotons fission) the 500 REM danger zone will be 50 miles long, and 8 or 9 miles wide. Higher wind speeds will enlarge the danger zone, lower winds decrease it.

The 600 REM zone can also be taken to correspond to the area which will be effectively closed to infantry movements in a tactical nuclear war for several days after the last, nearby, nuclear burst. Calculating its maximum extent in a European tactical nuclear war is a rather chancy business. Modern NATO TNW are said to be very clean (low fission yield) and capable of such accurate delivery that bursts could be made high enough, over most targets, to keep the fireball clear of the ground. Soviet TNW, especially if we include some of the 600 ballistic missiles they nominally hold in readiness for strategic use in the European theatre, are larger in yield, probably dirtier and less accurate. NATO admits to 7,000 TNW and they probably average about 50 kilotons each. We will assume that they average 20 kilotons of fission yield each. If they were all used in a ground burst mode (which is unlikely, but gives an idea of what the upper limit of contamination might be), the 600 REM and greater zone could cover 50,000 square miles, over one-third the entire land area of the two Germanys. But unless winds were freakishly high, fallout would not extend eastward in dangerous amounts for more than about 15 miles from the most easterly burst (assuming a prevailing west wind is blowing), provided the largest tactical nuclear warhead used is less than 100 kilotons (50 kiloton fission).

Civilian casualties due to fallout will depend on circumstances. A tactical nuclear war in Europe will not be fought in such a way as to enable many civilians to do much better than obtain the factor of protection from gamma radiation provided by ordinary day-to-day living. NATO's

7,000 TNW evenly distributed over East Germany, Poland and Czechoslovakia as surface bursts could kill nearly 10 million people by radioactive fallout alone, but because of the use of airbursts, regional variations in weather, and the concentration of use on military targets which will not be evenly spread about these Warsaw Pact countries, this casualty figure is very much an upper limit. And if maximum yield employed is below 100 kilotons, under normal wind conditions bursts would have to be made within 15 miles of thickly populated areas before fallout became a really serious hazard to civilians.

A similar (and more reliable) calculation can be made of the effects of fallout in a limited strategic nuclear war. Because more is publicly known about where the Americans base their ICBMs and in what numbers, we shall assume a Soviet ICBM attack on US ICBM sites. The Soviets will presumably want their attack to be a telling one, so they will devote enough throw weight to each silo to give themselves a 90% chance of destroying it. At 1978 Soviet accuracies, this will mean either 5×1 megaton warheads per silo, or 1×10 megaton or 2×4 megaton, with the warheads surface-burst. Assuming the Soviets used the 2×4 megaton option, which is the most probable given the general Soviet preference for large warheads, and that each warhead gets 50% of its yield from fission, the attack would amount to four megatons of fission per silo.

Each of the six US Minuteman ICBM bases contains on average 166 silos. The Whiteman Air Force Base, just east of Kansas City, has 150 silos placed in an irregular pattern covering about 5,500 square miles. An attack on the Whiteman base, of the kind envisaged, would involve a total of 600 megatons of fission. Scaling up the calculation done earlier, assuming a 15 mph westerly wind, the 600 REM danger zone will extend almost 500 miles downwind in the shape of a broad cigar 140 miles wide

(the distance between the most northerly Whiteman ICBM silo and the most southerly is about 80 miles). The total 600 REM danger zone from similar attacks on all six silos would extend for over 400,000 square miles, some of which would lie in Canada.

A crude estimate of the death toll can be obtained by multiplying this area by 66 (the average population per square mile of the United States, excluding Alaska) and then by three-quarters, because of the 50% fatality rate of a 600 REM dose spread over several months. (The average dose *inside* the 600 REM contour will be higher than 600 REM and we have assigned it a fatality rate of 75%.) The answer obtained is 19,000,000. In one way this is an overestimate in its assumption that no advantage will be taken of the 30 hours between the bursts and the settling of fallout on the more remote downwind regions to get people into good gamma ray shelters such as basements. But it is an understimate in another way, since the population density of the United States in the zone to the east of the bursts is much above the national average.

It may be that this very large fatality figure is the clearest indication we have that the large warheads of Soviet ICBMs are probably not seen by the Soviets as of much good for would-be limited acts of war of this kind. A comparable American attack on Soviet ICBM sites would use less throw weight, since American accuracies are higher: and since Soviet ICBM sites lie for the most part to the east of the most densely populated areas fallout would put a much smaller percentage of the population at risk.

We are now in a position to sketch in the extent of destruction resulting from a nuclear war that was not held at the shopping places of a tactical nuclear war in Europe or of an attack on ICBM silos in the United States or Soviet Union, but resulted from a sudden or gradual breakdown of first-level deterrence between the superpowers. Since there are no developments in sight capable of objectively undermining first-level deterrence, any breakdown, if it came about in the near future, would to some extent be accidental: perhaps, if the breakdown was sudden, as a consequence of a true accident of the kind referred to earlier; and if the breakdown was gradual, as the result of a miscalculation in the heat of a limited nuclear war. And if the objective conditions for first-level deterrence are, as we assume, intact, then each superpower, in the event of a large-scale nuclear attack by one on the other and in the retaliation that would follow, will suffer enormous casualties (if the objective conditions were not met on either side, retaliation would, by definition, be too feeble to do much damage).

No attempt will be made to target everyone in even a large-scale nuclear attack. The 25% of Americans who live in rural areas are essentially safe from nuclear attack, since to bring them within the range of the blast wave and heat pulse it would be necessary to allocate almost one warhead per family (rural population density is less than 1 per square mile). But the 75% living in urban areas are a different matter. The total area of urban areas in the United States is only 45,000 square miles (1.5% of the total). The area of the 5 psi zone of a one megaton warhead is 80 square miles, so somewhere between 400 and 600 one megaton warheads would have a combined destructive area equal to the entire urban area of the United States, killing by blast and fire alone one third to one half of the urban population. A few hundred of these same warheads will, at the same time, account for the bulk of American industrial capacity. Simultaneous attacks will be made on military targets such as ICBM sites and quasi-military targets such as nuclear power stations, and these will be particularly heavy in an attack, as opposed to a retaliation when ICBM silos at any rate will be mostly empty and not worth hitting.

Some attacks on urban areas will be by surface burst, as will most attacks on military targets, and these will push up casualty figures both in the cities and in the rural areas. The nearest thing to an official estimate of the death toll of a central nuclear war was released by the US Defense Department during the late 1960s, and in spite of being based on a smaller Soviet attack potential than is now the case, it is plainly of the right order.

American deaths were estimated at 110 million (just over half the total population) in the event of a Soviet attack, and at 120 million as a result of Soviet retaliation to an American attack. The first figure is lower than the second because it is assumed in the latter case that a substantial proportion of available warheads will be directed against military targets. Developments since these estimates were made are likely to have pushed the two figures closer together. Soviet megatonnage has grown in the interim, and urban targets will no longer need to be spared to free capacity for military strikes; at the same time the American capacity to weaken Soviet ability to retaliate has also grown.

Soviet deaths were estimated at 80 million (just under a third of the total population) in the event of an American retaliation to a Soviet attack. Later developments are unlikely to have altered these figures much: the Soviets have many more ICBMs for the Americans to target but the accuracy of American warheads has improved, and any improvement in Soviet capacity to knock out American ICBMs has been offset by improvements in the retaliatory potential of the American submarine missile forces.

The smaller percentage of the Soviet population dying in a central nuclear war is partly because the Soviet Union is less urbanized than the United States (but its industrial capacity, is if anything, more centralized), and partly because Soviet attacks on American military targets will cause a large number of deaths through fallout. Even so, we cannot speak of a significant difference in the vulnerability of the two states to nuclear attack.

If nuclear attacks are confined to the United States and the Soviet Union, apart from Canada no other country will be seriously affected by fallout. Strontium 90 and Caesium 137 will be the only active components in the long-term fallout that will settle, thinly and evenly, on most of the Northern Hemisphere; but the hazard to health involved could be coped with by careful monitoring, and some temporary changes in eating habits – hugely inconvenient, certainly, but a long way from the end of the world.

In the superpowers themselves, survivors will be concentrated in the rural areas and this seems likely to remain a feature of any nuclear war in which active defences are unimportant. Civil defence of urban areas does not seem to have much of a future; too much warning of attack will be needed and conspicuous attempts to implement civil defence arrangements that rely on long warning will not only irritate the electorate (mock evacuation practice once a year) but can also promote suspicion on the other side that a nuclear attack is being planned. Civil defence of rural areas, on the other hand, makes a great deal of sense, although no government will find it easy to make explicit preparations for postwar life in rural areas without appearing to write off the towns.

IAN BELLANY

HIROSHIMA'S LEGACY

'Apart from the shadows of living creatures
and of objects turned to charcoal by the heat of the atomic flash,
one professor also collected hundreds of other specimens –
materials which had not been destroyed, but only transmuted
or changed in the huge blast furnace that had been the explosion.
These included weirdly coloured earthenware tiles,
bottles twisted into extraordinary shapes,
singed fragments of cloth, and an ever-increasing quantity of stones.
And what stones! Stones such as existed nowhere else on earth.
In the uniquely high temperature produced by the atom bomb
they had begun to 'weep' or to 'bleed'.
This was clearly apparent when one of these stones was dissected.
The deep black centre remained intact, but part of this core
had forced its way through the light grey surface to emerge as boils or sores.
It was as if the very stones had contracted mange or leprosy . . .'
[From 'Children of the Ashes' by Robert Jungk,
published by Heinemann]

THE AUTHORS
BIBLIOGRAPHY
INDEX

THE AUTHORS

SHELFORD BIDWELL

In World War 2 Brigadier Shelford Bidwell commanded a battery in North Africa, landed in Italy at Salerno and was a staff officer in an armoured division in Italy. In 1946 he was an instructor at the Staff College. Later he became Chief Instructor Tactical Development at the Royal School of Artillery and on promotion Commander, Royal Artillery in the 2nd Division of the British Army of the Rhine. In both these two appointments he was actively concerned with the increasing problems of land tactics in the nuclear age, which he later analysed in his controversial book *Modern Warfare*. After Germany he served in the Far East during the war in Borneo. This wide experience was valuable to him when he turned to military history and the problems of contemporary defence. He was elected Fellow of the Royal Historical Society in 1974 and member of Council of the Royal United Services Institute for Defence Studies in 1978.

IAN BELLANY

Ian Bellany was educated at Balliol College, Oxford, where he received a MA, D Phil (Atomic Physics) in 1966. He was a member of Arms Control Research Unit 1965-68 and then from 1968-70, a Research Fellow for the Australian National University, Canberra. In 1970 he became a lecturer and later, Senior Lecturer in Politics at Lancaster University. He is author of *Australia in the Nuclear Age* and many pamphlets and articles on international strategic and nuclear affairs. Ian Bellany was elected fellow of the Inter-University Seminar on Armed Forces and Society (Chicago) 1976.

LAWRENCE FREEDMAN

Lawrence Freedman is currently a research fellow at the Royal Institute of International Affairs, Chatham House. He has previously held research appointments at Nuffield College, Oxford, and the International Institute for Strategic Studies. In addition to many articles in European and American journals, he has written a book entitled *US Intelligence and the Soviet Strategic Threat*.

REAR-ADMIRAL E. F. GUERITZ

Rear-Admiral E. F. Gueritz joined the Navy in 1937 and served throughout World War 2 in destroyers and Combined Operations. He was severely wounded as a beachmaster in the Normandy landing. He was Naval Force Logistics Officer in the Suez Operation in 1956 and Captain of the Fleet during the Confrontation with Indonesia in 1965-66. He was Director of Defence Plans (Navy) in 1967 and became Admiral President of the Royal Naval College, Greenwich, in 1968. Admiral Gueritz was Commandant of the Joint Warfare Establishment at Old Sarum, Salisbury, England from 1970-72. He is Director of Studies at the Royal United Services Institute for Defence Studies.

RONALD T. PRETTY

Ronald T. Pretty flew as an observer with Coastal Command during World War 2. On leaving the RAF in 1947, he spent several years at the Royal Aircraft Establishment, Farnborough, Hants. This was followed by a period with a company specializing in electronics and control systems, before becoming Aviation and

Defence Correspondent for the journal *Electronics Weekly*, a position held for fourteen years. Since 1969 Ronald Pretty has been Contributing Editor for the American publication *Electronic Warfare/Defense Electronics*, and Editor of *Jane's Weapon Systems*. He has contributed to a major US encyclopaedia, and also writes and broadcasts on military technology. He is author of *Jane's Pocket Book of Missiles*.

ANTHONY VERRIER

Anthony Verrier has for many years written about strategic issues, as a journalist, broadcaster and the author of two books: *An Army for the Sixties*, and *The Bomber Offensive*. As a former senior Associate member of St Anthony's College, Oxford, and frequent contributor to seminars at its Middle East Centre, Anthony Verrier has studied strategic, political and economic issues in this area with particular care. His personal knowledge of the Middle East is extensive and he is currently engaged in advising commercial concerns about conditions there.

PHIL WILLIAMS

Phil Williams is lecturer in International Relations in the Department of Politics and an Associate of the Centre for Defence Studies at the University of Aberdeen. His publications include *Crisis Management: Confrontation and Diplomacy in the Nuclear Age* and *Contemporary Strategy: Theories and Policies*. At the moment, he is also completing a book on the Senate and U.S. troops in Europe between 1945–75. He was a NATO Research Fellow from 1974–75.

BILL GUNSTON

Bill Gunston was an RAF flying instructor during World War 2. In December 1951 he joined the staff of *Flight International*, being appointed Technical Editor in April 1955. He has written 44 books, countless magazine articles and handled editorial assignments for 129 publishers. He is European Editor of *Aircraft* and Assistant Compiler of *Jane's All the World's Aircraft*.

KENNETH HUNT

Kenneth Hunt is Director of the British Atlantic Committee. He was a regular officer in the British Army for some thirty years. In 1967, he resigned from the Army to become Deputy Director of the International Institute for Strategic Studies, a post he held until October 1977. For some five years he has been specialist advisor to the British House of Commons Defence and External Affairs Sub-Committee, and has been Visiting Professor at the Fletcher School of Law and Diplomacy, Cambridge, Mass., U.S.A. He is a frequent broadcaster and has travelled widely, including numerous visits to the Far East, including Korea, Japan and China.

CAPTAIN JOHN MOORE

Captain John Moore was born in Genoa, Italy and educated in New Zealand. In September 1939, he entered the Royal Navy and served in Submarines during World War 2. After the war he continued in submarines in the Mediterranean and Far East. After having held six commands he was promoted to Commander in 1957. He served in Turkey, Admiralty, Portsmouth and Singapore and was again promoted in 1967 to Captain. From 1967–69 he served as Chief-of-Staff in Naval Home Command and from 1969–72 was in charge of Soviet Naval Intelligence. After voluntary retirement, Captain Moore became editor of *Jane's Fighting Ships*. He is a member of the U.S. Strategic Studies Institute, and author of *Major Warships*, *Ships of the Royal Navy,* and *Submarine Development*.

PICTURE SOURCES

Page 11, 26-7, 29-30, 34, 40, 43, 58 - Keystone; 14 - McDonnell-Douglas, USA; 16 - US Navy/J.G. Moore Collection, London; 17 - North American Rockwell, USA/J.G. Moore Collection; 18 - Novosti Press Agency; 19 - US Air Force; 24 - United Press; 43 - US Army; 44 - NAC Military Aircraft Division/J.G. Moore Collection; 69 - Marconi Company Ltd/Ronald T. Pretty; 71 - Jane's Weapons/Ronald T. Pretty; 74 - Hawker Siddeley Dynamics Ltd/Ronald T. Pretty; 88 - Martin Marietta Aerospace, USA/J.G. Moore Collection; 89 - Bundesministerium der Verteidigung; 96 - Ministry of Defence; 99 - Fairchild Industries, USA/J.G. Moore Collection; 101 - Ministry of Defence; 109 - Royal Air Force; 115 - Novosti Press Agency; US Navy/J.G. Moore Collection; 119 - US Air Force; 122 - General Dynamics, Groton/ J.G. Moore Collection; 125 - British Aircraft Corporation; 128 - J.G. Moore Collection; 145 - Novosti Press Agency; 149 - Camera Press; 151 - Fairchild Industries, USA/J.G. Moore Collection; 155 - US Air Force; 160 - British Aerospace Aircraft Group/J.G. Moore Collection; 162 - Boeing Aerospace Co, Washington/J.G. Moore Collection; 167 - Fairchild Industries, USA/J.G. Moore Collection; 170 - Novosti Press Agency; 175 - Ministry of Defence; 178 - Novosti Press Agency.

YEARBOOKS

International Institute for Strategic Studies (18 Adam St, London WC2N 6AL)
The Military Balance
Strategic Survey
Jane's Yearbooks (Paulton House, 8 Shepherdess Walk, London N17LW)
Fighting Ships (ed. John E. Moore)
All the World's Aircraft (ed. John W. R. Taylor)
Weapon Systems (ed. Ronald T. Pretty)
Infantry Weapons (ed. Denis H. R. Archer)

RECOMMENDED FURTHER READING

Bell, C., *The October Middle East War: A Case Study in Crisis Management during Detente* (*International Affairs,* Vol. 50, No 4, Oct. 1974, pp 531-43)
The Conventions of Crisis: A Study in Diplomatic Management (Oxford University Press, 1971)
Bidwell, Shelford, *Modern Warfare* (Allen Lane, 1973)
Fisher, R., *International Conflict for Beginners* (Harper & Row, 1969)
Glasstone, S., *The Effects of Nuclear Weapons* (US Atomic Energy Commission, 1962)
Holsti, O. R., *Crisis, Escalation, War* (McGill - Queen's University Press, 1972)
Johnson, L. B., *The Vantage Point - Perspectives of the Presidency* (New York Popular Library, 1971)
Kahn, H., *On Thermonuclear War* (Princeton University Press, 1961)
Kennedy, R. F., *Thirteen Days* (Pan Books 1969)
Osgood, R. E., and Tucker, R. W., *Force, Order and Justice* (Johns Hopkins Press, 1967)
Richardson, J. L., *Germany and the Atlantic Alliance* (Harvard University Press, 1968)
Sampson, Anthony, *The Arms Bazaar* (Coronet 1978)
Snyder, G., 'Crisis Bargaining', in *International Crises: Insights from Behavioural Research* (Collier Macmillan, 1972)
Sorensen, T. C., *Kennedy* (Pan Books 1966)
Spiegel, S. L., *Dominance and Diversity* (Little, Brown 1972)
Stanley, J., and Pearton, M., *The International Trade in Arms* (International Institute for Strategic Studies, 1972)
Vigor, P., *The Soviet View of War, Peace & Neutrality* (Routledge & Kegan Paul, 1975)
Williams, P., *Crisis Management; Confrontation and Diplomacy in the Nuclear Age* (Martin Robe6tson, 1976)
Willrich, M., and Rhinelander, J. B., eds, *SALT: The Moscow Agreements and Beyond* (Collier-Macmillan 1974)
The Arms Trade With The Third World (Stockholm International Peace Research Institute - SIPRI - 1971)
A Nuclear Middle East (Sept. 1977); *Israel's Nuclear Options and What a Fifth Arab-Israeli War might Look Like* (Nov. 1977) - University of California Center for Arms Control and International Security

INDEX